I0882314

The Long-Term Residence Status as a Subsidiary Form of EU Citizenship

Immigration and Asylum Law and Policy in Europe

Editors

Elspeth Guild
Kingsley Napley Solicitors, London,
Centre for Migration Law, Radboud University Nijmegen
Jan Niessen
Migration Policy Group, Brussels

VOLUME 23

The Long-Term Residence Status as a Subsidiary Form of EU Citizenship

An Analysis of Directive 2003/109

By

Diego Acosta Arcarazo

BRILL

LEIDEN • BOSTON
2011

This book is printed on acid-free paper.

Library of Congress Cataloging-in-Publication Data

Acosta Arcarazo, Diego.
The long-term residence status as a subsidiary form of EU citizenship : an analysis of directive 2003/109 / by Diego Acosta Arcarazo.
p. cm. -- (Immigration and asylum law and policy in Europe ; v. 23)
Includes bibliographical references and index.
ISBN 978-90-04-20412-6 (hardback : alk. paper) 1. Council of the European Union. Council Directive 2003/109/EC of 25 November 2003 concerning the status of third-country nationals who are long-term residents. 2. Citizenship--European Union countries. 3. Aliens--Civil rights--European Union countries. 4. Immigrants--Civil rights--European Union countries. 5. Freedom of movement--European Union countries. 6. European Union countries--Emigration and immigration--Government policy. I. Title.

KJE5124.A928 2011
342.2408'3--dc22

2011011844

ISSN 1568-2749
ISBN 978 90 04 20412 6

Copyright 2011 by Koninklijke Brill NV, Leiden, The Netherlands.
Koninklijke Brill NV incorporates the imprints Brill, Global Oriental, Hotei Publishing, IDC Publishers, Martinus Nijhoff Publishers and VSP.

All rights reserved. No part of this publication may be reproduced, translated, stored in a retrieval system, or transmitted in any form or by any means, electronic, mechanical, photocopying, recording or otherwise, without prior written permission from the publisher.

Authorization to photocopy items for internal or personal use is granted by Koninklijke Brill NV provided that the appropriate fees are paid directly to The Copyright Clearance Center, 222 Rosewood Drive, Suite 910, Danvers, MA 01923, USA.
Fees are subject to change.

To the memory of Profesor Rafael Acosta Patiño

Contents

Section III. The Content of the Long-Term Residence Directive

Section IV. The Integration Conditions

Abbreviations

ACP	African, Caribbean and Pacific
CEEC	Central and Eastern European Countries
CESEDA	Code de l'Entrée et du Séjour des Étrangers et du Droit d'Asile
CJEU	Court of Justice of the European Union
EC	European Community
ECR	European Court Reports
ECHR	European Convention of Human Rights and Fundamental Freedoms
ECtHR	European Court of Human Rights
EEA	European Economic Area
EEC	European Economic Community
EU	European Union
FYROM	Former Yugoslav Republic of Macedonia
IGC	Intergovernmental Conference
MEP	Member of the European Parliament
NGO	Non-Governmental Organization
OJ	Official Journal
SAA	Stabilisation and Association Agreement
SEA	Single European Act
TCN	Third-Country National
TEC	Treaty establishing the European Community
TEU	Treaty on European Union
TFEU	Treaty on the Functioning of the European Union
UK	United Kingdom
USSR	Union of Soviet Socialist Republics

Acknowledgements

This book constitutes my PhD dissertation that I defended at King's College University in London in October 2010. My interest in the area of immigration dates back to the time I spent as an Erasmus student in Brussels in 2001 when I read the book "Les Identités Meurtrières" by Amin Maalouf. That was the first time I reflected upon issues of European identity and how it is influenced by the free movement of citizens. It was only later though, in 2003, when I was studying at FIU in Miami, when I started to be interested on migration issues. That time it was the book "City on the Edge. The Transformation of Miami" by Alejandro Portes and Alex Stepick which made me think about the role of migrants in their new societies. Those thoughts evolved during the next years due to my personal experiences living in different places such as New York, Stockholm, Madrid, Bogota and London.

It was indeed in London where I found the support to pursue my PhD at King's College University. Its Centre for European Law granted me a 3 year scholarship and I am tremendously indebted to Andrea Biondi and Piet Eeckhout as well as Sir Francis Jacobs for their generous support and encouragement in all my endeavours and projects. I owe my greatest thanks to Alexander Türk and Elspeth Guild who, in their role as my thesis supervisors, have been invaluable in their guidance, expertise and enthusiasm for the subject of European law and immigration. I tremendously enjoyed the monthly meetings that the three of us had together to discuss my work and their help and advice on my professional career. My PhD colleagues with whom I spent so many hours at the Melbourne house in London as well as Annette Lee and Christine Copping at King's College also deserve my special thanks. My thesis examiners, Dora Kostakopoulou and Cristina Gortázar, were instrumental in helping to refine the arguments presented here and for this I am extremely grateful.

I would like to extend my gratitude to Kees Groenendijk for his warm welcome at the Centre for Migration Law at Radboud University in Nijmegen. He has been, together with my two supervisors, the most important person in shaping my understandings of integration and immigration in the European Union. I would also like to thank other colleagues like Kristine Kruma, Jürgen Bast, Sara Iglesias, Cian Murphy, Yves Pascouau, Sergio Carrera, Anja Wiesbrock and many others who gave me their advice and help at different stages of my research, as well as Irene Blázquez Navarro and Antonio Remiro Brotóns at Universidad Autónoma in Madrid where I began my Law studies.

Finally, the School of Law, University of Sheffield, has offered me a fantastic place to continue my research and my academic career.

On a more personal level, I would like to thank my mother, grandmother and sister for their love and support behind all my initiatives. I would like to dedicate this book to the memory of my father, Profesor Rafael Acosta Patiño, who will remain a source of inspiration in anything I will do in my life.

Section I

Introduction, Methodology and Key Concepts

Chapter 1

Preliminary Concepts

1. *Introduction*

Immigration has become one of the most fiercely contested issues on the political agenda of many governments in Europe and throughout the world. In the case of the European Union (EU) there are 20 million third-country nationals residing within its borders.[1] It is essential to see the legal treatment that these third-country nationals receive as it will have very important consequences for the future of the EU. Thus, the purpose of this study is to see how the EU deals with those third-country nationals who have resided in a Member State for a period of, at least, five years, through the implementation of the Long-term Residence Directive.

The EU has had a clear immigration competence since the entry into force of the Treaty of Amsterdam in 1999. In the same year, five months later, the Tampere European Council Conclusions, which included the Tampere programme,[2] drew up the guidelines stating how the EU should deal with this issue. This represented a turning point in the Union's pledge to work in the area of immigration. These two events constitute the starting point of my study of a period of ten years, which I will close with the entry into force of the Treaty of Lisbon and the adoption of the new Stockholm programme in December 2009.[3]

The interest of this book lies in the fact that this has been a period of constant and radical changes. The concept of change is indeed one of the most important aspects and motivations for this research. Throughout the following pages I will illustrate how this concept affects many of the issues analysed. For instance, in the last years there have been procedural and competency changes. In addition, there are nationals of countries which did not enjoy free movement rights in the EU in the past, who now have these rights. This is due

---

[1] K. Vasileva (2010), "Statistics in Focus", Eurostat, 45/2010, p. 1.

[2] This programme will be analysed in Chapter 2 below.

[3] For the sake of comprehensiveness I will also include in my analysis some relevant national and European legislative developments which took place until 1 December 2010.

to two enlargement processes[4] and the signature of other agreements. Finally, there has been a constant legislative process with the adoption of new Directives which have an impact on both European citizens and third-country nationals. This process has produced numerous modifications in the immigration legislations of Member States as they have had to implement various Directives in the area. All these changes need reflection and they will be appropriately examined in the following pages. Suffice it to anticipate here that the concept of change creates a remarkable paradox since the actors claim a stability into which the "Other" would integrate.

This book studies the implications for third-country nationals of the adoption of the Long-term Residence Directive. The Long-term Residence Directive is extremely important as it has the potential to become a subsidiary form of EU citizenship which escapes direct control by Member States. Hence, this Directive brings the prospect of transforming Member States' control over the relationship between territory and population.

In order to arrive at this conclusion, the book looks at its content and at the way in which Member States have implemented some of the most controversial provisions in the Directive. It then explores how the Court of Justice of the European Union (CJEU) could interpret those provisions, taking into account its previous jurisprudence on Turkish workers, European citizens and other immigration Directives such as the one on family reunification. Chapter 8 tackles the political motivations for the introduction of integration conditions, in order to acquire the long-term residence status, in many Member States, by looking at the debates that preceded those legislative developments. These integration conditions, almost non-existent in 1999, have become a widespread practice and constitute the central issue of the Directive's implementation. Their future interpretation by the CJEU is key for understanding the way in which the EU will deal with its third-country nationals.

The extent to which long-term residence status will become a subsidiary form of EU citizenship is central in seeing whether the EU, through the implementation of the Long-term Residence Directive, is creating a "Legal Other" or, if it is, on the contrary, bridging the gap between the rights of European citizens and those of third-country nationals. In other words, through the implementation and interpretation of the Long-term Residence Directive, the "Legal Other" could be in the process of transforming into the "Legal Us".

---

[4] As Groenendijk points out, it took certain politicians and public opinion sometime to get used to this transformation from "irregular" workers into Union citizens. See K. Groenendijk (2009), "Forty Years of Free Movement of Workers: Has it been a Success and Why?" in P. Minderhoud and N. Trimikliniotis (eds.) (2009), *Rethinking the Free Movement of Workers: The European Challenges Ahead*, Wolf Legal Publishers: Nijmegen, pp. 11–24, at 17.

As mentioned above, these questions are analysed in a period of time which spans 1999 to 2009. In fact, the transfer of immigration to EU competence took place with the entry into force of the Treaty of Amsterdam in 1999. That same year, the European Council meeting in Tampere highlighted the importance of giving third-country nationals, regularly residing in the different Member States, a comparable treatment to European citizens. The EU consequently legislated extensively on immigration in those ten years. It adopted several measures on visas, border control and irregular immigration. Its activity on regular migration was less impressive, including only five Directives: the Long-term Residence Directive,[5] the Family Reunification Directive,[6] the Highly Skilled Workers Directive,[7] the Students Directive[8] and the Researchers Directive.[9] Of those five, it can be argued that the most important is the one on long-term residence. In fact, this Directive gives the best measurement of how the EU approaches third-country nationals, specifically their rights and security of residence. The other four Directives are relevant as well but they deal with closed categories of third-country nationals (family members, students, researchers and highly skilled workers). By contrast, the Long-term Residence Directive applies to any migrant who has regularly resided for a period of five years in a Member State.

Several authors have provided an in-depth and detailed analysis of the Directive and its adoption, as well as its different aspects.[10] Some scholars have

---

[5] Directive 2003/109/EC of 25 November 2003 of the Council concerning the Status of Third-country Nationals who are Long-term Residents, OJ 2004 L 16/44, 23.1.2004.

[6] Directive 2003/86/EC of 22 September 2003 of the Council on the Right to Family Reunification, OJ 2003 L251/12, 3.10.2003.

[7] Directive 2009/50/EC of 25 May 2009 of the Council on the Conditions of Entry and Residence of Third-country Nationals for the Purposes of Highly Qualified Employment, OJ 2009 L 155/17, 18.6.2009.

[8] Directive 2004/114/EC of 13 December 2004 of the Council on the Conditions of Admission of Third-country Nationals for the Purposes of Studies, Pupil Exchange, Unremunerated Training or Voluntary Service, OJ 2004 L375/12, 23.12.2004.

[9] Directive 2005/71/EC of 12 October 2005 of the Council on a Specific Procedure for Admitting Third-country Nationals for the Purpose of Scientific Research, OJ 2005 L289/15, 3.11.2005.

[10] See S. Guèvremont (2009), *Vers un Traitement Équitable des Étrangers Extracommunautaires en Séjour Régulier. Examen des Directives sur le Regroupement Familial et sur les Résidents de Longue Durée*, Wöhrmann Print Service : Zutphen ; K. Groenendijk (2007), "The Long-Term Residents Directive, Denizenship and Integration", in A. Baldaccini, E. Guild and H. Toner (eds.), *Whose Freedom, Security and Justice? EU Immigration and Asylum Law and Policy*, Hart Publishing: Oxford, pp. 429–450; S. Boelaert-Suominen (2005), "Non-EU Nationals and Council Directive 2003/109/EC on the Status of Third-country Nationals who are Long-term Residents: Five Paces Forward and Possibly Three Paces Back", *Common Market Law Review*, Vol. 42(4), pp. 1011–1052; S. Peers (2004), "Implementing Equality? The Directive on Long

paid special attention to some elements such as the rights granted to third-country nationals[11] or the possibility to reside in other Member States.[12] Still others have compared the rights of long-term residents under the Directive with those of European citizens,[13] or have explored other issues such as the concept of civic citizenship.[14]

Despite the large amount of literature there are some important gaps that I propose to fill with this work by looking at the implementation and possible interpretation by the CJEU of selected Articles. These two steps will help to measure the potential of long-term residence to become a subsidiary form of EU citizenship.

With regard to the first issue, there is little written on the implementation of the Directive in the different Member States. Some authors have done some work on particular countries[15] but comparative analysis is largely missing.[16] This book uses a comparative research method to investigate the implementation of four key Articles in different Member States. These Articles determine who may acquire the long-term residence permit (Article 3), how it can be obtained (Article 5), what the protection against expulsion is once the status is granted (Article 12) and, lastly, what the possibilities to move in order to reside

Term Resident Third Country Nationals", *European Law Review*, Vol. 29(4), pp. 437–460; J. Handoll (2003), "The Status of Third-Country Nationals Residing on a Long-term Basis", in P. de Bruycker (ed.), *The Emergence of a European Immigration Policy*, Bruylant: Brussels, pp. 269–362.

11 L. Halleskov (2005), "The Long-term Residents Directive: A Fulfilment of the Tampere Objective of Near Equality?", *European Journal of Migration and Law*, Vol. 7(2), pp. 181–201.

12 A. Kocharov (2008), "What Intra-Community Mobility for Third Country Workers?", *European Law Review*, Vol. 33(6), pp. 912–26; A. Skordas (2006), "Immigration and the Market: The Long Term Residence Directive", *Columbia Journal of European Law*, Vol. 13, pp. 201–229; S. Iglesias Sánchez (2009), "Free Movement of Third Country Nationals in the European Union? Main Features, Deficiencies and Challenges of the New Mobility Rights in the Area of Freedom, Security and Justice", *European Law Journal*, Vol. 15(6), pp. 791–805.

13 K. Groenendijk (2006), "Citizens and Third Country Nationals: Differential Treatment or Discrimination?", in J.Y. Carlier, E. Guild & B. Coulie (eds.), *The Future of Free Movement of Persons in the EU*, Collection du Centre des Droits de L'Homme de l'Université Catholique de Louvain, Bruylant: Brussels, pp 79–101.

14 M. Bell (2007), "Civic Citizenship and Migrant Integration", *European Public Law*, Vol. 13(2), pp. 311–333.

15 See, for example, on France S. Carrera (2009), "Nationality, Immigration and 'the Republican Integration' in France", in K. Groenendijk, S. Carrera and E. Guild (eds.), *Illiberal Liberal States: Immigration, Citizenship and Integration in the EU*, Ashgate: Surrey, pp. 315–335.

16 See, however, on the Netherlands, Germany and Sweden A. Wiesbrock (2010), *Legal Migration to the European Union*, Martinus Nijhoff: Leiden.

and work in a second Member State are, for those third-country nationals who have already acquired this status in one Member State (Article 14). I will devote one Chapter to each one of these provisions in order to identify problems in their interpretation or implementation in different Member States, paying special attention to four case studies: Spain, Italy, Sweden and Latvia, which were selected for reasons that are explained below. However, there is the need not to restrict my analysis to the four above-mentioned countries. In fact, the information on the implementation of the Directive in other Member States enriches the research by revealing specific problems which are not necessarily present in the four case studies. This is very significant as the different approaches in the implementation of these provisions prove the unwillingness of some Member States to have a harmonised approach to immigration, despite having granted the EU powers to legislate in this area under the Amsterdam Treaty. This is the consequence of Member States' "'lowest common denominator' approach to convergence, which results in low minimum standards" and which gives a "wide margin of discretion to the national legislators in the process of transposing Community rules".[17] Some authors have advocated a more extensive use of the so-called open method of coordination in order to overcome these problems.[18] However, the use of soft law will not be discussed in this book, as there is already hard law in the area of permanent residence, even if it might be argued that some of the provisions have the characteristics of soft law. Nonetheless, the margin of discretion enjoyed by Member States has its limits when the transposition into the national legal order runs contrary to the provisions in the Directive, or when the final objective of the Directive is endangered. Consequently, it is important to analyse the implementation together with the possible interpretation by the Commission and, especially, by the Court of Justice.

With reference to this second issue of the possible interpretation of the Directive, this work brings a new perspective by looking at how the Court has interpreted parallel provisions for Turkish workers, European citizens and

---

[17] M.C. Foblets (2009), "The Fragmented Development of EU Immigration and Integration Policy. Which Status for Third-Country Nationals in Europe?", in J. Wouters, L. Verhey, P. Kiiver et al., *European Constitutionalism beyond Lisbon*, Intersentia: Mortsel, pp. 81–109, at 83 and 90.

[18] See M.C. Foblets (2009) *Ibid.*; S. Velluti (2007), "What European Union Strategy for Integrating Migrants? The Role of OMC Soft Mechanisms in the Development of an EU Immigration Policy", *European Journal of Migration and Law*, Vol. 9(1), pp. 53–82; A. Caviedes (2004), "The Open Method of Coordination in Immigration Policy: A Tool for Prying Open Fortress Europe?", *Journal of European Public Policy*, Vol. 11(2), pp. 289–310.

in other immigration Directives, in order to later establish some possible analogies. The research method is also comparative and tries to identify similarities that provide guidance on how the Court could interpret the implementation and practice of the four Articles that I scrutinise. The underlying organising principle of choosing the four Articles that I examine is further revealed when looking at the possible interpretation by the Court. In fact, the discrepancies in implementation in the different Member States reveal the resistance to harmonisation (Europeanisation) in the field. This results in incoherent practices that the CJEU will have to interpret, especially since after Lisbon, all national courts may refer a question. The CJEU has two different options of judicial interpretation. On the one hand, it can opt for a purposive or teleological interpretation of the Directive in which it would leave little discretion for Member States.[19] On the other hand, it can follow a literal interpretation of the Directive which may allow more leeway for Member States.[20] I will however argue, in the following Chapters, that it is important for the Court to lean towards the first option. There are several reasons for that. First, an in-depth examination of the implementation of certain provisions in different Member States shows a lack of harmonisation. Second, that lack of harmonisation might produce a downgrade in certain areas in the rights of third-country nationals. Finally, the larger the EU becomes, the more important is the need to have a coherent immigration regime in Europe. In fact, the CJEU has already adopted this approach in *Chakroun* as will be analysed in Chapter 9.

As mentioned earlier, I will consistently analyse in more depth four case studies: Spain, Italy, Sweden and Latvia. These countries have been selected because of a combination of different factors. First, these countries joined the EU in different periods: Italy was a founding Member State whereas Spain joined in 1986, Sweden in 1995 and Latvia in 2004. Second, these countries have a significant number of third-country nationals residing in their territories. According to the most reliable estimates there were 2,987,489 third-country nationals in Italy on 1 January 2009,[21] 2,562,032 in Spain on 31 December

---

19 See on the teleological method of interpretation T. Tridimas (1996), "The Court of Justice and Judicial Activism", *European Law Review*, Vol. 21, pp. 199–210.

20 See on this K.J. Alter (1998), "Who are the 'Masters of the Treaty'?: European Governments and the European Court of Justice", *International Organization*, Vol. 52, pp. 121–147; G. de Búrca and J.H.H. Weiler (2001), *The European Court of Justice*, Oxford University Press: Oxford.

21 ISTAT (2010), *Italia in Cifre 2010,* Istituto Nazionale di Statistica: Roma, p. 6.

2009,[22] 265,182 in Sweden on 31 December 2008[23] and 351,435 non-citizens and around 40,000 third-country nationals in Latvia on 1 July 2009.[24] Most of the third-country nationals in Latvia are non-citizens, which resulted from the Latvian authorities' decision after independence to grant citizenship, almost uniquely, to those who had been Latvian nationals on 17 June 1940 and their descendants. Non-citizens are those who were nationals of the Union of Soviet Socialist Republics (USSR) before 1991, but who did not qualify for Latvian citizenship after independence and did not obtain the nationality of any other country.[25] Non-citizens are considered long-term residents in accordance with Directive 2003/109 in the EU framework.[26] Third, these countries represent a good sample of different population sizes. There are around 60 million people residing in Italy, almost 46 million in Spain, slightly more than nine million in Sweden and about two million two hundred thousand in Latvia.[27] Fourth, geography is also important with two countries being located

[22] Ministerio de Trabajo e Inmigración (2010), *Extranjeros con Certificado de Registro o Tarjeta de Residencia en Vigor y Extranjeros con Autorización de Estancia por Estudios en Vigor a 31 de Diciembre de 2009*, Ministerio de Trabajo e Inmigración: Madrid, p. 6. There would be another 229,000 third-country nationals family members of Spanish, EU citizens or third-country nationals. Those who are family members of third-country nationals are included in the number provided above of 2,562,032. However, those who are family members of Spanish or European citizens are not included as they have the right to enter in order to reside in Spain and their status is not regulated by Spanish Immigration law but by the one relating to EU citizens (Real Decreto 240/2007, de 16 de febrero, sobre entrada, libre circulación y residencia en España de ciudadanos de los estados miembros de la Unión Europea y de otros estados parte en el acuerdo sobre el espacio económico europeo, (BOE núm. 51, de 28 de febrero), en su redacción dada por el Real Decreto 1161/2009, de 10 julio (BOE núm. 177, de 23 de julio)).

[23] Statistics Sweden (2009), *Tables on the Population in Sweden 2008*, Statistiska centralbyrån, pp. 62–71.

[24] Information retrieved from the Office of Citizenship and Migration Affairs Latvia *at* http://www.pmlp.gov.lv/lv/statistika/dokuments/2009/2ISVP_Latvija_pec_VPD.pdf (accessed 01 December 2010).

[25] See on these policies and on the status of non-citizens in Latvia: K. Kruma (2009), "Checks and Balances in Latvian Nationality Policies: National Agendas and International Frameworks", in R. Bauböck, B. Perchinig and W. Sievers (eds.) (2009), *Citizenship Policies in the New Europe*, Amsterdam University Press: Amsterdam, pp. 67–96.

[26] *Ibid.*, at 73. See also K. Kruma, I. Indans and L. Meijere (2008), "Enacting EU Citizenship in Latvia: the case of noncitizens", *ENACT, Enacting European Citizenship*, at 11–15; K. Kruma (2009), "Country Report: Latvia", *Eudo Citizenship Observatory*.

[27] G. Lanzieri (2009), "Data in Focus", Eurostat: Brussels, *at* http://epp.eurostat.ec.europa.eu/cache/ITY_OFFPUB/KS-QA-09-047/EN/KS-QA-09-047-EN.PDF (accessed 01 December 2010).

in the Baltic Sea and two in the Mediterranean, with the implications that has in terms of neighbouring non-European or EU countries. Fifth, these countries have different stories of immigration. Sweden, which was an emigration country before the Second World War, has been an old destination for migrants and asylum seekers since the 1940s.[28] In contrast, Spain and Italy only started receiving immigration in the late 1980s and early 1990s, as they were emigration countries until the late 1970s and beginning of the 1980s.[29] Latvia represents a different case as immigration is not important in numbers but it has a large group of non-citizens due to the restrictive citizenship legislation that was passed after its independence.[30] Finally, the approach that the four countries have adopted in implementing the Long-term Residence Directive as well as, more generally, their views on immigration, vary considerably as it will be seen in the Chapters that follow.

This book thus examines the implementation and possible interpretation of the Long-term Residence Directive in order to see its potentiality to become a subsidiary form of EU citizenship. That would help in assessing whether the rights of third-country nationals might be comparable to those of EU citizens or whether there is a new "Legal Other" in the making.

This introductory Chapter will first provide some conceptual clarifications as regards key concepts that will be used throughout the book. First, it will be explained what is meant by the EU when this particular area is analysed, since the views of the European Commission, Parliament, Council, Court of Justice and European Council may differ greatly. Second, it will be seen what is meant by "Legal Other". "Legal Other" means those third-country nationals who do not have an independent right of entry to work in the EU. Hence I will look at which nationals of what countries enjoy that right. Next, I will spell out that the concept of "Legal Other" that will be developed in this book affects only regular migrants, mainly exercising an economic activity, who have prospects to stay in the host State. To conclude this Chapter, I will sketch the outline of the book and I will pose the main questions that I will attempt to answer in the next Chapters.

---

[28] C. Westin (2006), "Sweden: Restrictive Immigration Policy and Multiculturalism", Migration Policy Institute, June 2006.

[29] C. González-Enríquez and A. Triandafyllidou (2009), "Introduction: Comparing the New Hosts of Southern Europe", *European Journal for Migration and Law,* Vol. 11(2), pp. 109–118.

[30] K. Kruma (2010), "Latvian Integration Policy: Lost in Translation", in R. van Oers, E. Ersbøll and D. Kostakopoulou (eds.), A Re-definition of Belonging? *Language and Integration Tests in Europe*, Martinus Nijhoff: Leiden, pp. 241–249.

2. *What is meant by European Union?*

The main research question for this book is to see to what extent the EU is constructing a new "Legal Other" through the implementation of the Long-term Residence Directive. This Directive has however, I argue, the potential to become a subsidiary form of EU citizenship which escapes direct control by Member States. Thus, it seems appropriate, before advancing any further, to provide some clarification as to the significance of certain terms. I will begin with the meaning of the EU. The EU is not a single consistent actor. On the contrary, it has different institutions with diverse ideas and interests in the area. The concept of change plays a remarkable role here since the balance of power of the different institutions shifts with every new Treaty. In addition, the ideas inside each institution evolve as well. Hence, a review of the position of the different actors is relevant at this point, especially in the light of the changes that the Lisbon Treaty has brought.

2.1. *The European Commission*

It can be argued that the European Commission has, in general, played a proactive role in immigration matters.[31] It has done so with a variety of policy initiatives some of which will be acknowledged in the following Chapter. These initiatives have come from an understanding of migration as a positive economic factor. Sometimes, these proposals have also come with a big push towards the integration of migrants whether of a non-community origin or not.[32] In addition to the economic motivations, two other factors are acknowledged by Geddes in order to understand the Commission's stance. First, Commissioners and the Commission staff are less vulnerable to pressure for supporting tougher immigration policies as they do not have to face

---

[31] It is acknowledged, however, that the different Directorates General inside the Commission may sometimes have divergent approaches with regard to immigration. See on this G. Papagianni (2006), *Institutional and Policy Dynamics of EU Migration Law*, Martinus Nijhoff Publishers: Leiden/Boston, at 249.

[32] In 1985, the Commission stated the following: "Migrant communities, whether of Community or non-Community origin, face much the same problems in their social and working lives. It is a constant factor of the Community approach to these problems that the aim should be equality of treatment in living and working conditions for all migrants, whatever their origin, and workers who are not nationals". Commission Communication, Guidelines for a Community Policy on Migration, COM (1985) 48 final, Bulletin of the European Communities, Supplement 9/85, 7.3.1985. Quoted in P. Oliver (1985), "Non-Community Nationals and the Treaty of Rome", *Yearbook of European Law*, Vol. 5, p. 57–92, at 77.

re-election.[33] Hence, it is also easier for non-governmental organizations (NGOS) and pro-migrant groups to lobby them. Second, it is important to understand that:

> Pro-migrant Commission activity need not arise because the Commission has a positive view about the rights of migrants (it may or may not), but because it has a positive view about the role of the Commission (it certainly does).[34]

In that way, the Commission's activity may have important and positive spillover effects for third-country nationals within the EU. The Commission will have a very important role in the transposition of European Directives.[35]

2.2. *The European Parliament*

Turning now to the European Parliament, its role has always been diminished by its lack of legal power. Its stance has always been positive towards immigration and immigrant rights, more aligned with the Commission's,[36] as opposed to the Council's views. This positive attitude is explained by some commentators by the Parliament's sensitivity to human rights.[37] This lack of legal power has definitively changed with the Lisbon Treaty. In fact, the European Parliament has gained co-decision power in many areas from which it was previously excluded. Among them, legal migration[38] and integration of third-country nationals[39] are the most important ones. Whether this will lead to less restrictive legislation at an EU level or not is something which will require further empirical analysis.[40] Suffice it to say here that the second important

---

33 A. Geddes (2000), *Immigration and European Integration. Towards Fortress Europe?*, Manchester University Press: Manchester, at 139.

34 *Ibid.*, at 139–40.

35 G. Papagianni (2006), *Institutional and Policy Dynamics of EU Migration Law*, Martinus Nijhoff Publishers: Leiden/Boston, at 245.

36 However, it is important to note that on many occasions the European Parliament has gone further in its demands than what the European Commission was willing to propose.

37 G. Papagianni, (2006), *Institutional and Policy Dynamics of EU Migration Law*, Martinus Nijhoff Publishers: Leiden/Boston, at 252.

38 It was previously governed by unanimous voting. See S. Peers (2007), "EU Reform Treaty: Analysis 1: Version 3 JHA Provisions", Statewatch Analysis 22 October 2007, *at* http://www.statewatch.org/news/2007/oct/eu-refrom-treaty-jha-anal-1-ver-3.pdf (accessed 1 December 2010).

39 The integration of third-country nationals constitutes a new legal base.

40 Juss warns about the danger of considering supranationalisation as a "self-evident antidote to the exclusionary and securitized migration policy that has been enacted through intergovernmental cooperation". In S. Juss (2005), "The Decline and Decay of European Refugee Policy", *Oxford Journal of Legal Studies*, Vol. 25, 749–792, at 751.

piece of immigration legislation in which the European Parliament has participated,[41] the Returns Directive,[42] has been tremendously criticised,[43] not least because of the poor performance of the European Parliament.[44] This could have been expected if one had borne in mind that the institutional struggles in Europe between the Parliament and the Council to gain more legal power may have contributed to a certain parliamentary consensus, giving the impression that ideological factors were not important in migration matters.[45] In fact, Monar showed that there were important discrepancies along ideological lines in the positions of the Parliament and how sometimes these positions were only adopted with exiguous majorities.[46] This might change with co-decision being the normal procedure and consequently ideology on immigration might regain its importance, as has been seen with the adoption of the Returns Directive. Furthermore, as the European Parliament has co-decision power in this matter, many Member States' governments may see this as an opportunity to encourage their own Members of the European

---

[41] The Schengen Borders Code was the first immigration measure to be adopted by co-decision. See Regulation (EC) No 562/2006 of the European Parliament and of the Council establishing a Community Code on the rules governing the movement of persons across borders (Schengen Borders Code), 15 March 2006, OJ 2006 L 105/1.

[42] Directive 2008/115/EC of the European Parliament and of the Council of 16 December 2008 on common standards and procedures in Member States for returning illegally staying third-country nationals, OJ 2008 L 348/98.

[43] D. Acosta Arcarazo (2009), "Latin American Reactions to the Adoption of the Returns Directive", Centre for European Policy Studies, CEPS: Brussels, 13 November 2009.

[44] See on the negotiations for adopting the Directive, D. Acosta (2009), "The Good, the Bad and the Ugly in EU Migration Law: Is the European Parliament Becoming Bad and Ugly (The Adoption of Directive 2008/115: The Returns Directive)", *European Journal of Migration and Law*, Vol. 11(1), pp. 19–39; See on the Directive, A. Baldaccini (2009), "The Return and Removal of Irregular Migrants under EU Law: An Analysis of the Returns Directive", *European Journal of Migration and Law*, Vol. 11(1), pp 1–17; D. Acosta (2010), "Migration and Borders in the European Union: The Implementation of the Returns Directive on Irregular Migrants in Spain and Italy", in E. Zapata (ed.), *Shaping the Normative Contours of the European Union: a Migration-Border Framework*, Cidob Foundation: Barcelona, pp. 81–95.

[45] G. Lahav (1997), "Ideological and Party Constraints on Immigration Attitudes in Europe", *Journal of Common Market Studies*, Vol. 35(3), pp. 377–406, at 395.

[46] J. Monar (1995), "The European Parliament and Immigration Policy: its Positions and Possibilities of Control", in P.M. Twomey and G.D. Korella (eds.), *Towards a European Immigration Policy: Current Situation-Perspectives*, European Interuniversity Press: Brussels, pp. 123–137. See also on this, G. Lahav (2004), *Immigration and Politics in the New Europe. Reinventing Borders*, Cambridge University Press: Cambridge, at p. 126–135; S. Hix (2001), "Legislative Behaviour and Party Competition in the European Parliament: An Application of Nominate to the EU", *Journal of Common Market Studies*, Vol. 39(4), pp. 663–88.

Parliament (MEPs) to vote in favour of their position in the Council.[47] Once again, this occurred in the adoption of the Returns Directive.[48]

2.3. *The Council of the European Union*

When referring to Member States and the Council, generalisations are always inadequate. First, because not all of the Member States have opposed the "communitarisation" of immigration policy, with most of them being in favour at least some of the time. In fact, they all agreed to include an EU immigration competence in the Treaty of Amsterdam. Second, because a change of government represents in many cases an alteration of stance of a particular State with regard to these matters. Third, Member State's positions may also be influenced by historical factors. However, even taking due account of all these factors, it seems clear that Member States coped better with the loss of discretion over other EU nationals than with the prospects of losing it over other third-country nationals.[49] Member States have been reluctant to give up power in this area, as they consider it a core part of their sovereignty.[50] It is obvious that unanimity voting in the Council has made the adoption of Directives a slow process. The outcome has always been, as mentioned earlier, closer to a lowest common denominator.[51] The introduction of the qualified majority voting rule with the Treaty of Lisbon, combined with the new powers of the European Parliament, might change this situation. Once again, it is important to be careful with certain assumptions as "it is not certain that a qualified majority voting system would be more efficient than unanimity".[52] In fact, it has been argued, that qualified majority voting requires alliances that are difficult to obtain for long legal texts.[53]

---

47 H. Farrell and A. Héritier (2003), "The Invisible Transformation of Codecision: Problems of Democratic Legitimacy", Report No. 7, Swedish Institute for European Policy Studies (SIEPS): Stockholm, at 9.

48 See D. Acosta (2009), "The Good, the Bad and the Ugly in EU Migration Law: Is the European Parliament Becoming Bad and Ugly (The Adoption of Directive 2008/115: The Returns Directive)", *European Journal of Migration and Law,* Vol. 11(1), pp. 19–39, at 38.

49 E. Guild (2001), *Immigration Law in the European Community,* Kluwer Law International: The Hague, at 17.

50 B. Melis (2001), *Negotiating Europe's Immigration Frontiers*, Kluwer Law International: The Hague, at 124.

51 G. Papagianni (2006), *Institutional and Policy Dynamics of EU Migration Law*, Martinus Nijhoff Publishers: Leiden/Boston, at 204.

52 *Ibid.*, at 225.

53 G. Elkaïm (2005), "Quelques Remarques du Point de Vue du Négociateur" in F. J. Laferriere, H. Labayle and O. Edström, *La Politique Européenne d'Immigration et d'Asile : Bilan Critique Cinq Ans après le Traité d'Amsterdam*, Bruylant : Bruxelles, at 85–91.

2.4. *The Court of Justice of the European Union*

In turn, the CJEU had minimum involvement in immigration matters up until the Maastricht Treaty.[54] Apart from an important case regarding Commission's Decision 85/381,[55] the rest of the cases involved family members of EU nationals exercising free movement rights, employees of a firm providing services in another Member State and the rights of foreign nationals under the third-country agreements.[56] This first jurisdiction of the Court was well received by academic commentators.[57] However, since Maastricht, the distrust that certain judgments created in some Member States led to the Court limiting its jurisdiction over immigration matters.[58] According to Article 68(1) of the Treaty establishing the European Community (TEC), Article 234 EC on preliminary rulings was restricted to be used before tribunals against whose decisions there was no judicial remedy under national law. During the period in which Amsterdam applied, the Court decided some important judgments on European citizens which also had an impact on third-country nationals; *Metock* is certainly the most important one in that sense.[59] With the Lisbon

---

[54] W. Alexander counted 13 judgments affecting the legal status of nationals of third countries up until 1992. See W. Alexander (1992), "Free Movement of Non-EC Nationals. A Review of the Case-Law of the Court of Justice", *European Journal of International Law*, Vol. 3(1), pp 53–64.

[55] Case 281, 283–5 & 287/85, *Germany and others v. Commission* [1987] ECR 3203.

[56] With regard to the last category, it is important to mention Case C-192/89 *Sevince* [1990] ECR I-3461 and Case C-18/90, *Kziber* [1991] ECR I-199. The first one provides for the direct effect of certain provisions of Decisions Nos. 2/76 and 1/80 of the Association Council with Turkey. The second one concerns the possibility of direct application of the discrimination clause contained in the cooperation agreement with Morocco. See W. Alexander (1992), "Free Movement of Non-EC Nationals. A Review of the Case-Law of the Court of Justice", *European Journal of International Law*, Vol. 3(1), pp 53–64, at 60–63.

[57] There are, nevertheless, some critics. See for instance, J.H.H. Weiler (1992), "Thou Shalt Not Oppress a Stranger. On the Judicial Protection of the Human Rights of Non-EC Nationals- A Critique" European *Journal of International Law*, Vol. 3, pp 65–91.

[58] See E. Guild and S. Peers (2001), "Deference or Defiance? The Court of Justice's Jurisdiction over Immigration and Asylum" in E. Guild and C. Harlow (eds.), *Implementing Amsterdam. Immigration and Asylum Rights in EC Law*, Hart Publishing: Oxford, pp. 267–290. According to Guild and Peers, the Court would have appeased the fears of some Member States, reassuring them of their powers in the immigration area. See also W. Alexander (1992), "Free Movement of Non-EC Nationals. A Review of the Case-Law of the Court of Justice", *European Journal of International Law*, Vol. 3(1), pp 53–64, at 64, who mentions Case 12/86 *Demirel* [1987] ECR 1573.

[59] See on *Metock*: D. Acosta (2009), "Immigration in the European Union: Family Reunification after the Metock Case", *UCD Law Review*, Vol. 9, pp. 64–88; C. Costello (2009), "*Metock*: Free Movement and "Normal Family Life" in the Union", *Common Market Law Review*,

Treaty, the Court gains a new impetus. In fact, its regular jurisdiction applies to immigration without any further limitations, as all national Courts can refer a question, and not only those of last instance.[60] This is obviously a great step forward. Consequently, the main interest of this research lies in seeing how the Court could interpret some of the provisions in the Long-term Residence Directive in light of its previous jurisprudence on Turkish workers, European citizens and on other immigration Directives such as the family reunification one. In that sense, it is important to mention that the CJEU has favoured a teleological interpretation taking seriously the intentions of the legislator by carefully analysing the operative part as well as the preambles.

2.5. *The European Council*

The European Council defines the general political direction and priorities of the EU and has become a Union institution since the entry into force of the Treaty of Lisbon. It consists of the Heads of State or Government of the Member States, together with its President and the President of the Commission and meets four times per year. The European Council as an actor in migration matters in the EU gained importance in 1999 when it adopted the Tampere conclusions which contained the dogma of almost equal treatment for third-country nationals with European citizens, as will be seen below in Chapter 2.[61] However, the European Council has not always been consistent in this approach. This can be seen in the differences present between the European Pact on Asylum and Immigration, adopted in 2008, and the Stockholm programme, endorsed by the European Council in 2009.[62] The role that the Presidency plays is

---

Vol. 46, pp. 587–622; A. Tryfonidou (2009), "Family Reunification Rights of (Migrant) Union Citizens: Towards a More Liberal Approach", *European Law Journal*, Vol. 15(5), pp. 634–653; S. Peers (2009), "Free Movement, Immigration Control and Constitutional Conflict", *European Constitutional Law Review*, Vol. 5, pp. 173–196; S. Currie (2009), "Accelerated Justice or a Step too Far? Residence Rights of non-EU Family Members and the Court's Ruling in Metock", *European Law Review*, Vol. 34(2), pp. 310–326; J. Handoll (2009), "The Metock Case. Union Citizenship, Family Reunion and the Abuse of Rights" in P. Minderhoud and N. Trimikliniotis (eds.) (2009), *Rethinking the Free Movement of Workers: The European Challenges Ahead*, Wolf Legal Publishers: Nijmegen, pp. 173–187.

60 See S. Peers (2007), "EU Reform Treaty: Analysis 1: Version 3 JHA Provisions", Statewatch Analysis 22 October 2007, *at* http://www.statewatch.org/news/2007/oct/eu-refrom-treaty-jha-anal-1-ver-3.pdf (accessed 1 December 2010, at 2; S. Carrera and F. Geyer (2007), "The Reform Treaty & Justice and Home Affairs. Implications for the Common Area of Freedom, Security & Justice", CEPS Policy Brief No. 141, Centre for European Policy Studies, CEPS: Brussels, at 3.

61 See Chapter 2 below.

62 See Chapter 2 below.

important in understanding these differences in the position of the European Council throughout the years.[63] The fact that the European Council now has a permanent president might be important in giving more stability to its position. Moreover, the European Council's power has been reinforced in various areas to the detriment of the Council, as Monar has pointed out.[64]

The Stockholm programme recalls once again the Tampere dogma of almost equal treatment for third-country nationals, as will be seen below in the next Chapter.[65] This seems an unconscious recognition that such a principle has yet to be achieved and shows the tension between the direction that the European Council is sometimes willing to take and the final result once legislation has been adopted by the Council.[66] This divergence can only be solved by the interpretation of the CJEU.

3. *The "Legal Other"*

The main question of this work is to assess the potential of the long-term residence status to become a subsidiary form of EU citizenship escaping direct control by Member States. In other words, it examines whether the EU is constructing a "Legal Other" through the implementation of the Long-term Residence Directive, or if on the contrary, third-country nationals are getting closer in status to European citizens. Hence, it is key to understand what is meant by "Other" from a legal point of view.

This study defines "Legal Other" to mean those third-country nationals who do not have an independent right of entry to reside and work in the EU. This concept is constantly changing. There are two different processes which have provided for this change since 1999. First, there is enlargement. Citizens of the 12 new Member States were part of the "Legal Other" before 2004 and 2007. However, after both enlargements, these citizens were automatically transformed, with limitations in some cases, into the privileged group. Hence, there is a transition between third-country nationals and European citizens.[67]

---

63 See on the role of the Presidency A. Schout (1998), "The Presidency as a Juggler- Managing Conflicting Expectations", Eipascope, No 2, 1998, p. 2–10.

64 See J. Monar (2010), "The Institutional Balance after the Treaty of Lisbon", Global Jean Monnet/ECSA-World Conference, Brussels, 25–26 May 2010.

65 See Chapter 2 below.

66 This relationship between the European Council and the Justice and Home Affairs Council has been well depicted by Papagianni. See G. Papagianni, (2006), *Institutional and Policy Dynamics of EU Migration Law*, Martinus Nijhoff Publishers: Leiden/Boston, at 219–220.

67 E. Guild (2007), "Citizens without a Constitution, Borders without a State: EU Free Movement of Persons" in A. Baldaccini, E. Guild and H. Toner (eds.) *Whose Freedom, Security and Justice?*, Hart Publishing: Oxford, pp. 25–55, at 25–26.

Second, there are agreements signed between the EU and other countries which will be analysed in the following pages. These agreements may have the effect of transforming the "Other" into "Us", as in the case of the agreement with Switzerland, or of improving the situation of the "Other" from a particular country, as in the case of the agreement with Croatia for instance.

For the sake of coherence, it is important to see who the third-country nationals who can be considered as "Other" are. Those third-country nationals are precisely the ones interested in the effects of the Long-term Residence Directive. The only plausible way to do this from a legal perspective is by seeing, country by country, those who are inside and those who are outside. This distinction is made at a European level. At a national level, there are different rules that could apply with reference to, for example, acquisition of nationality. Finally, it is also important to understand that both groups, "Us" and "Other", are not legally consistent. Therefore, there are different gradations within both. Hence a classification approach is needed.[68]

3.1. *Who is inside the "Us" Group?*

Who is inside? Which third-country nationals cannot be considered from a legal point of view as an "Other"? The following groups of nationals are inside although different layers exist between them. Hence, it is possible to establish an imperfect hierarchy (see Diagram I). This hierarchy is imperfect for two reasons. First, the closeness to the core of "Us" varies depending on the aspect that is examined (e.g. nationals of one Member State might have more difficulty being reunited with family members than other European citizens residing in that same Member State). Second, the hierarchy changes with time (e.g. nationals of the new Member States which joined the EU in 2004 and 2007 will soon have the same rights as nationals of the Member States already part of the Union in 2004).

Nationals of a Member State residing in their own Member State

They constitute the first of the concentric circles inside the "Us" group. These persons have certain rights which other European citizens residing in that Member State do not have. These include the right to vote in the national elections or the right not to be expelled from their own country. However,

[68] There are other authors who use a different way of categorising the groups. Layton-Henry distinguishes for instance between insiders who are really insiders, insiders who are outsiders, outsiders who are insiders and outsiders who are beyond the Pale. See Z. Layton-Henry (1999), "Insiders and Outsiders in the European Union: The Search for a European Identity and Citizenship", in E. Guild (ed.), *The Legal Framework and Social Consequences of Free Movement of Persons in the European Union*, Kluwer Law International: The Hague, pp. 49–58.

there are certain areas in which European citizens might have better rights than nationals, such as family reunification. This phenomenon is known as reverse discrimination.[69]

European citizens

Nationals of the ex EU15[70] form the core of the inside group. They enjoy their free movement rights without any further limitations.[71]

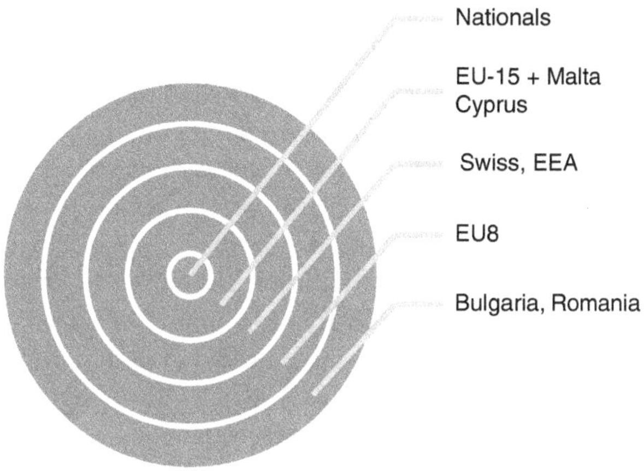

Diagram I: *The "Us" hierarchy*

European citizens of the new Member States which have entered the EU since 2004

These citizens have been labelled as "insiders yet outsiders".[72] They enjoy the right of movement to become self-employed in any other Member State if

[69] See on this A. Walter (2008), *Reverse Discrimination and Family Reunification*, Wolf Legal Publishers: Nijmegen.

[70] These are Austria, Belgium, Denmark, Finland, France, Germany, Greece, Ireland, Italy, Luxembourg, the Netherlands, Portugal, Spain, Sweden and the UK.

[71] The only limitations applicable are those of public policy, public security and public health, and some economic limitations not to become a burden on the social security system of another Member State. See Directive 2004/38/EC of the European Parliament and of the Council of 29 April 2004 on the right of citizens of the Union and their family members to move and reside freely within the territory of the Member States [2004] OJ L158/77. See on this S. Carrera (2005), "What Does Free Movement Mean in Theory and Practice in an Enlarged EU?", *European Law Journal*, Vol. 11(6), pp. 699–721.

[72] N. Rollason (2007), "Citizenship and the Expanding European Union: the Rights of New EU Nationals" in A. Baldaccini, E. Guild and H. Toner (eds.) *Whose Freedom, Security and Justice?*, Hart Publishing: Oxford, pp. 517–28.

they have entered and remained regularly in that State.[73] However, with regard to free movement of workers, a distinction must be made between the following countries:

• *Nationals of Malta and Cyprus*: their nationals enjoy, from the date of accession, free movement of workers without any further limitation. Therefore, they can be considered as forming part of the core as well.

• *Nationals of the other eight countries (EU8) that entered the EU in 2004*:[74] the free movement of workers is limited by transitional arrangements. These countries had a changing regime with the passing of the years. During the first two years following their accession, access to the labour markets depended on the national law as well as the bilateral agreements that they had with the old Member States. Basically, only Sweden, Ireland and the United Kingdom (UK)[75] granted unlimited free movement of workers to these citizens. At the end of these first two years, each Member State decided whether to continue with national law measures for three more years or whether to apply the Union law[76] regime of full free movement of workers. Essentially, only Germany, Austria, Denmark and Belgium kept the restrictions, with France,[77] Luxembourg,[78] the Netherlands,[79] Italy,[80] Greece, Spain, Portugal and Finland[81] joining the three Member States which had already granted free movement of workers. After this period of five years (2+3), a Member State

[73] E. Guild (2004), "Who is an Irregular Migrant?" in B. Bogusz, R. Cholewinski, A. Cygan and E. Szyszczak (eds.), *Irregular Migration and Human Rights: Theoretical, European and International Perspectives*, Martinus Nijhoff Publishers: Leiden/Boston, pp. 3–28, at 8.

[74] These are Czech Republic, Estonia, Hungary, Latvia, Lithuania, Poland, Slovakia and Slovenia.

[75] In the UK, citizens coming from the EU8 who wanted to work for an employer for more than one month had to register under the Worker Registration Scheme. Once they had been working in the UK legally for 12 months without a break in employment, they no longer had to register on the Scheme and were able to obtain a residence permit confirming the right to live and work in the UK. Interestingly, non-citizens from Latvia did not have the right to work in the UK under the Worker Registration Scheme but had to apply for permission to enter the UK before going to work there. This scheme ended at the end of April 2011.

[76] I will use the term Union law to refer to European Union law even when it predates 1 December 2009.

[77] France lifted the restrictions from 1 July 2008.

[78] Luxembourg lifted the restrictions from 1 November 2007.

[79] The Netherlands lifted the restrictions from 1 May 2007.

[80] Italy lifted the restrictions from 27 July 2006.

[81] Greece, Spain, Portugal and Finland decided to open their labour markets from 1 May 2006.

could ask the Commission to extend the period for two more years but only if it experienced serious disturbances within its labour market. This was the case in Germany and Austria where citizens from these eight Member States still had to apply for a work permit prior to commencing employment although the conditions for obtaining such a permit were eased in some sectors or professions.[82] These national measures irrevocably ended on 30 April 2011 at the latest as the transitional arrangements could not be extended beyond an absolute maximum of seven years.[83]

• *Nationals of Bulgaria and Romania*: A similar 2+3+2 scheme is in place with regard to workers from these two countries that joined the EU on 1 January 2007. All EU15 countries, with the exception of Finland and Sweden, restricted the free movement of workers from Bulgaria and Romania. The new ten Member States liberalised access of Romanian and Bulgarian workers to their markets, except for Hungary and Malta. After the first two years, only Greece, Spain, Hungary and Portugal lifted all the barriers from 1 January 2009. Denmark followed them from 1 May 2009. The remaining ten EU25 Member States went on applying some restrictions although they simplified their procedures or reduced restrictions in some sectors or professions.

Citizens of Norway, Iceland and Liechtenstein

These citizens have basically the same rights as citizens of Member States with regard to freedom of movement for workers, freedom of establishment and free movement for the economically inactive. This comes as a result of the 1994 European Economic Area (EEA) Agreement.[84] Moreover, Iceland is also a candidate to join the EU, as will be analysed below. Thus, it can be argued that they are more privileged than citizens of the EU8 and those from Bulgaria and Romania. This is also the case for Swiss citizens. However, once the transitional arrangements come to an end, they will be at the same level as citizens from the new EU Member States.

---

[82] In the UK, as has been seen above, they had to register under the Workers Registration Scheme.

[83] E. Guild (2009), "Free Movement of Workers: From Third Country National to Citizen of the Union" in P. Minderhoud and N. Trimikliniotis (eds.) (2009), *Rethinking the Free Movement of Workers: The European Challenges Ahead*, Wolf Legal Publishers: Nijmegen, pp. 25–38.

[84] Agreement signed in Porto on 2 May 1992, OJ 1994 L1. See on this N. Rogers and R. Scannell (2005), *Free Movement of Persons in the Enlarged European Union*, Sweet and Maxwell: London, especially at 249–252.

Citizens of Switzerland

Switzerland never became part of the EEA because of a negative referendum result in 1992. However, seven agreements with the Community entered into force on 1 June 2002.[85] One of them concerned free movement of persons.[86] As is the case with the citizens of Norway, Iceland and Liechtenstein, Swiss nationals have free movement of workers and establishment and also free movement for the economically inactive.[87] A referendum held in Switzerland in 2009 on the free entry of Romanian and Bulgarian citizens confirmed the validity of these agreements.[88] The concept of citizenship is excluded.[89]

Family members of European citizens residing in another Member State

Directive 2004/38 affects family members (even if they are third-country nationals) of Union citizens who move to another Member State for the purpose of working, studying or who have sufficient resources. Hence, it does not cover internal situations, which are regulated by national law.[90] The family members affected by this Directive are identified in Article 2 which differentiates between those who absolutely have to be granted access to the territory of the Member State[91] and those whose entry and residence must be facilitated.[92] The Directive makes an important advancement in the sense that it provides

85 Decision of the Council, and of the Commission as regards the agreement on Scientific and Technological cooperation of April 4 2002 on the conclusion of seven agreements with the Swiss Confederation, OJ 2002 L 114/1.

86 OJ 2002 L114/6.

87 N. Rogers and R. Scannell (2005), *Free Movement of Persons in the Enlarged European Union*, Sweet and Maxwell: London, at 251–52.

88 International Herald Tribune, *Swiss Referendum Favours Wider Economic Ties to EU*, 9 February 2009.

89 See S. Peers (2000), "The EC-Switzerland Agreement on Free Movement of Persons: Overview and Analysis", *European Journal of Migration and Law*, Vol. 2(2), pp. 127–142.

90 Cases C-64/96 & 65/96, *Land Nordrhein-Westfalen v. Uecker and Jacquet v. Land Nordhein-Westfalen* [1997] ECR I-3171. Also see Cases 35&36/82, *Morson and Jhanjan v. Netherlands* [1982] ECR 3723.

91 Notably the spouse, the registered partner (if the host Member State treats registered partnerships as equivalent to marriage), the direct descendants who are under 21 or are dependants (as well as those of the spouse or partner) and, finally, the dependent direct relatives in the ascending line (and those of the spouse or partner).

92 Any other family members who, in the country from which they have come, are dependants or members of the household of the Union citizen, or where serious health grounds require the personal care of the family member by the Union citizen, and the partner with whom the Union citizen has a durable relationship, duly attested.

for an independent right of residence[93] in the event of death or departure of the Union citizen (Article 12), in the event of divorce, annulment of marriage or termination of registered partnership (Article 13), or after five years of residence (Article 16). This independent right is subject to the fulfilment of some requirements (of which the most important is that the marriage has lasted for three years).[94] This right of residence is complemented by the related rights to work and to receive equal treatment with nationals of the Member State (Articles 23 and 24).[95] Hence, from a legal point of view, these persons can be considered as part of the inside group regardless of their nationality, as they have a family link with an EU citizen who has exercised his[96] free movement rights.

3.2. *Who is the "Legal Other"?*

Once the "Us" is considered, attention must be paid to the "Other". Which third-country nationals have an interest in the Long-term Residence Directive? The EU has signed different types of agreements with various countries. These agreements are based on Article 217 of the Treaty on the Functioning of the EU (TFEU)[97] that allows the Union to conclude agreements with other countries or international organisations. Hence, as before, these kinds of agreements produce differences among the diverse third-country nationals; as in the case with the "Us", there is a hierarchy here too, which is also both imperfect and changeable (e.g. Turkish citizens are more privileged today than Croatians but that will change if Croatia joins the Union before Turkey). (See Diagram II.)

[93] This was not the case before as was made clear by Case 267/83, *Diatta v. Land Berlin* [1985] ECR 567.

[94] This requirement comes within the framework of the Council Resolution of 4 December 1997 on measures to be adopted on the combating of marriages of convenience [1997] OJ C382/01. See B. de Hart (2006), "The Marriage of Convenience in European Immigration Law", *European Journal of Migration and Law*, Vol. 8(3), pp. 251–62.

[95] These rights are also complemented by Council Regulation 1408/71, [1971] OJ L149.

[96] He, him or his will be used to denote both the masculine and the feminine gender.

[97] Art 217 provides that: "The Union may conclude an agreement with one or more third countries or international organisations agreements establishing an association involving reciprocal rights and obligations, common action and special procedure".

Citizens of candidate countries for accession to the EU

• *Turkey:*[98] The European Economic Community (EEC)-Turkey Association agreement signed in 1963 (the Ankara Agreement)[99] was the first step towards the accession of Turkey. It was the second agreement of its kind and replicated much of a previous agreement between the Community and Greece. An Additional Protocol to the agreement was signed in 1970.[100] One of the most important provisions in the Ankara Agreement was the establishment of an Association Council capable of making decisions with regard to the agreement. This Association Council promulgated Decisions from 1976[101] to 1980[102] to give effect to the ongoing accomplishment of free movement.[103] Decision 1/80 provides Turkish workers and their families with important rights, subject to previous legal residence in one Member State. Among them it is central to note that after one year of lawfully residing and working in a Member State, a Turkish national will have the right to remain and work if his position in the labour force is secure and stable. After three years, and subject to the priority to be given to workers of Member States of the Union, the Turkish worker will be able to respond to another offer of employment, with an employer of his choice, made under normal conditions and registered with the employment services of that State, for the same occupation. After four years he will have free access to the labour market. There is extensive case law on these provisions.[104] There are also provisions dealing with establishment (Articles 13 and 14 of the Ankara Agreement and 41 of the Additional Protocol), family members (Article 7 of Decision 1/80) and expulsion (Article 14 of Decision 1/80). Finally, Article 13 of the Decision

[98] The Helsinki European Council of December 1999 granted the status of candidate country to Turkey. Accession negotiations with Turkey were opened in October 2005.

[99] 64/732/EEC: Council Decision of 23 December 1963 on the conclusion of the Agreement establishing an Association between the European Economic Community and Turkey OJ 1964 217/3685.

[100] Additional Protocol and Financial Protocol signed on 23 November 1970, annexed to the Agreement establishing the Association between the European Economic Community and Turkey and on measures to be taken for their entry into force - Final Act – Declarations Signed on 23 November 1970, OJ 1972 L 293/4.

[101] Decision 2/76.

[102] Decisions 1/80 and 3/80.

[103] E. Guild (2001), *Immigration Law in the European Community,* Kluwer Law International: The Hague, at 96.

[104] See N. Rogers (2000), *A Practitioner's Guide to the EC-Turkey Association Agreement*, Kluwer Law International: The Hague; N. Rogers and R. Scannell (2005), *Free Movement of Persons in the Enlarged European Union*, Sweet and Maxwell: London.

prohibits within the fields of its application the introduction of new restrictive measures, including those which have to do with family members of Turkish workers.

• *Croatia*[105] *and the Former Yugoslav Republic of Macedonia (FYROM):*[106] They have both signed a Stabilisation and Association Agreement (SAA) with the EU.[107] Article 44 of the agreement with FYROM contains a clause which provides for a right to non-discrimination.[108] According to the case law of the Court of Justice, with regard to the previous agreements between the European Community (EC) and the Central and Eastern European Countries (CEEC), this clause has direct effect.[109] Article 45 from the Croatian SAA provides a clause that mirrors the one in the Macedonian agreement. Freedom of establishment for natural persons is also contemplated in the agreements and these provisions have entered into force, although no decision has been taken.[110] Consequently, the Court will have to decide on whether or not they have direct effect.

---

105 The European Council of June 2004 granted the status of candidate country to Croatia and accession negotiations were opened in October 2005.

106 The European Council of 17 December 2005 granted the status of candidate country to the Former Yugoslav Republic of Macedonia.

107 The one with Croatia was signed in October 2001 and entered into force in February 2005. The one with Former Yugoslav Republic of Macedonia was signed April 2001 and entered into force in April 2004. See SAA between the European Communities and their Member States, of the one part, and the Republic of Croatia, of the other part, OJ 2005 L 26/3; SAA between the European Communities and their Member States, of the one part, and the former Yugoslav Republic of Macedonia, of the other part, OJ 2004 L 84/13.

108 According to this Article: "Treatment accorded to workers who are nationals of the former Yugoslav Republic of Macedonia and who are legally employed in the territory of a Member State shall be free of any discrimination based on nationality, as regards working conditions, remuneration or dismissal, compared to its own nationals;
– the legally resident spouse and children of a worker legally employed in the territory of a Member State, with the exception of seasonal workers and of workers coming under bilateral agreements, within the meaning of Article 45, unless otherwise provided by such agreements, shall have access to the labour market of that Member State, during the period of that worker's authorised stay of employment".

109 See Case C-162/00, *Land Nordrhein-Westfalen v Beata Pokrzeptowicz-Meyer* [2002] ECR I-01049.

110 According to Article 49(4) of the Croatian agreement, four years after the entry into force the Stabilisation and Association Council will establish the modalities to extend this freedom to natural persons. In the Macedonian agreement, the same provision comes in Article 48(4) but the period is five years.

• *Iceland*: Iceland submitted its application for EU membership to the Council in July 2009. The European Council decided to open negotiations with Iceland on 17 June 2010. Citizens from Iceland already enjoy a privileged status under the EEA Agreement, as has just been explained above.

Potential candidate countries
Albania,[111] Serbia,[112] Bosnia and Herzegovina,[113] Montenegro[114] and, eventually, Kosovo. These SAA provide citizens of these countries with the same non-discrimination clauses as those present in the agreements with Croatia and Macedonia. These clauses provide for a right to equal treatment. However, they do not grant any residence right.

Partnership and cooperation agreements
The formalisation of bilateral relations between the EU and individual partner countries has been achieved through the negotiation of these agreements, now in force in ten of the Eastern European and Central Asian countries, while two others have been signed but not yet ratified. Those in force are with Russia,[115] Ukraine,[116] Moldova,[117] Armenia, Azerbaijan, Georgia, Kazakhstan, Kyrgyz

[111] The SAA between Albania and the EU was signed in June 2006. An Interim Agreement remained in force from December 2006 as the association agreement had not been ratified. Finally, on 14 January 2009 the agreement was ratified. It entered into force on 1 April 2009. This agreement makes provision in Article 46 for a clause on non-discrimination with the same terms as the ones for Macedonia and Croatia.

[112] Negotiations on a SAA between Serbia and the EU were officially opened in October 2005. The agreement was signed on 29 April 2008. Serbia submitted its candidacy for EU membership on 22 December 2009. The EU Member States decided to start the ratification process of the SAA on 14 June 2010.

[113] Negotiations on a SAA between Bosnia and Herzegovina and the EU were officially opened in November 2005. The agreement was signed on 16 June 2008.

[114] The SAA between Montenegro and the EU was signed in October 2007. An Interim Agreement was also signed on the same date and entered into force in January 2008. The SAA entered into force on 1 May 2010. Montenegro submitted its application for EU membership on 15 December 2008.

[115] This agreement entered into force on 1 December 1997. Article 23 provides for a non-discrimination clause for legally employed Russian workers: "1. Subject to the laws, conditions and procedures applicable in each Member State, the Community and its Member States shall ensure that the treatment accorded to Russian nationals, legally employed in the territory of a Member State shall be free from any discrimination based on nationality, as regards working conditions, remuneration or dismissal, as compared to its own nationals".

[116] The agreement entered into force on 1 March 1998. The same non-discrimination clause is found in Art 24.

[117] This agreement entered into force on 1 July 1998. Art 23 mirrors the one in the Russian agreement on non-discrimination.

Republic, Uzbekistan[118] and Tajikistan.[119] Those which have not yet been ratified are with Belarus and Turkmenistan. All of them have a non-discrimination clause. The CJEU has already given a pronouncement on its meaning in the case of *Simutenkov*.[120] It is very important to mention that the Court held that:

> Article 23 (1) of the Communities-Russia Partnership Agreement has direct effect, with the result that individuals to whom that provision applies are entitled to rely on it before the courts of the Member States.[121]

This case reaffirms the right to equal treatment in working conditions. However, that right is premised on the fact that third-country nationals have already acquired a residence right.

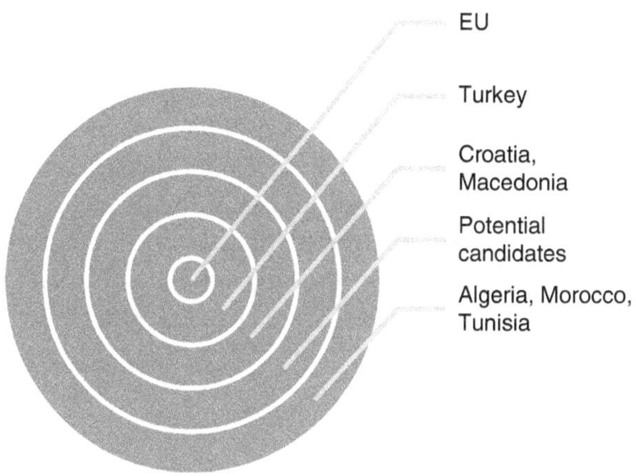

Diagram II: *The "Other" hierarchy*

Algeria, Morocco and Tunisia

The original cooperation agreements with these three countries (the Maghreb Agreements),[122] which contained some clauses on non-discrimination based

---

[118] The agreements with Armenia, Azerbaijan, Georgia, Kazakhstan, Kyrgyz Republic, and Uzbekistan all entered into force on 1 July 1999. The same non-discrimination clauses are found in Art 20, in the case of the first three countries, and in Art 19 in the other three.

[119] The agreement with Tajikistan entered into force on 1 January 2010. The same non-discrimination clause is found in Article 17.

[120] Case C-265/03 *Simutenkov v. Abogado del Estado, Real Federación Española de Fútbol and Ministerio Fiscal* [2005] ECR I-02579.

[121] *Ibid.*, at paragraph 29.

[122] Council Regulation (EEC-Algeria) No 2210/78 of 27/9/78, Council Regulation (EEC-Morocco) No 2211/78 of 27/9/78 and Council Regulation (EEC-Tunisia) No 2212/78 of 27/9/78.

on nationality,[123] have now been supplemented by the Moroccan Euro-Mediterranean agreement,[124] the Euro-Mediterranean agreement with Tunisia[125] and the Euro-Mediterranean agreement with Algeria.[126] They all contain some provisions in terms of non-discrimination in the working conditions, salary and social security for legally resident workers.[127] It is in the field of social security that the CJEU has pronounced more judgments.[128]

Chile

The agreement establishing an association between the European Community and its Member States and the Republic of Chile[129] entered into force on 1 March 2005. It sets out in Article 132 certain establishment rights for natural persons in some sectors, subject to limitations.[130]

The other Mediterranean countries

These agreements are an essential feature of the implementation of the Euro-Mediterranean partnership. In some of them, there are some vague and weak clauses regarding the importance of conducting a social dialogue to improve the working conditions of the nationals of the Mediterranean countries in the EU, especially with regard to equal treatment and social integration. However, the main bulk of the agreements in the migration field have to do with the readmission of irregular migrants. There are agreements with migration

---

123 See J. Apap (2002), *The Rights of Immigrant Workers in the European Union*, Kluwer Law International: The Hague, at 92–93.

124 It entered into force on 1 March 2000, OJ 2000 L70/2.

125 It entered into force on 1 March 1998, OJ 1998 L97/2.

126 It entered into force on 1 September 2005, OJ 2005 L 265/2.

127 See Articles 64–68 of the first two agreements and Articles 67–68 of the Algerian agreement. See on this P.J. Cardwell (2009), *EU External Relations and Systems of Governance. The CFSP, Euro-Mediterranean Partnership and Migration*, Routledge: Oxon.

128 See on this T. Eicke (1999), "The Third Country Agreements: The Right to Work and Reside in the First Generation Agreements", in E. Guild (ed.), *The Legal Framework and Social Consequences of Free Movement of Persons in the European Union*, Kluwer Law International: The Hague, pp 89–103, especially at 100–103. The CJEU has held that the provisions on non-discrimination are capable of having direct effect. See Case C-416/96, *Nour Eddline El-Yassini v Secretary of State for Home Deparment*, [1999] ECR I-01209; Case C-97/05, *Mohamed Gattoussi v Stadt Rüsselsheim*, [2006] ECR I-11917.

129 OJ 2002 L 352/3.

130 N. Rogers and R. Scannell (2005), *Free Movement of Persons in the Enlarged European Union*, Sweet and Maxwell: London, at 264–65.

clauses in force with Egypt,[131] Jordan[132] and Lebanon.[133] The agreement with Israel also contains some migration clauses.[134]

The African, Caribbean and Pacific (ACP) countries

The ACP comprises 79 countries from these three regions in the world. Article 13 of The Cotonou Agreement[135] is devoted to immigration. Notably, Article 13(3) establishes non-discrimination in working conditions. However, in the rest of the clauses in Article 13, the biggest emphasis is on the readmission by these countries of irregular immigrants.

What happens with the rest of third-country nationals? Their status is in the hands of the Member States as their countries of origin do not have any specific agreement with the EU. However, according to my perception, there are two more groups of countries which cannot be included in either the "Us" group or the "Other". They are what Guild labels as "invisible migrants".[136] The following paragraphs explore the legal reasons why these third-country nationals can be considered to come within a grey area, by dividing them into two groups:

Citizens of the European micro-States

These are Andorra, Monaco, San Marino and the Vatican. The citizens of these countries cannot be considered completely as part of the "Us" group, but they resist all attempts to be considered as "Legal Others", although from a purely legal point of view they ought to be. However, one might argue that they are more inside than outside for various reasons. First, with regard to Schengen, three of them have an open border with the EU, with the exception

---

131 The agreement entered into force on 1 July 2004. See Articles 62 to 70 for matters related to immigration, OJ 2004 L 304/39.

132 This agreement entered into force on 1 May 2002. See Articles 80 to 84 for migration related issues. OJ 2002 L 129/3.

133 It entered into force on 1 April 2006. See Article 64 on immigration. OJ 2006 L143/2.

134 The agreement entered into force on 1 June 2000. Article 57 refers to cooperation in migration matters, while Art 64 requires the coordination of social security regimes of legal workers in each other's territory. OJ 2002 L 147/3.

135 Partnership Agreement between the members of the African, Caribbean and Pacific Group of States on the one part, and the European Community and its Member States, on the other part, signed in Cotonou on June 23, OJ 2000 L 317/3.

136 E. Guild (2005), "Cultural and Identity Security. Immigrants and the Legal Expression of National Identity" in E. Guild and J. Van Selm (eds.) *International Migration and Security. Opportunities and Challenges*, Routledge: Oxon, pp. 101–112, at 103.

of Andorra. Second, according to Council Regulation 539/2001,[137] citizens of these countries are exempted from the requirement to obtain a visa to enter the EU for stays of less than three months. Finally, and most importantly, citizens of these States[138] have preferential entrance treatment for work purposes in different EU Member States: France,[139] Germany,[140] Spain[141] and the Netherlands.[142]

Citizens of the USA, Canada, Australia, New Zealand and Japan
Citizens of these countries are not considered as a complete legal "Other" either. This is due to several reasons. First, they do not need a visa to enter the EU for less than three months as in the case above. Second, there are some provisions deriving from national law which benefit the citizens of these countries. For example, there are some Member States which grant them preferential treatment with regard to access to their job market. These include Germany[143] and the Netherlands.[144] Also, they do not have to fulfil certain integration requirements in some countries. For example, citizens of these countries do not have to take the civic integration examination abroad[145] in order to reside

[137] Council Regulation (EC) No 539/2001 of 15 March 2001 listing the third countries whose nationals must be in possession of visas when crossing the external borders and those whose nationals are exempt from that requirement [2001] OJ L 81/1. This Regulation has been amended several times.

[138] The fact that Vatican citizens are not included in the following examples is due to its very small population of around 800 citizens, which consists mainly of the clergy and the Swiss Guard.

[139] Nationals of Andorra and Monaco do not require a work permit. This is according to Art R212-1, 3rd of the Code de l'Entrée et du Séjour des Étrangers et du Droit d'asile (CESEDA).

[140] Citizens of Andorra, Monaco and San Marino are privileged by law for the purposes of taking up employment. See Ecotec Research and Consulting (2000), *Admission of Third Country Nationals for Paid Employment or Self-Employed Activity*, Ecotec: Brussels, p. 109.

[141] Nationals of Andorra have the same treatment as any other EU citizen in Spain. This is according to Article 4 of the 'Convenio entre el Reino de España, la República Francesa y el Principado de Andorra, relativo a la entrada, circulación, residencia y establecimiento de sus nacionales' hecho "ad referendum" en Bruselas el de diciembre de 2002 (BOE núm 153, de 27 de junio de 2003).

[142] Citizens of Monaco have an easier access to the employment market in the Netherlands. Ecotec Research and Consulting (2000), *Admission of Third Country Nationals for Paid Employment or Self-Employed Activity*, Ecotec: Brussels, at 183.

[143] Citizens of Australia, Canada, Japan, New Zealand and the USA have preferential treatment by law with regard to taking up employment. *Ibid.*

[144] Citizens of Australia, Canada, Japan, New Zealand and the USA have better access to the Dutch market. *Ibid.*, at 183.

[145] For an explanation of the civic integration examination abroad see Chapter 7 below.

in the Netherlands.[146] This is also the case in Germany, where spouses of a third-country national wishing to move to Germany need to speak basic German. This requirement does not apply however to citizens of these five countries.[147] In Estonia, citizens of the USA and Japan are exempted from the limitation of the quota system that is imposed on other third-country nationals.[148] In addition, there are also some easier processes with regard to working holidays, for example, in Estonia,[149] Finland,[150] Ireland[151] and Sweden.[152] Finally, it is worth mentioning that these countries have different social security agreements with various countries in Europe. These agreements facilitate the process of working in another country. The analysis of the precise terms of these agreements is outside the scope of this work. EU Member States that have signed some of these Treaties include Austria,[153] Belgium,[154] Cyprus,[155] Czech Republic,[156] Estonia,[157] Poland[158] and the UK.[159]

---

146 C. Adam and A. Devillard (2008), *Comparative Study of the Laws in the 27 EU Member States for Legal Immigration*, IOM: Brussels, at 62.

147 German Residence Act, Art 28(1) sentence 5 and Art 30(1) sentence 1 no. 2 and the exceptions in Art 30(1) sentence 2 and 3 and Art 41 of the Residence Ordinance. See Chapter 7 below. The German Federal Administrative Court decided that foreign policy considerations, which have the effect of treating nationals of certain countries more favourably than others, are within the margin of appreciation of a Member State. See German Federal Administrative Court (BVerwG), judgment of 30 March 2010, case 1 c 8.09.

148 Estonian Aliens Act, Art 6(3).

149 Australia and New Zealand have a Working Holiday Scheme with Estonia. C. Adam and A. Devillard (2008), *Comparative Study of the Laws in the 27 EU Member States for Legal Immigration*, IOM: Brussels, at 219.

150 Finland has a Holiday Agreement with Australia and New Zealand. *Ibid.*, at 231.

151 Australia, Canada, Japan and New Zealand have reciprocal schemes with Ireland to facilitate young people undertaking working holidays.

152 There is an exchange of trainees programme with the US and Canada. Ecotec Research and Consulting (2000), *Admission of Third Country Nationals for Paid Employment or Self-Employed Activity*, Ecotec: Brussels, at 223.

153 These concerned social insurance law with Australia and the USA. C. Adam and A. Devillard (2008), *Comparative Study of the Laws in the 27 EU Member States for Legal Immigration*, IOM: Brussels, at 140.

154 These are related to the field of social security and have been concluded with Australia, Canada and the USA. *Ibid.*, at 155.

155 These are reciprocal agreements in social security with Australia and Canada. *Ibid.*, at 179.

156 There is a bilateral agreement with Canada with regard to pension rights. *Ibid.*, at 191.

157 There is an agreement concerning reciprocal provision of social security with Canada. *Ibid.*, at 219.

158 Poland is negotiating agreements on social security and pension rights with Australia, Canada and the USA. *Ibid.*, at 379.

159 The UK has retirement pension agreements with Canada, New Zealand and the USA. *Ibid.*, at 463.

4. *The Concept of the "Legal Other" in this Book*

Once this distinction between nationalities has been made, and before concluding this part, further clarification is necessary. The concept of the "Legal Other" that I will attempt to develop in this work affects only regular migrants who have prospects to stay in the host State, mainly performing a paid activity. In other words, it embraces regular labour migration (employment or self-employment) with the intention of permanency, that is, migrants who could acquire the long-term residence status provided by Directive 2003/109. Thus, I am focusing on migrants who have been admitted by a Member State, usually in order to work.

Once again, the concept of change plays a notable role here. The subject of my work has no clear-cut boundaries. For example, a third-country national could enter the EU as a student. During that time he would not be the subject of my investigation. However, if, at the end of his studies, he enters the workforce through a process established by the Member State which is willing to retain him, he would be part of my analysis. He would have changed from being a student to being a third-country national regularly working in the EU with a prospect to stay. The same could be said of an undocumented migrant who entered into the EU with a tourist visa and then overstayed the period that he was allowed to stay. He could find his situation regularised by virtue of a campaign. Consequently, he could enter the regular labour force with prospects to remain in that country as that Member State willingly changed his situation. Thus, it can be inferred that the key point is not when the Member State accepted the permanency of that third-country national, but the acceptance of his stay per se. To summarise it can be said that there are two prerequisites for the third-country national to be considered in this work: first, he has the possibility of obtaining a long-term residence permit in the future. Second, he usually performs an economic activity for which he has been admitted into that country.

Accordingly, by *a contrario* reasoning, this book is not about the following categories of third-country nationals:

Family reunification migrants

In this work, family reunification is understood as a right of the sponsor. This has been the case in European law from the very beginning. In fact, the preamble to Regulation 1612/68[160] stated the following:

[160] Regulation (EEC) No 1612/68 of the Council of 15 October 1968 on freedom of movement for workers within the Community, OJ 1968 L 257/2.

> Obstacles to the mobility of workers shall be eliminated, in particular as regards the worker's right to be joined by his family and the conditions for the integration of that family into the host country.

Directive 2003/86 on the right to family reunification[161] for third-country nationals provides for the right of the sponsor to be reunited with certain family members, but there is no independent right for any family member to enter a Member State. If the family member acquires an independent status with the possibility of permanent residence, usually by entering the workforce, he becomes the subject of this work as well.

Asylum seekers

Asylum is a form of protection given by a State on its territory, based on the principle of non-refoulement and internationally or nationally recognised refugee rights. It is granted to a person who is unable to seek protection in his/her country of citizenship and/or residence in particular for fear of being persecuted for reasons of race, religion, nationality, membership of a particular social group or political opinion.[162] The reason for the entry has nothing to do with the economic necessities of the host country or of the person himself as it is involuntary. Hence my analysis will not deal with this category. It will not deal either with those who enjoy other forms of subsidiary or temporary protection.[163] Moreover, people under this kind of protection could not obtain the long-term residence permit under Article 3 of the Directive until 2011. That has however changed with the adoption of a new Directive amending Directive 2003/109 and extending long-term resident status to refugees and persons with subsidiary protection.[164] Once a refugee or a person with subsidiary protection obtains long-term residence he also becomes the subject of this work.

Short-term economic migrants

Temporary or seasonal workers are an important part of the labour force in many countries. Their contribution is essential in many sectors like agriculture,

161 Council Directive 2003/86 of 22 September 2003 on the right to family reunification, OJ 2003 L251/12

162 G. Goodwin Gill and J. Mc Adam (2007), *The Refugee in International Law*, Oxford University Press: Oxford, third edition.

163 J. Mc Adam (2007), *Complementary Protection in International Refugee Law*, Oxford University Press: Oxford.

164 That Directive had not yet been adopted by 1 December 2010. See on this S. Peers (2010), "Extending EU long-term Resident Status to Refugees and Persons with Subsidiary Protection Status", Statewatch Analysis, *at* http://www.statewatch.org/analyses/no-114-ltr.pdf (accessed 1 December 2010).

tourism or construction. Different Member States have agreements with sending countries to implement temporary and circular migration of this workforce. When these kinds of agreements are not put in place there is the risk of an increase in irregular work under precarious conditions. At an EU level, the Commission has proposed a Directive on the conditions of entry and residence of seasonal workers.[165] Taking into account that these workers lack the permanency element of my definition they will not be considered in this work. Seasonal workers are also excluded from the scope of the Long-term Residence Directive under Article 3(2)(e).

Students or researchers
Students and researchers constitute an important proportion of the number of third-country nationals entering Europe every year. Higher education centres and universities are very keen to attract them. These two categories come within the framework of two different Directives.[166] The first concerns the admission of third-country nationals for the purposes of study, pupil exchange, unremunerated training or voluntary service.[167] The second relates to the admission of third-country nationals for the purpose of scientific research.[168] With regard to the first category, students do not constitute labour migration. However, a student could work in the EU after attaining his degree. In that case, it is important to mention that the period of residence as a student would only count as half the time for acquiring long-term residence status.[169] By and large, once a student enters the workforce and has the possibility of acquiring the long-term resident status, he also becomes the subject of this work. Whilst his main purpose is to study he is not taken into consideration here.

With reference to the second category, that of researchers, their status is somewhat controversial. The Directive on their admission does not make any reference to the Long-term Residence Directive. In that Directive, it is not said either if time spent as a researcher will count towards obtaining the long-term residence status or not. It can be presupposed that:

---

165 Proposal for a Directive of the European Parliament and of the Council on the conditions of entry and residence of third-country nationals for the purposes of seasonal employment, COM (2010) 379 final, Brussels, 13.7.2010.

166 See on this A, Wiesbrock (2010), *Legal Migration to the European Union*, Martinus Nijhoff: Leiden, at Chapter 4.

167 Council Directive 2004/114/EC of 13 December 2004 on the conditions of admission of third-country nationals for the purposes of studies, pupil exchange, unremunerated training or voluntary service, OJ 2004 L375/12.

168 Council Directive 2005/71/EC of 12 October 2005 on a specific procedure for admitting third-country nationals for the purpose of scientific research, OJ 2005 L289/15.

169 Article 4(2) of Directive 2003/109.

> In the absence of any explicit derogation in either Directive … researchers will ultimately be able to qualify for long-term residence status, particularly because their residence permits under the researchers' Directive are expressly renewable as long as the conditions for their issue are still met, and therefore should not be considered as "limited" permits taking them outside the scope of the long term residents' Directive.[170]

Considering this, they are to be taken into account as part of the economic labour migration with a permanency element.

Irregular migrants

The challenge of irregular or undocumented migration in Europe[171] is important not in terms of numbers but in terms of the highly politicised debate surrounding it.[172] Irregular migrants are the least protected of the different groups, although they obviously still have certain rights.[173] Irregular migration arises from the lack of legal channels to enter a country, linked with the existence of an unregulated job market in certain sectors. To improve the situation of these workers and to introduce them into the regular workforce, Member States[174] have used regularisation processes in the past.[175] In fact, many of the irregular migrants legally entered the EU, losing their authorisation at a later stage. Once an undocumented migrant regularises his administrative situation in the host country and has prospects of staying for a long period, he becomes the subject of this work as well. In fact, one of the requirements that the

---

170 S. Peers and N. Rogers (2006), *EU Immigration and Asylum Law. Text and Commentary*, Martinus Nijhoff Publishers: Leiden/Boston, at 686–87.

171 See M. Le Voy, N. Verbruggen and J. Wets (eds.) (2004), *Undocumented Migrant Workers in Europe*, PICUM: Brussels.

172 According to the most reliable statistics, there were only between 1.9 and 3.8 million irregular migrants present in the EU in 2008, which merely represented between 0.39 and 0.77 per cent of the total EU population. See V. Kovacheva and D. Vogel (2009) "The Size of the Irregular Foreign Resident Population in the European Union in 2002, 2005 and 2008: Aggregated Estimates", *Hamburg Institute of International Economics*. Database on Irregular Migration. Working Paper No.4/2009.

173 See L. Bicocchi and M. Le Voy (2007), *Undocumented Migrants Have Rights! An Overview of the International Human Rights Framework*, PICUM: Brussels; M. Le Voy and N. Verbruggen (2005), *Ten Ways to Protect Undocumented Migrant Workers*, PICUM: Brussels.

174 For example Belgium, France, Germany, Greece, Italy, Spain, the Netherlands, Portugal, Luxembourg, the UK or Poland. For the Polish case see K. Iglicka, P. Kazmierkiewicz and A. Weinar (2005), "Poland" in J. Niessen, Y. Schibel and C. Thompson (eds.), *Current Immigration Debates in Europe: A Publication of the European Migration Dialogue*, Migration Policy Group: Brussels.

175 See on this: M. Baldwin-Edwards and A. Kraler (eds.) (2009), *REGINE. Regularisations in Europe*, Pallas Publications: Amsterdam; P. de Bruycker (2000) (ed.), *Regularisations of Illegal Immigrants in the European Union*, Bruylant: Brussels.

migrant has to fulfil in order to take advantage of the provisions in the Long-term Residence Directive is to be regularly residing in a Member State (Article 4(1)). The difficulty is that regular migrants do sometimes move in and out of an irregular status.

Naturalised citizens
Citizens who have acquired the citizenship of a Member State are not considered in this work. This is regardless of whether or not they have retained a second nationality. Citizenship in this book is understood as the end of the legal struggle for the immigrant, although he can still be subject to discrimination or racism.[176] Also, citizens returning home are not within the scope of this work nor are possible internal migrations within the different Member States.

5. *Outline of the Book and Research Questions*

In order to conclude this introductory Chapter, an overview of the following Sections is necessary. This book is divided into five Sections and ten Chapters. This introductory Section in which the research topics have been outlined, the main themes and questions summarised and the key concepts and methodology clarified, will give way to the following Chapters in which the main arguments of the book will be developed.

Section II is entitled "Historical Evolution of EU Migration Law" and comprises Chapters 2 and 3. Chapter 2 looks at the historical developments in the area of migration regulation in the EU. It provides a brief chronological overview of the origins of the legislative process in the area before the entry into force, in 1999, of the Treaty of Amsterdam. It then looks in more depth at the policy and legislative developments in the period 1999–2009. The Chapter concludes with a note on the changes brought by the Treaty of Lisbon and the Stockholm programme adopted in 2009.

Chapter 3 examines the genealogy of the Long-term Residence Directive. It commences by assessing the importance of adopting an instrument on long-term residents, as well as the historical legislative antecedents which led to its approval. It then explores the process of adoption, paying significant attention to how the integration conditions entered the negotiations. This illustrates the struggle between Europeanisation and some Member States' willingness to keep their prerogatives. The Chapter concludes by laying down the main

[176] G. Avci (1999), "Immigrant Categories: The Many Sides of the Coin?", *European Journal of Migration and Law*, Vol. 1 (2), pp. 199–213, at 207.

elements in the Directive and introducing the most important Articles, which are consequently critically evaluated in Sections III and IV.

Section II addresses the following research questions:

1. What was the state of migration regulation before the entry into force of the Treaty of Amsterdam? What were the main elements which made the EU realise the suitability of having a common immigration policy?
2. What have been the legislative and policy developments in the area since the entry into force of the Treaty of Amsterdam in 1999 until the end of 2009? What will the entry into force of the Lisbon Treaty, as well as the 2009 programme in the area of Justice and Home Affairs (the Stockholm programme) for the years 2010–2014 mean for migration regulation?
3. Why was it important to adopt a Directive on long-term residents? What were the legislative antecedents?
4. What was the process for adopting the Directive? How did the integration conditions enter the negotiations?
5. What are the main features of the Directive and what are the elements to be analysed in more depth in the following Section?

Section III constitutes a central part of my analysis and comprises Chapters 4 to 6. They deal with three different Articles in the Long-term Residence Directive: Articles 3, 12 and 14. As mentioned before, the rationale for selecting these Articles is that they are arguably the most important in the Directive as they determine who may acquire the long-term residence permit (Article 3), what the protection against expulsion is once the status is granted (Article 12) and, lastly, what the possibilities to move in order to reside and work in a second Member State are, for those third-country nationals who have already acquired this status in one Member State (Article 14). Article 5 which determines how long-term residence may be obtained will be analysed in Section IV where I will consider integration conditions. Each of the Chapters in Section III will deal with one of the Articles and will have a similar structure. The three Chapters begin by explaining the respective Article and its limitations. Those limitations are consequently assessed by summarising the main critiques by other scholars and by seeing whether those limitations were present in the Commission proposal or are applicable to European citizens. The next step is to see how Member States have implemented those provisions and limitations in order to measure if there has been any change with regard to the situation before the approval of the Directive. Finally, the three Chapters look at the way in which the CJEU could interpret the Directive paying special attention to its previous jurisprudence on Turkish workers and European citizens. Following this key analysis, it is possible to draw some conclusions as to the validity of the Long-term Residence Directive in approaching the status of third-country nationals to that of European citizens and becoming a subsidiary form of EU citizenship, or not.

Chapter 4 examines the scope of the Directive paying special attention to Article 3(2). It explores which third-country nationals are excluded from the possibility to obtain the long-term residence permit. Chapter 5 turns to the analysis of Article 12 on the security of residence that a status-holder obtains. It investigates the reasons that Member States may put forward when expelling a long-term resident. Finally, Chapter 6 examines the possibilities under Article 14 that a status-holder has of moving to reside in order to work in another Member State. Hence, the analysis in these three Chapters follows a chronological rationale by answering several questions: Which third-country nationals can acquire the long-term residence status? What is their security of residence once they have obtained that status? What are their free movement possibilities? As mentioned above, the conditions required in order to obtain long-term residence will be analysed in a separate Section below, due to its centrality in understanding the importance of the Directive and its implementation by Member States.

The questions for the three Chapters are similar and can be summarised as follows:

1. What does the Directive say with regard to the scope, security of residence and movement to other Member States?
2. What are the limitations to these provisions? Were those limitations present in the Commission proposal? What have been the main criticisms to those limitations? Are there any similar limitations applicable in any way to European citizens?
3. How are Member States implementing the Directive? Are there any changes with regard to the situation before the adoption of the Directive?
4. What could be the interpretation of the different Articles by the CJEU? Are there any parallelisms that could be drawn from its previous case law on Turkish workers and European citizens?

Section IV consists of Chapters 7, 8 and 9. Chapter 7 deals with the integration conditions in Article 5. Hence, it looks at the conditions that a third-country national, who has already resided for five years in a Member State, has to fulfil before obtaining the status. It also explores the origins of those integration conditions in certain citizenship legislations. It then looks at how integration has been implemented in another European instrument: the Family Reunification Directive. Chapter 8 summarises and categorises the political motivations for the introduction of integration conditions, in order to acquire the long-term residence status, in different Member States, by looking at the political debates preceding those legislative developments. It ends by considering whether those political motivations could be seen as valid for the introduction of integration conditions, or if the rationale behind them runs contrary to the main objective of the Directive, which is to grant those third-country nationals who have regularly resided for a period of five years in a Member State a more secure status. The possible response of the CJEU to these integration conditions is key to assessing the importance of the Directive for third-country nationals as will be seen in Chapter 9.

The main questions for this Section are:

1. What are the origins of the integration conditions in order to obtain a permanent residence status?
2. How are integration requirements implemented in the Family Reunification Directive?
3. Which are the conditions in order to obtain a long-term residence permit? How have Member States implemented the integration conditions?
4. What are the political motivations for introducing integration conditions?
5. Are those political motivations valid or do they run contrary to the final objective of the Directive of granting a more secure status to third-country nationals who have resided for five years in a Member State? How could the CJEU interpret these integration conditions, especially in light of the general principles of Union law?

To conclude, Section V contains Chapter 10. In this last Chapter the main findings are summarised. I also propose some policy recommendations on how to implement and interpret the Long-term Residence Directive. Those recommendations might be relevant for various actors both at a European level (European Commission, CJEU and European Parliament) as well as a national level (national Ministries, national Courts and national practitioners).

Section II

Historical Evolution of EU Migration Law

Chapter 2

The Involvement of the EU in Migration Regulation: From Amsterdam and Tampere to Lisbon and Stockholm

1. *Introduction*

This second Chapter aims to provide the reader with a comprehensive but brief historical framework, in order to understand how the EU became involved in migration regulation. This analysis attempts to illustrate the difficulties encountered in establishing a common immigration policy, due to the different interests and priorities of the actors involved.

The Chapter begins by briefly sketching the reasons that made the engagement of the EU in migration issues inevitable. Following this overview of the motivations, the Chapter will divide the historical analysis into four different periods. The first one covers the years 1957–1999. During that period, there was little activity by the Community on migration issues and everything was dealt with by the Member States acting independently or at an intergovernmental level. That changed in 1999 with the entry into force of the Treaty of Amsterdam and the adoption of a five-year programme for Justice and Home Affairs: the Tampere Programme. Both developments brought a new impetus to the area and there was important legislative activity during the five years of the Tampere Programme, including the adoption of the Long-term Residence Directive in 2003. The years 1999–2004 constitute the second period of analysis. By the end of 2004, the Hague Programme, which replaced the Tampere Programme, was adopted, introducing new priorities and a legislative timetable for the period 2005–2009. Finally, the Chapter will conclude by highlighting the innovations enshrined in the Treaty of Lisbon and the Stockholm Programme, which replaced the Hague Programme, and which marked the beginning of a new period for the years 2010–2014.

In order to pursue this analysis, both policy and legislative developments will be considered, as policy developments have sometimes set the direction of European legislation subsequently adopted. They are also useful for understanding the positions of the different actors.

The questions for this Chapter are thus the following:

1. Why was the involvement of the EU in migration regulation inevitable?
2. What were the struggles between the different actors and the developments in the area during the 40 years of Community activity which preceded the adoption of the Amsterdam Treaty?
3. What changes did the Amsterdam Treaty and the Tampere Conclusions bring with regard to migration and the treatment of third-country nationals?
4. What was the development of migration regulation during the period of the Hague Programme (2005–2009)?
5. What are the main innovations under the Stockholm Programme for the period 2010–2014?

2. *Why the EU Became Involved in Migration Regulation*

The phenomenon of immigration is not new in Europe. Historically, Europe has been a continent of immigration. In the last century, this phenomenon gained importance from the 1940s onwards when, after the end of World War II, some countries started to recruit foreign workers. The Federal Republic of Germany, for instance, looked for workers in countries such as Italy, Spain, Greece, the former Yugoslavia, Turkey and Iran; France, by contrast, sought workers from her former colonies in North Africa, and also from Spain and Portugal.[1] After the oil crises in 1973, more stringent immigration controls were introduced in Europe and as a result family reunification became the easiest way of arriving in Europe. Later, in the 1990s asylum gained importance, largely as a consequence of the war in the former Yugoslavia.[2] At the same time, the new Member States which joined the Community in the 1980s, as well as Ireland and Italy, shifted from being countries of emigration to being countries of immigration.[3] In total, the EU has around 20 million

[1] N. Harris (2002), *Thinking the Unthinkable, the Immigration Myth Exposed*, IB Tauris: London, at 14.

[2] C.U. Schierup, P. Hansen and S. Castles (2006), *Migration, Citizenship and the European Welfare State. A European Dilemma*, Oxford University Press: Oxford, especially at Chapter 2; S. Castles and M.J. Miller (2003), *The Age of Migration. International Population Movements in the Modern World*, MacMillan: Basingstoke, especially at Chapter 5.

[3] See on this R. King, G. Lazaridis and C. Tsardanidis (2000), *Eldorado or Fortress Europe? Migration in Southern Europe*, Macmillan: Basingstoke; C. González-Enríquez and A. Triandafyllidou (2009), "Comparing the New Hosts of Southern Europe", *European Journal of Migration and Law*, Vol. 11(2), pp. 109–118; M. Pajares (1999), *La Inmigración en España*, Icaria: Barcelona.

third-country nationals out of almost 500 million citizens; around 4 percent of the total population.[4]

From the turn of the century onwards Europe has faced a renewed need for third-country nationals workers. This is due to three main reasons: First, Europe's population is getting smaller. In 2005, Eurostat forecasted that, from 2010, population growth in the 25 Member States of the EU (EU25)[5] would be due to net migration, as total deaths in the EU25 would outnumber total births.[6] Second, Europe's population is getting older. According to some estimates, the number of people of working age is expected to fall by 15 percent or about 50 million between 2008 and 2060.[7] Moreover, the proportion of elderly people (aged 65 or more) is expected to double while the share of the population of those aged between 0 and 14 will be reduced.[8] Third, and as a consequence of these two factors linked with increased competition in a globalised world, the EU needs to attract both highly skilled workers and low-skilled ones to be able to keep up in the world economy. The European Commission has stressed this on numerous occasions.[9] This is also part of the Europe 2020 strategy which aims at turning "the EU into a smart, sustainable and inclusive economy delivering high levels of employment, productivity and social cohesion".[10] The Commission reminded in 2010 of the need to "improve labour matching and skills recognition" in order to promote a comprehensive labour migration policy under the 2020 strategy, which will also help in meeting the demographic challenges.[11]

---

4 There has been a historical problem with obtaining reliable data on non-EU citizens residing in Europe. To overcome this drawback, the Council and the European Parliament passed Regulation (EC) No. 862/2007 of the European Parliament and of the Council of 11 July 2007 on Community Statistics on Migration and International Protection and repealing Council Regulation (EEC) No. 311/76 on the Compilation of Statistics on Foreign Workers, OJ 2007 L 199/23, 31.07.2007. See on this M. Poulain, N. Perrin and A. Singleton (2006), *THESIM: Towards Harmonised European Statistics on International Migration*, Presses Universitaires de Louvain: Louvain.

5 In 2005 Bulgaria and Romania were not Member States of the EU.

6 Eurostat News release, STAT/05/48, 8 April 2005.

7 See European Commission Communication, An Area of Freedom, Security and Justice Serving the Citizen, COM (2009) 262 final, Brussels, 10.6.2009.

8 Eurostat News release, STAT/05/48, 8 April 2005.

9 See for example Commission Communication, First Annual Report on Migration and Integration, COM (2004) 508, 16.7.2004; Green Paper on an EU Approach to Managing Economic Migration, COM (2004) 811 final, 11.1.2004; Commission Communication, Study on the Links between Legal and Illegal Migration, COM (2004) 412, 4.6.2004.

10 Commission Communication, Europe 2020, a Strategy for Smart, Sustainable and Inclusive Growth, COM (2010) 2020, 3.3.2010, p. 3.

11 Commission Report, First Annual Report on Immigration and Asylum (2009), COM (2010) 214 final, 6.5.2010, p. 3.

The fact that the EU needs foreign workers would anticipate open legislation. The following chapters will analyse to what extent this is the case taking into account that immigration regulation in Europe is not only about the economic interests of the receiving country, the sending one and the migrant himself. It also enters into the realm of the sovereignty of the Member States, which is closely linked to questions of membership and identity.[12]

Two questions need to be analysed and answered at the outset: how did the EU become involved in this issue and why? When considering the latter, three reasons can be mentioned:

First, the establishment and completion[13] of a European Internal Market and the abolition of internal border controls produced as a logical conclusion the need for a common immigration policy.[14] This reason has to do with the internal border as it is obvious that Member States could not keep their powers to control the movement of third-country nationals,[15] as otherwise freedom of movement of EU citizens would be aggravated as they would be controlled at the border as well.

Second, if third-country nationals are free to move from one country to another once they have entered this common area, there is the need for a common border control regime and a common visa system.[16] This explanation refers to the consistency of the external border.

Finally, in order to establish the EU as an area of freedom, security and justice it is necessary to harmonise the basic immigration rules.[17] In other words, this area of freedom, security and justice can never be achieved without proper harmonisation of the area for everyone, European citizens or not.[18]

---

12 A. Geddes (2000), *Immigration and European Integration. Towards Fortress Europe?* Manchester University Press: Manchester, at 17.

13 White Paper on the Completion of the Internal Market, COM (1985)310, 14.6.1985.

14 K. Hailbronner (2000), *Immigration and Asylum Law and Policy of the European Union*, Kluwer Law International: The Hague, at 1.

15 B. Melis (2001), *Negotiating Europe's Immigration Frontiers*, Kluwer Law International: The Hague, at 11.

16 K. Hailbronner (2000), *Immigration and Asylum Law and Policy of the European Union*, Kluwer Law International: The Hague, at 1.

17 *Ibid.*, at 1.

18 P. Boeles (2001), "Introduction: Freedom, Security and Justice for All" in E. Guild and C. Harlow (eds.), *Implementing Amsterdam. Immigration and Asylum Rights in EC Law*, Hart Publishing: Oxford, pp. 1–12, at 1. See also about the Area of Freedom, Security and Justice: B. Van Simaeys and J.Y. Carlier (1998) "Le Nouvel Espace de Liberté, de Securité et de Justice" in Y. Lejeune (ed.) *Le Traité d'Amsterdam-Espoirs et Déceptions*, Bruylant: Brussels, p. 227–285; H. Labayle (1997), "Le Traité d'Amsterdam: Un Espace de Liberté, de Securité et de Justice", *Revue Trimestrielle de Droit Européen*, Vol. 4, p. 813–881.

Once the reasons for the involvement of the EU in migration regulation had been considered, one would have expected that involvement to be pragmatic and straightforward. However, this is far from being the case. The EU has faced a continuous struggle between two opposite positions with more or less clear actors: those who wanted EU involvement in the issue and who advocated an open policy (notably the Parliament and the Commission); and those who did not wish that involvement and had a more restrictive view (some Member States and the Council), with the Court of Justice playing an independent role and the European Council varying its position along the years as has been seen in the previous Chapter.[19] That struggle seemed to end when the Amsterdam Treaty entered into force in 1999. Moreover, the Tampere Programme, adopted in the same year by the European Council, gave the impression that the different institutions were reaching a point of convergence in their opinions, with regard to how immigration should be managed and how third-country nationals should be treated.

Nevertheless, before analysing what has happened in the ten-year period since the adoption of the Amsterdam Treaty and the Tampere Conclusions, it is necessary to properly grasp this historical contradiction in the positions of the actors involved. This will help to better understand the present debates at a European level. My intention is not to cover this contradiction in great detail since other authors, whose studies will be acknowledged in the following pages, have already extensively explained the historical aspects and developments in the subject. I will limit myself to briefly depicting the positions of the actors and the most important developments in the area which preceded the adoption of the Amsterdam Treaty.

3. *The Regulation of Immigration in the European Community before Amsterdam (1957–1999)*

During its first years of existence after the adoption of the Rome Treaty,[20] the European Community (EC) made little attempt to deal with immigration.[21] EC law regulated only the movement of specific categories of EC nationals

[19] See Chapter 1 above.

[20] Treaty establishing the European Economic Community (EEC), signed 25 March 1957, entered into force 1 January 1958.

[21] J.M. Pérez de Nanclares (2002), *La Inmigración y el Asilo en la Unión Europea. Hacia un Nuevo Espacio de Libertad, Seguridad y Justicia*, Editorial Colex: Madrid, at 32–35.

and, briefly, the legal status of third-country nationals, notably answering to an economic logic.[22]

Free movement of workers was one of the four freedoms provided by the EC Treaty of 1957. Article 3(c) of the EEC Treaty envisaged "the abolition of obstacles…to freedom of movement". Although this right was applicable only to nationals of Member States, secondary EC legislation began to grant some rights indirectly to third-country nationals in two ways:

First, by Regulation 15/61 which addressed in Articles 11–14 the issue of family members of workers.[23] This was reaffirmed in Regulation 38/64.[24] Finally, Regulation (EEC) No 1612/68 of the Council on freedom of movement for workers within the Community[25] also provided those third-country nationals who were family members of European workers with different rights: the right to residence, the right to education, the right to work and other rights.[26] This was restated in Directive 360/68.[27] These ancillary rights were obtainable only when a European worker had travelled from one Member State to another to work. Hence it did not apply to purely internal situations.[28] Directive 73/148 on the self-employed[29] is also worth mentioning. With minor

22 B. Melis (2001), *Negotiating Europe's Immigration Frontiers*, Kluwer Law International: The Hague, at 10.

23 Regulation (EEC) No. 15/61 relatif aux première s mesures pour la réalisation de la libre circulation des travailleurs à l'intérieur de la Communauté, OJ 1961 1073/61.

24 Regulation (EEC) No. 38/64 du Conseil du 25 mars 1964 relatif à la libre circulation des travailleurs à l'intérieur de la Communauté, OJ 1964 965/64. See on these two Regulations E. Guild (2001), *Immigration Law in the European Community*, Kluwer Law International: The Hague, at 121–145.

25 Regulation (EEC) No. 1612/68 of the Council of 15 October 1968 on freedom of movement for workers within the Community, OJ 1968 L 257/2.

26 See P. Oliver (1985), "Non-Community Nationals and the Treaty of Rome", *Yearbook of European Law*, Vol. 5, p. 57–92, especially at 62–78; See also E. Guild (2001), *Immigration Law in the European Community*, Kluwer Law International: The Hague; S. A. W. Goedings (2005), *Labour Migration in an Integrating Europe. National Migration Policies and the Free Movement of Workers, 1950–1968*, Sdu Uitgevers: The Hague.

27 Council Directive 68/360/EEC of 15 October of 1968 on the abolition of restrictions of movement and residence within the Community for workers of Member States and their families, OJ 1968 L 257. This Directive aimed, according to its first Article, to "abolish restrictions on the movement and residence of nationals of the said States and of members of their families to whom Regulation (EEC) No 1612/68 applies".

28 See joined Cases 35 and 36/82 *Jhanjan and Morson v Netherlands* [1982] ECR 3723.

29 Directive 73/148 EEC of 21 May 1973 on the abolition of restrictions of the movement and residence within the Community for nationals of Member States with regard to the establishment and the provision of services, OJ 1973 L 173/14.

differences, the same rights applied to family members as in the previous Regulation.[30]

Second, the 1963 ECC-Turkey association agreement[31] and its 1970 Additional Protocol[32] are also relevant.[33] An Association Council was created, under the agreement, which promulgated some Decisions to give effect to the ongoing accomplishment of free movement.[34] Later the EC signed other agreements with North African countries.[35] These latter agreements extended social rights applicable to community workers.

Immigration matters began to gain importance by the mid-1970s. There are certain elements worth highlighting which anticipated later developments, especially with regard to the difference in discretion between the three main institutions (Council, Commission and European Parliament).[36] It was soon seen, indeed, that harmonisation would not come from the supranational sphere at a European level.[37] Immigration was to be considered "on a

---

30 See P. Oliver (1985), "Non-Community Nationals and the Treaty of Rome", *Yearbook of European Law*, Vol. 5, p. 57–92, at 79–80. In order to implement both measures with regards to social security there was Council Regulation No 1408/71 of 14 June 1971 on the application of social security schemes to employed persons, to self-employed persons and to members of their families moving within the Community, OJ 1971 L149. Council Regulation (EC) No 859/2003 of 14 May 2003 extended Regulation (EEC) No 1408/71 to the nationals of third countries who were not already covered by those Regulations solely on the ground of their nationality. Regulation (EC) No 883/2004 of the European Parliament and of the Council of 29 April 2004 on the coordination of social security systems replaced Regulation (EEC) No 1408/71.

31 64/732/EEC: Council Decision of 23 December 1963 on the conclusion of the Agreement establishing an Association between the European Economic Community and Turkey, OJ 1964 217/3685.

32 Additional Protocol and Financial Protocol signed on 23 November 1970, annexed to the Agreement establishing the Association between the European Economic Community and Turkey and on measures to be taken for their entry into force - Final Act – Declarations Signed on 23 November 1970, OJ 1972 L 293/4.

33 The EC also signed an association agreement with Greece in 1961. See on this F. Werner (1965), "The Association Agreements of the European Communities: A Comparative Analysis", *International Organization¸* Vol. 19(2), pp. 223–249.

34 See Chapter 1 above.

35 Council Regulation (EEC-Algeria) No 2210/78 of 27/9/78, Council Regulation (EEC-Morocco) No 2211/78 of 27/9/78 and Council Regulation (EEC-Tunisia) No 2212/78 of 27/9/78.

36 K. Hailbronner (2000), *Immigration and Asylum Law and Policy of the European Union*, Kluwer Law International: The Hague, at 35.

37 A. Geddes (2000), *Immigration and European Integration. Towards Fortress Europe?* Manchester University Press: Manchester, at 55.

co-operative basis…in different intergovernmental fora outside the EC framework"[38] predicting the problems that arose after the adoption of the Single European Act (SEA).

Indeed, in July 1985 before the adoption of the SEA, the Commission adopted Decision 85/381 setting up a prior communication and consultation procedure on migration policies in relation to non-member countries.[39] Some Member States (Germany, France, The Netherlands, Denmark and UK) reacted to this Decision with an application for annulment. The CJEU declared the Decision void[40] "in so far as the Commission lacked competence" (paragraph 42) but, at the same time, showed itself less than sympathetic to the Member States' arguments in favour of complete national control over the immigration sphere based on Article 118. In that sense, the Court stated that:

> Migration policy is capable of falling within the social field within the meaning of Article 118 only to the extent to which it concerns the situation of workers from non Member countries as regards their impact on the community employment market and on working conditions (paragraph 23).

The Court went on to state that this did not mean that "the whole field of migration policy in relation to non Member countries falls necessarily within the scope of public security" (paragraph 25).

The SEA changed the whole context by obliging Member States to remove all internal frontiers by 1992. The Act was signed in 1986 (and came into force from July 1987) to establish a single European market, defined as an area without frontiers in which free movement of goods, services, people, and capital was ensured (Article 26 TFEU).[41] Article 26 (which was then Article 8b) stated:

> The Commission shall report to the Council before 31 December 1988 and again before 31 December 1990 on the progress made towards achieving the internal market within the time limit fixed in Article 8a.
>
> The Council, acting by a qualified majority on a proposal from the Commission, shall determine the guidelines and conditions necessary to ensure balanced progress in all the sectors concerned.

---

38 B. Melis (2001), *Negotiating Europe's Immigration Frontiers*, Kluwer Law International: The Hague, at 11.

39 Commission Decision of 8 July 1985 setting up a prior communication and consultation procedure on migration policies in relation to non-member countries, OJ 1985 L 217/25.

40 Case 281, 283–5 & 287/85, *Germany and others v. Commission* [1987] ECR 3203.

41 The SEA introduced into the EC Treaty Article 8(a), which was renumbered Article 7a by the Treaty on European Union (TEU) and once again renumbered Article 14 by the Amsterdam Treaty. Finally it has been renumbered by the TFEU as Article 26. I will refer to it as Article 26.

This was actually the most controversial article in the SEA and it confirmed a "struggle" between, on the one hand, the Member States and the Council, and, on the other, the Parliament and the Commission. Guild mentions this problem when she acknowledges that:

> The package was a whole: barriers of all kinds had to be abolished and where those barriers included obstacles to the movement of persons then these too had to be abolished...Whether the Member States wanted it or not, the determination to succeed in economic integration symbolized by the abolition of border controls meant a sudden and for some Member States disconcerting loss of control over the entry of non-nationals be they third country nationals or nationals of other Member States.[42]

Tensions between the different institutions grew during these years. Thus, it is easy to understand that the only possible way to coordinate immigration policy was outside the Community system, via an intergovernmental agreement. The Schengen agreement provided a good solution, although it excluded the European Parliament, Commission and CJEU.[43] Signed on 15 June 1985 between Belgium, France, Germany, Luxembourg and the Netherlands, it established a framework for the abolition of border controls between the participant Member States, setting out some compensatory measures to be adopted such as checks at external borders, police and judicial cooperation, harmonisation of visa and immigration policies, etc.[44] The Schengen agreement came into effect in 1995, ten years after it was signed, when it was implemented by the five original members plus two new ones, Spain and Portugal.

---

[42] E. Guild (2001), *Immigration Law in the European Community*, Kluwer Law International: The Hague, at 220.

[43] D. O'Keeffe, (1995), "The Emergence of a European Immigration Policy", *European Law Review*, Vol. 20(1), pp. 20–36.

[44] On 19 June 1990, the Schengen implementation agreement was signed. Italy signed the agreement on 27 November 1990, Spain and Portugal signed the agreement on 25 June 1991, Greece followed on 6 November 1992, Austria on 28 April 1995 and finally, Denmark, Finland and Sweden signed the agreement on 19 December 1996. A Schengen cooperation agreement was complemented with the non-EU members of the Nordic Passport Union (Norway and Iceland) in 1996, which have also implemented the Schengen regime in full since 25 March 2001. As from 21 December 2007, nine new Member States (all of the 2004 enlargement except Cyprus) entered into the Schengen area as well. Switzerland joined the Schengen area on 12 December 2008. Cyprus, Bulgaria and Romania are also expected to play a full part in the Schengen acquis. Liechtenstein is also expected to implement the Schengen laws in the future as it has an open border with Switzerland. In addition to that, Monaco, San Marino and The Vatican are considered as de facto members. Andorra, by contrast, is not integrated into the Schengen area and border controls remain between it and both France and Spain.

Later, the Treaty of Amsterdam incorporated the decisions which had been taken since 1985 by the Schengen Group members and the associated working structures into EU law on 1 May 1999. This is known as the "Schengen acquis".[45]

This cooperative way of policy making was also reflected in other intergovernmental groups outside the EC structure such as the Trevi Group (1985), the *ad hoc* Group on Immigration (1986) and the Co-ordinators' Group on the Free Movement of Persons (1988).[46]

It is in this legal environment that the opening of the Intergovernmental conference, which led to the Maastricht Treaty,[47] occurred on 14 December 1990. The same dichotomy as before was present here. On the one hand, the Commission proposed that immigration should be dealt with within a Union law framework, as there had been important problems with the cooperation adopted in the SEA.[48] On the other hand, the Council arrived at a different conclusion and stressed the importance of keeping immigration matters intergovernmental.[49] As Peers mentions:

> Despite the argument that with the Single European Act, the Community gained competence over some or all aspects of immigration...law, the Member States firmly resisted this suggestion and instead held purely intergovernmental discussions on possible conventions, resolutions or recommendations of Immigration Ministers. The Maastricht Treaty (TEU) confirmed this approach for most aspects of immigration...law, providing that the Council could adopt intergovernmental third pillar measures...governing these issues.[50]

As a matter of fact, after the entry into force of the Maastricht Treaty, the law on immigration at a European level was basically divided between the First

45 See E. Wagner (1998), "The Integration of Schengen into the Framework of the European Union" *Legal Issues of European Integration*, Vol. 25(2), p. 1–60; M. Den Boer and L. Corrado (1999), "For the Record or Off the Record: Comments about the Incorporation of Schengen into the EU", *European Journal of Migration and Law*, Vol.1(4), p. 397–418.

46 For an explanation of the creation of the different groups see E. Guild and J. Niessen (1996), *The Developing Immigration and Asylum Policies of the European Union. Adopted Conventions, Resolutions, Recommendations, Decisions and Conclusions*, Kluwer Law International, The Hague, at 31–33.

47 The TEU, signed at Maastricht on 7 February 1992, entered into force on 1 November 1993 OJ 1992 C 191.

48 There were three inadequacies of the SEA intergovernmental cooperation, according to Geddes: Inadequate decision making procedures, exacerbation of the democratic deficit and lack of accountability. See A. Geddes (2000), *Immigration and European Integration. Towards Fortress Europe?*, Manchester University Press: Manchester, at 88.

49 Report of the Ministers of Immigration to the Council 3 December 1991.

50 S. Peers (1998), "Building Fortress Europe: The Development of EU Migration Law", *Common Market Law Review*, Vol. 35, pp. 1235–1272, at 1236.

and Third Pillars.[51] Under the First Pillar, the Community had responsibility with regard to visas under Article 100c and d (repealed by the Amsterdam Treaty). The Third Pillar, ex Article K.1 of the TEU, provided for intergovernmental cooperation with respect to immigration policy and policies regarding third-country nationals. However, Third Pillar cooperation experienced many problems that eventually led to its failure.[52]

Considering that the system was not working, it is not hard to realise that there was a need to change to yet a different method, not least because some Member States were not satisfied with the solutions adopted so far.

4. *The Adoption of the Treaty of Amsterdam and the Tampere Programme (1999–2004)*

Many of the problems mentioned were improved with the Amsterdam Treaty, which entered into force on 1 May 1999.[53] This Treaty marks the beginning of my research period and represented a profound change of direction that will be described in the following pages.

The Treaty introduced a new Title IV of Part III of the EC Treaty (dealing with visas, immigration and asylum), which incorporated a large part of the previous policy areas of the Third Pillar and repealed Articles 100(c) and (d). The Intergovernmental Conference (IGC) and the Amsterdam Treaty were set to prepare the EU for the challenges of the 21st century. A new approach was inevitable but cautious nevertheless.[54] The fact that it was unstoppable was

---

51 The Treaty of Maastricht brought a very important institutional change for what was henceforth known as the EU. The Treaty divided the EU into three pillars. The Communities was the first of these pillars. The second one dealt with Common Foreign and Security Policy whereas the third laid down cooperation in the field of Justice and Home Affairs. See on this P. Craig and G. de Búrca (2003), *EU Law. Text, Cases and Materials*, Oxford University Press: Oxford, at 14–18.

52 See for example A. Geddes (1995), "Immigrant and Ethnic Minorities and the EU's 'Democratic Deficit'", *Journal of Common Market Studies*, Vol.33 (2), pp. 197–217. Among the problems that can be cited are: the irrelevance of the European Parliament, the loss by the European Commission of its exclusive right of initiative and the avoidance of the European Court of Justice.

53 The Treaty of Amsterdam, amending the TEU, the TEC and certain related acts, signed on 2 October 1997, entered into force on 1 May 1999, OJ 1997 C 340.

54 K. Hailbronner, (2000), *Immigration and Asylum Law and Policy of the European Union*, Kluwer Law International: The Hague, at 37. See also K. Hailbronner (1998), "European Immigration and Asylum Law under the Amsterdam Treaty", *Common Market Law Review*, Vol. 35, pp. 1047–1067.

already clear in the Presidency Paper issued by the Conference Secretariat on "an area of freedom and security: introduction of Community methods and procedures for certain aspects".[55] It stated in its second paragraph that:

> It is a constant feature that matters affecting our security and individual freedoms are not at present being handled adequately. The choice of a forum of enhanced intergovernmental cooperation has failed to produce tangible results.

There was also certain boredom with the obstructionist UK's attitude:

> By the time of the 1996–97 Intergovernmental Conference (IGC) it was clear that the majority of the EU Member States ... were frustrated by the fact that the UK's rejection of a single immigration regime for the EU was effectively holding up the completion of the personal dimension of the internal market, namely free movement of persons.[56]

Hence, there was an essential "reconstruction"[57] which was reflected in Article 2 TEU which mentioned as one of its objectives:

> to maintain and develop the Union as an area of freedom, security and justice, in which the free movement of persons is assured in conjunction with appropriate measures with respect to external border controls, asylum, immigration and the prevention and combating of crime.

This objective was reinforced with the prerogative included in Article 3(d) of the TEC of adopting "measures concerning the entry and movement of persons as provided for in Title IV". Thus, the first important change that the Amsterdam Treaty brought is that the exclusive competence of the Member States to decide on the entry of third-country nationals ended. Even so, Member States adopted many precautions with the result that the

---

[55] Note, Conference of the Representatives of the Governments of the Member States, 14 November 1996. Quoted in E. Guild (2001), *Immigration Law in the European Community*, Kluwer Law International: The Hague, at 298.

[56] M. Hedemann-Robinson (1999), "The Area of Freedom, Security and Justice with Regard to the UK, Ireland and Denmark: The Opt-in Opt-outs? Under the Treaty of Amsterdam" in D. O'Keeffe and P. Twomey (eds.) *Legal issues of the Amsterdam Treaty*, Hart Publishing: Oxford, p. 289–302, at 290. Monar mentions this problem as well: "it was very much the frustration of the Schengen members over British opposition against the 'communitarisation' of major parts of the third pillar which made 'flexibility' one of the key issues of the ICG from October 1996 on". J. Monar (1998), "Justice and Home Affairs in the Treaty of Amsterdam: Reform at the Price of Fragmentation", *European Law Review*, Vol. 23, pp. 320–335, at 332. This concept of flexibility will, nevertheless, lead to numerous drawbacks while adopting measures under this Title.

[57] S. Langrisch (1998), "The Treaty of Amsterdam: Selected Highlights", *European Law Review*, Vol. 23(1), pp. 3–19, at 19.

never-ending dichotomy/tension persisted. All this makes the analysis of this area a complex task. Barbara Melis described accurately the situation:

> The Amsterdam Treaty does not represent a U-turn in this area but a further confirmation of the tendency of exclusion of the extra-Community population, although some important concessions have been made. Unexpected evolution can nonetheless occur by the extension of Community competence in these areas, from pressure coming from the European Commission but, especially, from the European Parliament. In this respect it should be noted that Member States… committed themselves in the European Council held in Tampere (15–16 October 1999) to adopt a more liberal and generous policy in the area of immigration.[58]

Indeed, the European Council agreed in Tampere (Finland) on the creation of an area of freedom, security and justice, in order to make full use of the opportunities opened by the new Treaty. To achieve this goal, the Tampere Council established a five-year programme for Justice and Home Affairs. As part of this programme, it stated the elements and drew up the guidelines required for an EU immigration policy. These elements were: partnerships with the countries of origin, a common European asylum system, fair treatment of third-country nationals and management of migration flows.[59] The Tampere Council remarked in paragraph 18 of its Conclusions that:

> The European Union must ensure fair treatment of third country nationals who reside legally on the territory of its Member States. A more vigorous integration policy should aim at granting them, rights and obligations comparable to those of EU citizens. It should also enhance non-discrimination in economic, social and cultural life and develop measures against racism and xenophobia.[60]

The European Council also acknowledged "the need for approximation of national legislations on the conditions of admission and residence of third country nationals"[61] and that "the legal status of third country nationals should be approximated to that of Member States' nationals".[62]

It is within this framework that the Commission adopted a Communication on a Community immigration policy in 2000.[63] The Communication begins by stating that there is a common understanding that zero immigration

[58] B. Melis (2001), *Negotiating Europe's Immigration Frontiers*, Kluwer Law International: The Hague, at 3.

[59] See paragraphs 10–27 of the Tampere Council Conclusions.

[60] *Ibid.*, paragraph 18.

[61] *Ibid.*, paragraph 20.

[62] *Ibid.*, paragraph 21.

[63] Commission Communication, on a Community Immigration Policy, COM (2000) 757, 22.11.2000.

policies are not realistic.[64] With that premise in mind, the Commission points out three things: first, there is a need for a redefinition of the immigration policies with regard to the admission of third-country nationals. Second, economic migration needs to be dealt with differently.[65] Hence, and third, it is the view of the Commission that the admission of economic migrants should be dealt with in a more "flexible approach common to all Member States"[66] complemented with measures to facilitate the integration of the immigrants.

Considering the Tampere Council Conclusions and this Communication, it would seem that for the first time the Council would have been obliged to soften its initial position and in that sense reaching a point of compromise with the views of the Commission (and also of the European Parliament[67]). The reality was, however, different as Member States still kept various safeguards or limits to the Community action. In fact, the transfer of competences to the EU by Member States was not complete, thanks to the many prerogatives that they maintained.[68]

To begin with, the Third Pillar was still retained, albeit with a residual character.[69] Second, Member States emphasised the security aspects of the Treaty. This was well represented by the introduction of Article 64 TEC which included the exclusive competence of Member States to maintain law and order and the safeguarding of internal security.[70] In turn, Article 64(2) TEC provided for measures that could be taken in the event of a sudden influx of nationals of third countries. This prerogative was much more controlled since it was the Council, on a proposal from the Commission and by qualified majority, that could act and it had a time limit of six months.

---

64 *Ibid.*, at 3.

65 This is in view of the fact that "there is a substantial illegal immigration into the EU…" *Ibid.*, at 13.

66 A good solution, the Commission says, would be the "establishment of a special visa for job seekers from third countries". *Ibid.*, at 18.

67 In fact, the European Parliament produced a report in 2003 in which it welcomed the Commission's work while at the same time regretting the inactivity of the Council in this area. European Parliament, Report on the Commission Communication on an open method of coordination for the Community immigration policy, COM (2001)387, A5-0224/2003, 16 June 2003, Rapporteur: Ana Terrón i Cusí.

68 See on this T. Balzacq and S. Carrera (2005), *Migration, Borders and Asylum. Trends and Vulnerabilities in EU Policy*, CEPS: Brussels.

69 J.M. Pérez de Nanclares (2002), La Inmigración y el Asilo en la Unión Europea. Hacia un Nuevo Espacio de Libertad, Seguridad y Justicia, Editorial Colex: Madrid, at 61.

70 *Ibid.*, at 102.

More interesting for our purposes was the position of Denmark, the UK and Ireland. It should be noted that the UK and the Republic of Ireland opted out of the new measures on the free movement of persons provided for by the Treaty of Amsterdam. They had, therefore, the possibility to opt in for some measures on an ad hoc basis. Denmark, although a signatory to the Schengen agreements, was reluctant to apply the Community method in the area of the free movement of persons and did not apply any of the decisions adopted on the basis of the TEC in this field. Denmark could completely renounce the opt-out. Otherwise, Denmark could only participate in the Schengen follow-up process but under the framework of international law.[71]

Finally, there were some control and procedural limits which changed throughout this period. Article 67(1) of the Treaty provided that during the first five years following the entry into force of the Treaty of Amsterdam, the Council would act unanimously on a proposal from the Commission or on the initiative of a Member State and after consulting the European Parliament. This had various consequences:

1. To begin with, it created tremendous confusion. First because there were some subjects which were decided by the consultation process from the very beginning (Article 67(3) TEC). At the end of the five-year period, there were some subjects that were to be automatically decided by the co-decision process (Article 67(4) TEC). However, others were left for the Council to decide unanimously whether or not the co-decision process would apply (Article 67(2) TEC).[72]
2. Second, the Commission temporarily lost its power of initiative. Even after the five-year period, it had to take into account any request made by a Member State asking to submit a proposal to the Council (Article 67.2 TEC). Moreover, the Parliament was relegated to a subsidiary role of mere

[71] See C.D. Ehlermann (1998), "Differentiation, Flexibility, Closer Co-operation: The New Provisions of the Amsterdam Treaty", *European Law Journal*, Vol.4 (3), pp. 246–70, especially at 259–262.

[72] The council adopted Decision 2004/927 in which it was stated that "the Council should continue to act unanimously after consulting the European Parliament when adopting measures in the field of the legal migration of third-country nationals to and between Member States referred to in Article 63(3)(a) and (4) of the Treaty". Decision 2004/927/EC providing for certain areas covered by Title IV of Part Three of the Treaty establishing the European Community to be governed by the procedure set out in Article 251 of that Treaty, 22 December 2004, OJ 2004 L 396/45, recital seven of the preamble. This was deplored by the European Parliament in a report; see European Parliament, Report on the Links between Legal and Illegal Migration and Integration of Migrants, A6/0136/2005, 3 May 2005, Rapporteur: Patrick Gaubert.

consultant in some subjects (Article 67(1) TEC). It is fair to say, though, that Member States almost never used this possibility of proposing legislation, so it was more of a symbolic provision.[73]

3. Third, there was an excessive use of the unanimity rule in the Council, at least during the first five years (as has been mentioned). The Treaty of Nice changed this only with regard to asylum and the minimum standards for giving temporary protection to displaced persons from third countries.[74]
4. Finally, the control of the CJEU was limited in two different ways. First, Article 234 was restricted to be used before tribunals against whose decisions there was no judicial remedy under national law (Article 68(1) TEC). Second, Article 68(2) TEC provided that the Court had no jurisdiction to rule on any measure or decision taken pursuant to Article 62(1) TEC relating to the maintenance of law and order and the safeguarding of internal security.[75] Nevertheless, only the first limitation proved important.

Despite these procedural obstacles, there were some measures on regular migration adopted during the period under the Tampere Programme. The first important piece of legislation that, although not adopted, is worth mentioning is the 2001 proposal for a Directive dealing with "the conditions of entry and residence of third-country nationals for the purpose of paid employment and self-employed economic activities".[76] It envisaged determining common conditions and common procedural standards on the entry and residence of third-country nationals for the purpose of paid employment and self-employed economic activities. Whilst the other European Institutions gave positive opinions, discussion in the Council was limited to a first reading of the text and thus the Directive was not adopted.[77]

---

[73] France proposed the Council Directive 2001/40/EC of 28 May 2001 on the mutual recognition of decisions on the expulsion of third-country nationals, OJ 2001, L 149/34.

[74] With the Treaty of Nice there was only one change in this title. A further fifth point was added to Article 67. This point deals with the change in the process of co-decision to some of the asylum matters.

[75] See S. Peers (1998), "Who's Judging the Watchmen? The Judicial System of the Area of Freedom Security and Justice", *Yearbook of European Law*, Vol. 18, pp. 337–413.

[76] Proposal for a Council Directive on the Conditions of Entry and Residence for the Purpose of Paid Employment and Self-Employment Activities, COM (2001) 0386 final, Brussels, 11.7.2001.

[77] See S. Peers and N. Rogers (2006), *EU Immigration and Asylum Law. Text and Commentary*, Martinus Nijhoff Publishers: Leiden/Boston, at 661–86; B. Ryan (2007), "The EU and Labor Migration: Regulating Admission or Treatment?" in A. Baldaccini, E. Guild and H. Toner

It was only in 2003 that the Council adopted the first crucial measures in this area: Directives 2003/86 on the right to family reunification[78] and 2003/109 concerning the status of third-country nationals who are long-term residents.[79] They constitute the most important pieces of legislation already implemented by Member States in the area of regular migration.

With regard to the Family Reunification Directive, it is central to mention the action for annulment that the European Parliament brought before the CJEU in December 2003. Case *European Parliament v Council*[80] was finally delivered by the Court in June 2006 but it is interesting to mention it briefly as it is related to an instrument adopted in 2003. In fact, the European Parliament sought the annulment of certain provisions in the Directive as it claimed that some of the derogations from the obligations imposed were not in line with respect for fundamental rights. Interestingly enough, in this particular case, the Commission supported the Council before the Court, as did Germany. It is not necessary to consider the facts and findings of the Court in this case, as other authors have already done so.[81] Suffice it to say here that the Court did not find those provisions to be contrary to fundamental rights. However, and most importantly, it established some limits on how Member States can interpret the concept of integration, as will be seen below in Chapter 9.

Also in 2003 the Commission produced another Communication on immigration.[82] In this Communication the Commission set out proposals to support the development of integration policies. Also, interestingly, the Commission reintroduced the concept of civic citizenship which it had already put forward in 2000.[83] Civic citizenship, it was said, would enhance a successful settlement into society. The European Parliament, in turn, supported the

(eds.), *Whose Freedom, Security and Justice? EU Immigration and Asylum Law and Policy*, Hart Publishing: Oxford, pp. 489–515, at 500.

78 Council Directive 2003/86/EC of 22 September 2003, OJ 2003 L251/12.

79 Council Directive 2003/109/EC of 25 November 2003, OJ 2004 L 16/44.

80 Case C-540/03 European Parliament v Council of the European Union [2006] ECR I-5769.

81 See commentaries on this case: M. Bulterman (2008), *Common Market Law Review*, Vol. 45, pp. 245–259; D. Martin (2007), "Comments", *European Journal of Migration and Law*, Vol. 9 (1), pp. 141–157, at 144–153.

82 Commission Communication on Immigration, Integration and Employment, COM (2003) 336, 3.6.2003.

83 Commission Communication, on a Community Immigration Policy, COM (2000) 757, 22.11.2000. See also on this M. Bell (2007), "Civic Citizenship and Migrant Integration", *European Public Law*, Vol. 13(2), pp. 311–333.

Table I: *Developments years 1999-2004*

EU Law/Policy development	Actor adopting the measure	Significance
Tampere Programme, 15-16 October 1999.	European Council	It established the aim of granting third-country nationals treatment comparable to that of EU citizens.
Communication on a Community Immigration Policy, 22 November 2000, COM (2000) 757.	Commission	It established the necessity for migration and the need to deal with it with more flexibility. It mentioned the concept of civic citizenship.
Proposal for a Council Directive on the conditions of entry and residence for the purpose of paid employment and self-employment activities, 11 July 2001, COM (2001) 0386.	Commission	It envisaged determining common conditions and common procedural standards for the entry and residence of third-country nationals for the purpose of paid employment and self-employed activities.
Communication on Immigration, Integration and Employment, 3 June 2003, COM (2003) 336.	Commission	It set out proposals to support the development of integration policies.
Report on the Communication from the Commission on Immigration, Integration and Employment, 1 December 2003.	European Parliament	It supported the idea of civic citizenship as it would be important for increasing a sense of belonging in Europe.
Directive 2003/86 on the right to family reunification, 22 September 2003.	Council	Proposed by the Commission, it established the right to family reunification for third-country nationals.
Directive 2003/109 on the status of third-country nationals who are long-term residents, 25 November 2003.	Council	Proposed by the Commission, it established the conditions under which third-country nationals might be granted a long-term residence permit.

Table I: *(Cont.)*

EU Law/Policy development	Actor adopting the measure	Significance
Communication: Assessment of the Tampere programme, 02 June 2004, COM (2004) 401 final.	Commission	It took note of the implementation of the Tampere agenda and set new guidelines.
Directive 2004/114 on students, 13 December 2004.	Council	Proposed by the Commission, it established the conditions for the admission of third-country nationals mainly for the purpose of study.
Case C-540/03, *European Parliament v Council*, brought on 22 December 2003 and delivered on 27 June 2006.	Court	First ruling on a Title IV measure by the CJEU, specifically on the Family Reunification Directive.
Directive 2004/38 on the right of citizens of the Union and their family members to move and reside freely within the territory of the Member States, 29 April 2004.	European Parliament and Council	Proposed by the Commission, it lays down the conditions governing the exercise of the right of free movement and residence within the territory of the Member States by Union citizens and their family members.

idea of civic citizenship as it would be important for increasing a sense of belonging in Europe.[84]

A significant landmark in the area took place in May 2004. The nationals of ten new Member States[85] were transformed from third-country nationals into European citizens. This was the fifth enlargement and it was unprecedented due to the number of countries which entered the EU at once. Bulgaria and Romania also joined the EU later in 2007. Also in 2004, the European Council adopted a new Directive on third-country nationals entering the EU for the purpose of study.[86] This was followed by another Directive in 2005 for those third-country nationals entering the EU for the purpose of scientific research.[87] Finally, in 2004, the Council and the Parliament adopted Directive 2004/38 on the right of citizens of the Union and their family members to move and reside freely within the territory of the Member States.[88] The rights of family members of EU citizens are enshrined in Articles 2 and 3. However, although the rights of some family members who are third-country nationals are subsumed into the rights of EU citizens, some Member States struggle to treat them as less entitled, as will be seen below in the *Metock* case.

5. *The Adoption of the Hague Programme (2005–2009)*

In June 2004, the Commission presented a Communication[89] taking note of the implementation of the Tampere agenda and setting future guidelines for a new Justice and Home Affairs agenda for the years to come. Following Council

---

[84] European Parliament, Report on the Communication from the Commission on Immigration, Integration and Employment, A5-0445/2003, 1 December 2003, Rapporteur: Claude Moraes. It restated its support in another report in 2006: European Parliament, Report on Strategies and Means for the Integration of Immigrants in the European Union, A6-0190/2006, 17 May 2006, Rapporteur: Stavros Lambrinidis.

[85] Estonia, Latvia, Lithuania, Hungary, Slovakia, Czech Republic, Poland, Slovenia, Malta and Cyprus.

[86] Council Directive 2004/114/EC of 13 December 2004 on the Conditions of Admission of Third-country Nationals for the Purposes of Studies, Pupil Exchange, Unremunerated Training or Voluntary Service, OJ 2004 L375/12, 23.12.2004.

[87] Council Directive 2005/71/EC of 12 October 2005 on a Specific Procedure for Admitting Third-country Nationals for the Purpose of Scientific Research, OJ 2005 L289/26, 3.11.2005.

[88] Directive 2004/38/EC of the European Parliament and of the Council of 29 April 2004 on the right of citizens of the Union and their family members to move and reside freely within the territory of the Member States, OJ 2004 L158/77.

[89] Commission Communication, Area of Freedom, Security and Justice: Assessment of the Tampere programme and future orientations, COM (2004) 401 final, 2.06.2004.

discussions in July and October 2004, the Dutch Presidency produced a new programme for the area of freedom, security and justice for the years 2005–2009, to be known as the "Hague Programme".[90] This programme replaced the Tampere one and provided the policy schedule and legislative timetable for this period. The programme was endorsed by the Brussels European Council Conclusions in November 2004.[91] It had some specific orientations divided into areas. For the purpose of this book it is important to mention the second area (asylum, migration and border policy), the fourth one (legal migration and the fight against illegal employment) and the fifth (integration of third-country nationals). Later, in May 2005, the Commission produced another Communication[92] developing ten priorities for implementing the Hague Programme during the following five years. One of these priorities was immigration. The failure to adopt a Directive on economic migration led the Commission to re-launch the debate on the need for common rules for economic migration with a Green Paper issued in January 2005[93] and the subsequent adoption of a Policy Plan on legal migration in December 2005.[94] This document is interesting as the Commission acknowledges once again that Europe needs migrants with a full range of qualifications (unskilled and highly skilled workers).[95] It also highlights that the low birth rates and ageing population makes immigration "one of the available tools within a broader policy mix".[96]

Thus, the Commission announced that it would present several proposals which would consist of a general framework Directive defining the basic rights of all immigrant workers admitted into the EU (together with other horizontal measures) and of four specific Directives, addressing the conditions of entry and residence of certain categories of immigrants (highly skilled, seasonal workers, intra-corporate transferees and remunerated trainees).

---

[90] See on the Hague Programme: T. Balzacq and S. Carrera (eds.) (2006), *Security versus Freedom: A Challenge for Europe's Future?* Ashgate Publishing: Hampshire.

[91] Brussels European Council Conclusions 4/5 November 2004, paragraphs 14–20 and Annex I, 14292/1/04, Brussels, 8 December 2004.

[92] Commission Communication, The Hague Programme: Ten Priorities for the next Five Years. The Partnership for European Renewal in the Field of Freedom, Security and Justice, COM (2005) 184 final, 10.5.2005.

[93] Green Paper on an EU Approach to Managing Economic Migration, COM (2004) 811 final, 11.1.2004.

[94] Commission Communication, Policy Plan on Legal Migration, COM (2005) 669, 21.12.2005.

[95] *Ibid.*, at 4.

[96] *Ibid.*, at 5.

Table II: *Developments years 2004-2009*

EU Law/Policy development	Actor adopting the measure	Significance
Hague Programme, 4-5 November 2004.	European Council	It established the follow-up to the Tampere Programme.
Green Paper on an EU approach to Managing Economic Migration, 11 January 2004, COM (2004) 811 final.	Commission	It re-launched the debate on the need for common rules for economic migration.
Communication: The Hague Programme: Ten priorities for the next five years, 10 May 2005, COM (2005) 184 final.	Commission	It established the priorities for the implementation of the Hague Programme.
Directive 2005/71, 12 October 2005.	Council	Proposed by the Commission, it established a procedure for the admission of third-country nationals for the purpose of scientific research.
Policy Plan on Legal migration, 21 December 2005, COM (2005) 669.	Commission	It announced the future proposal of several Directives on legal migration.
Communication: A common immigration policy for Europe, 17 June 2008, COM (2008) 359 final.	Commission	It delivered the remaining elements of the Hague Programme.
Case 127/08, *Metock*, 25 July 2008.	Court	It interpreted family reunification under Directive 2004/38.
European Pact on Immigration and Asylum, 16 October 2008.	Council	It drew up the guidelines on migration management and prepared the Stockholm Programme.
Directive 2009/50, 25 May 2009.	Council	Proposed by the Commission, it established the conditions of entry and residence of third-country nationals for the purpose of highly qualified employment.

Two of these Directives, the general framework Directive and the highly skilled workers Directive, were presented in 2007,[97] with the later being adopted in 2009.[98] Two more were proposed in 2010.[99]

It is important to analyse more concisely two important documents that were presented by the Commission and by the Council respectively. As was previously mentioned, the adoption by the European Council in 1999 of the Tampere conclusions presupposed that the positions of the Commission and the Council would arrive to a point of agreement, through the mediation of the European Council. It has been seen how the rejection of the 2001 proposal for a Directive on legal economic migration made the Commission reassess its previous policy. In fact, in 2005 it proposed a less ambitious programme with a view to adopting a piecemeal approach with Directives for certain categories

---

97 The purpose of the horizontal Directive is, according to Article 1, to determine a "single application procedure for issuing a single permit for third country nationals to reside and work in the territory of a Member State" and "a common set of rights to third country workers legally residing in a Member State". Proposal for a Council Directive on a Single Application Procedure for a Single Permit for Third-country Nationals to Reside and Work in the Territory of a Member State and on a Common Set of Rights for Third-country Workers Legally Residing in a Member State, COM (2007) 638 final, Brussels, 23.10.2007. This Directive had not been adopted by 1 December 2010. The highly skilled workers Directive aims to attract them to the EU. It is known as the blue card initiative. Proposal for a Council Directive on the Conditions of Entry and Residence of Third-country Nationals for the Purposes of Highly Qualified Employment, COM (2007) 637 final, Brussels 23.10.2007.

98 Council Directive 2009/50/EC of 25 May 2009 on the conditions of entry and residence of third-country nationals for the purposes of highly qualified employment, OJ 2009 L 155/17. The adoption of this Directive has shown the contradictions in the positions of the institutions mentioned before. The European Parliament backed the Commission proposal while some Member States, notably Germany and Austria, expressed their concerns and doubts about it. This is regardless of the fact that Article 13(6) of the proposal emphasised the Community preference principle which established as follows: "Member States will consider requests for admission to their territories for the purpose of employment only where vacancies in a Member State cannot be filled by national and Community manpower or by non-Community manpower lawfully resident on a permanent basis in that Member State and already forming part of the Member State's regular labour force". Council Resolution of 20 June 1994, OJ 1996 C 274/3. See on the Directive: Y.K. Gümüs (2010), "EU Blue Card Scheme: The Right Step in the Right Direction? *European Journal of Migration and Law*, Vol. 12(4), pp. 435–454.

99 Proposal for a Directive of the European Parliament and of the Council on conditions of entry and residence of third-country nationals in the framework of an intra-corporate transfer, COM (2010) 378 final, Brussels, 13.7.2010; Proposal for a Directive of the European Parliament and of the Council on the conditions of entry and residence of third-country nationals for the purposes of seasonal employment, COM (2010) 379 final, Brussels, 13.7.2010.

of third-country nationals. Thus, it seems appropriate to compare again the positions of the European Council and the Commission in 2008, in order to see if they were closer or further away than they seemed to be in 1999. It seems as if the Commission took a less proactive approach in this area. However, there are still important differences when one looks at the last Commission's Communication in the field in 2008[100] and the European Council's European Pact on Immigration and Asylum[101] adopted on 16 October 2008 by the 27 Heads of State and Government.[102]

The first question that arises is what the relationship between both policy documents is. The aim of the Commission's Communication was to deliver the remaining elements of the Hague Programme concerning immigration.[103] In turn, the European Council's document seemed to be a preparation for the Stockholm Programme, which was adopted by the end of 2009.[104] However, both asked the other institutions to implement the principles proposed in the respective Communications. But, what happens when those principles are not in line? The European Council and the Commission seem to agree on certain things. For example both acknowledge that immigration into the EU is a reality.[105] They both also consider that immigration has to be managed with common policies.[106] It is in the meaning of those common policies though that they seem to disagree. I will focus on five different issues: Regular migration, treatment of third-country nationals, integration, the family reunification Directive and the issue of identity.

The Commission's document is articulated around ten common principles grouped under three headings: prosperity, security and solidarity. The first heading is important for this study. Under this heading the Commission mentions the importance of having clear rules promoting legal immigration and of giving third-country nationals fair treatment, which approximates their legal status to that of EU nationals.[107] With regard to integration[108] the Commission

[100] Commission Communication, A Common Immigration Policy for Europe: Principles, Actions and Tools, COM (2008) 359 final, 17.6.2008.

[101] Council of the European Union, European Pact on Immigration and Asylum, 13440/08, Brussels 24 September 2008, adopted on 16 October.

[102] See on this E. Guild and S. Carrera (2008), "The French Presidency's European Pact on Immigration and Asylum: Intergovernmentalism vs Europeanisation? Security vs Rights?", Centre of European Policy Studies (CEPS), 11 September 2008, *at* www.ceps.be.

[103] P. 4 of the Communication.

[104] Pact on Immigration and Asylum, p. 15.

[105] P. 2 of the Communication and p. 2 of the Pact.

[106] P. 2 of the Communication and p. 3 of the Pact.

[107] P. 5 of the Communication.

[108] In the field of integration there have also been many different policy developments, especially by the Commission, which took place during these years. They will not be examined

points out that it can be supported with different measures, e.g. facilitating the acquisition of language skills.[109] The Commission also mentions the possibility of assessing and, eventually modifying Directive 2003/86 on the right to family reunification. Most importantly, the Commission echoes the necessity of increased participation by third-country nationals in order to "reflect the multiple and evolving identities of European societies".[110]

The European Council's document revolves around five commitments. The first commitment is the one of interest for this research: to organise legal migration taking into account the priorities, needs and reception capacities of the Member States, and to encourage integration. Consequently this principle seems similar to the first heading of prosperity mentioned in the Commission's document. Under this commitment, the European Council also stresses the importance of giving third-country nationals fair treatment. Interestingly enough, it is never mentioned that this fair treatment should aim at approximating the status of third-country nationals to that of European citizens.[111] With regard to integration, the European Council also mentions the necessity to learn the language. However, it seems that the spirit of this necessity is more to oblige the third-country national rather than to encourage Member States to provide adequate conditions for this to happen, e.g. available language courses.[112] This is even clearer if the negotiations before the Pact was adopted are considered. The original idea in the Pact was to include a reference to the compulsory imposition of integration contracts for third-country nationals. The opposition of the Spanish Government to this measure was the cause for its elimination in the final text adopted.[113] With regard to family reunification, the position of the European Council seems to be in contradiction with that of the Commission. The European Council proposes to rethink family reunification in order to limit this right through the assessment of the resources and accommodation in the country of destination, and most importantly through the evaluation of the family members' knowledge of the host country's language.[114] Finally, the European Council stresses the importance of the respect

here as they have not produced any legislative measures. For a concise and exhaustive explanation and enumeration see S. Carrera (2009), *In Search of a Perfect Citizen? The Intersection between Integration, Immigration and Nationality in the EU*, Martinus Nijhoff: Leiden/Boston.

109 P. 7 of the Communication.

110 P. 8 of the Communication.

111 P. 5 of the Pact.

112 *Ibid.*, p. 6.

113 El País, *París renuncia al contrato de integración para satisfacer a España*, 1 July 2008; El País, *De la Vega confirma el pacto con París en inmigración*, 5 July 2008.

114 P. 6 of the Pact.

by third-country nationals for the identities of the Member States and of the EU.[115] This is completely opposed to what the Commission proposes. The Commission acknowledges that the identities of the Member States and of the EU are not a static concept. In contradiction, the European Council seems to take an "essentialist" view of what identities mean in the EU and in each Member State. In that sense it would be for the third-country national to integrate into a one-way process and not in a two-way one as the Tampere Conclusions in 1999 proposed.

Hence, a question arises: which one of the two positions has been enshrined in the new Stockholm Programme?

Just before I move to Section 6 I am going to do a little deviation to look at the activity of the CJEU in this period. The most important ruling it delivered was, without doubt, *Metock*[116] which resolved another important aspect of the treatment of third-country nationals by reducing the control exercised by Member States. The judgment arose out of an action by four third-country nationals, and their EU family members, who after having their asylum applications rejected in Ireland married non-Irish EU citizens. The ruling referred to the interpretation of Directive 2004/38 and its effects have been explained in detail elsewhere.[117] Out of the four applicants, the case of Mr Igboanusi is the most interesting one. He arrived in Ireland in 2004 in order to apply for asylum. However, his application was refused in 2005 and a deportation order was made against him on 15 September 2005. Nevertheless, he stayed in Ireland and met a Polish national in 2006 whom he married on 24 November 2006. He consequently applied for a residence card as the spouse of an EU citizen but his application was refused. Later, he was arrested and deported to Nigeria in 2007. The key question was whether Directive 2004/38 applied irrespective of how a third-country national entered the host Member State.

---

[115] *Ibid.*, p.6.

[116] Case C-127/08, *Metock and Others* [2008] ECR I-06241.

[117] D. Acosta (2009), "Immigration in the European Union: Family Reunification after the Metock Case", *UCD Law Review*, Vol. 9, pp. 64–88; C. Costello (2009), "*Metock*: Free Movement and "Normal Family Life" in the Union", *Common Market Law Review*, Vol. 46, pp. 587–622; A. Tryfonidou (2009), "Family Reunification Rights of (Migrant) Union Citizens: Towards a More Liberal Approach", *European Law Journal*, Vol. 15(5), pp 634–653; S. Peers (2009), "Free Movement, Immigration Control and Constitutional Conflict", *European Constitutional Law Review*, Vol. 5, pp. 173–196; S. Currie (2009), "Accelerated Justice or a Step too Far? Residence Rights of non-EU Family Members and the Court's Ruling in Metock", *European Law Review*, Vol. 34(2), pp. 310–326; J. Handoll (2009), "The Metock Case. Union Citizenship, Family Reunion and the Abuse of Rights" in P. Minderhoud and N. Trimikliniotis (eds.) (2009), *Rethinking the Free Movement of Workers: The European Challenges Ahead*, Wolf Legal Publishers: Nijmegen, pp. 173–187.

In other words, did Directive 2004 apply even if the third-country national marrying the Union citizen was irregularly present in the territory of the Member State? The CJEU answered in the positive. It explained that Member States could always make use of Article 35 of the Directive regarding marriages of convenience. That was however not the case here. Moreover, the Court declared that from the moment a third-country national family member derives rights of residence from Directive 2004/38, those rights can only be limited by Articles 27 and 35. Regarding Article 27, it allows Member States to penalise third-country nationals who entered or stayed in the territory of a Member State in breach of the national rules on immigration before becoming a family member of an EU citizen. However, these measures must be proportionate and expulsion on the ground of irregular entry or residence is only allowed if the person comes within the material criteria of Article 27. This final decision by the Court encountered fierce opposition by some Member States, notably the UK and Denmark.[118] However, the Commission resisted those attacks and upheld the ruling in *Metock* in its report on the implementation of the Directive.[119]

6. *The Lisbon Treaty and the Stockholm Programme: What Is the Future of Migration Regulation?*

The European Council meeting in Brussels on 11 December 2009 adopted the new multi-annual programme in the area of freedom, security and justice for the years 2010–2014, known as the Stockholm Programme.[120] It is interesting to compare the final outcome in the programme with the diverse positions, already analysed, that the European Council and the Commission maintained in 2008. The divergences in the position of the European Council between the Pact and the Stockholm programme, with only one year having passed between

[118] See S. Peers (2009), "The UK Proposals on EU Free Movement Law: an Attack on the Rule of Law and EU Fundamental Freedoms", *Statewatch Analysis*, *at* www.statewatch.org/analyses/no-72-eu-attack-on-fundamental-rights-08.pdf, (accessed 1 December 2010).

[119] Commission Report, On the Application of Directive 2004/38/EC on the Right of Citizens of the Union and their Family Members to Move and Reside Freely within the Territory of the Member States, COM (2009) 313 final, 2.7.2009.

[120] Council of the European Union, The Stockholm Programme: An Open and Secure Europe Serving and Protecting Citizens, 5731/10, Brussels, 3 March 2010. See European Commission, Communication on Delivering an Area of Freedom, Security and Justice for Europe's Citizens: Action Plan Implementing the Stockholm Programme, COM (2010) 171 final, Brussels, 20 April 2010.

both documents, might well be elucidated by the role played by the Presidency (French in 2008 and Swedish in 2009) and its agenda setting and structuring powers.[121]

I will again mention five issues here: regular migration, treatment of third-country nationals, integration, the Family Reunification Directive and identity.

The Stockholm Programme begins by acknowledging once again the continuous need for immigration in the EU.[122] In order to promote regular migration, it accepts the importance of creating "flexible admission systems that are responsive to the priorities, needs, numbers and volumes determined by each Member State". These systems should also allow "migrants to take full advantage of their skill and competence".[123] In this first point, the programme does not depart significantly from the positions of the European Council and Commission in 2008, which both call for mechanisms to permit regular migration. Moreover, it asks for the consolidation of all legislation in this area, especially on regular migration, and for "amendments needed to simplify and/or, where necessary, extend the existing provisions and improve their implementation and coherence".[124] This is certainly applicable to the Long-term Residence Directive as some Member States are probably incorrectly implementing and interpreting some of its provisions, as will be seen in Sections III and IV.

On the second issue, the Stockholm Programme leans towards the Commission's position of giving third-country nationals treatment comparable to that of EU citizens. In fact, it is extremely important to highlight that the Stockholm Programme recalls, word for word, the Tampere formula:

> The European Union must ensure fair treatment of third country nationals who reside legally on the territory of its Member States. A more vigorous integration policy should aim at granting them rights and obligations comparable to those of EU citizens.[125]

This is, the document goes on, "an objective of the common immigration policy and should be implemented as soon as possible, and no later than 2014."[126] This is a central point and has important consequences for the interpretation

---

[121] This has been well explained by J. Tallberg, (2003), "The Agenda-Shaping Powers of the EU Council Presidency", *Journal of European Public Policy*, Vol. 10(1), pp. 1–19.

[122] Stockholm Programme, Brussels, 2 December 2009, 17024/09, p. 59.

[123] *Ibid.*, p. 63.

[124] *Ibid.*, p. 64.

[125] *Ibid.*, p. 64.

[126] *Ibid.*, p. 64.

of the legislative provisions, as will be seen in Sections III and IV when analysing the Long-term Residence Directive. This also seems like an unconscious acknowledgement that the Tampere objective has not been achieved in the previous ten years.

With reference to integration, the Stockholm Programme puts forward again the old formula which describes integration as "a dynamic, two-way process of mutual interaction". This requires effort by the authorities (national, regional and local) and by the host community and migrants.[127] On the issue of language, the programme calls for the identification of joint practices to support integration, such as introductory courses and language classes.[128] There is no mention of a possible compulsory element to these kinds of courses, which was also erased, as has been seen, from the Pact.

With regard to family reunification, the European Council invites the Commission to submit proposals to review Directive 2003/36 on the right to family reunification, "taking into account the importance of integration measures".[129] This is in line with the Pact which advocated limitation of the right to family reunification and the integration of family members even before arriving in the country of destination. Three Member States (France, the Netherlands and Germany) have enshrined that requirement in their national legislations when implementing Directive 2003/86.[130] Interestingly, the European Commission has already adopted a report on the implementation of the Directive.[131] In that report, it pointed out certain practices by some Member States which may be incorrectly implementing the Directive. One of those practices was the requirement to fulfil certain integration conditions before arriving in the EU. The Commission clearly stated that the admissibility of such measures depends on whether or not they are proportionate. It also highlighted the importance of assessing how the courses or tests were organised (e.g. fees, materials, venue, etc.).[132] Some of the practices by Member States, especially the Netherlands, do not seem to be in line with the principle of proportionality.[133]

---

127 *Ibid.*, p. 64.

128 *Ibid.*, p. 65.

129 *Ibid.*, p. 64.

130 See on this Chapter 7 below.

131 Commission Report, On the Application of Directive 2003/86/EC on the Right to Family Reunification, COM (2008) 610 final, 8.10.2008.

132 *Ibid.*, p. 7–8.

133 See Human Rights Watch (2008), "The Netherlands: Discrimination in the Name of Integration. Migrants' Rights under the Integration Abroad Act", Briefing Paper Number 1 May 2008, *at* http://www.hrw.org/backgrounder/2008/netherlands0508/ (accessed 1 December 2010). See on these Chapters 7 and 9 below.

It seems as if some Member States do not agree with these observations as they are willing to further limit the numbers of family members joining third-country nationals in Europe. The validity of those integration conditions will be a matter for the CJEU to establish, as will be seen below in Chapters 7 and 9.

Table III: *The positions of the different actors*

Policy Area	European Commission	Pact on Immigration and Asylum (European Council)	Stockholm Programme (European Council)
Regular migration	Establish clear rules promoting regular migration.	Organise regular migration taking into account the priorities, needs and reception capacities of the Member States.	Need to encourage flexible admission systems that are responsive to the priorities, needs, numbers and volumes determined by each Member State and enable migrants to take full advantage of their skills and competence.
Treatment of third-country nationals	Give third-country nationals fair treatment which approximates their legal status to that of EU nationals.	Give third-country nationals fair treatment.	Ensure fair treatment of third-country nationals by granting them rights and obligations comparable to those of EU citizens (Tampere formula).
Integration	Support integration. E.g. facilitate acquisition of language skills.	Support integration. E.g. promote language learning.	Integration is a dynamic two-way process. Identification of joint practices to support integration such as introductory courses and language classes.

Table III (*Cont.*)

Policy Area	European Commission	Pact on Immigration and Asylum (European Council)	Stockholm Programme (European Council)
Family reunification	Assess and eventually modify Directive 2003/86 on the right to family reunification.	Rethink family reunification in order to limit this right through the assessment of the resources and accommodation in the country of destination, and the evaluation of the family members' knowledge of the host country's language.	Evaluate and review Directive 2003/86 taking into account the importance of integration measures.
Identity	Need to increase participation of third-country nationals in order to reflect the multiple and evolving identities of European societies.	Third-country nationals have to respect the identities of the Member States and the EU.	Enhance the democratic values and social cohesion in relation to immigration and integration of immigrants and promote intercultural dialogue and contacts at all levels.

Finally, with reference to identity, the programme only skims the surface of the issue, positioning somewhere in the middle of the views mentioned above, by inviting the Commission to support the Member States' efforts "to enhance the democratic values and social cohesion in relation to immigration and integration of immigrants and to promote intercultural dialogue and contacts at all levels".[134]

[134] Stockholm Programme, p. 65.

Thus, it seems as if the programme is ambiguous enough to establish a balance between what the Commission advocated in its Communication in 2008 and the views put forward in the Pact by the European Council in 2008. That conclusion is, however, endangered by the reaffirmation, contained in the Stockholm Programme, of the principles set out in the European Pact on Migration and Asylum.[135]

This raises some questions, which will only be answered by looking at the practice that the actors involved will follow. That practice will be certainly influenced by the Treaty of Lisbon which entered into force in December 2009. The main innovations brought to the roles of the different actors have already been discussed in Chapter 1 and their practice will establish how the new powers gained by the Court and the Parliament, as well as the European Council, affect the evolution of this area.

7. *Conclusion*

This Chapter has provided a necessary historical background for the forthcoming analysis of the Long-term Residence Directive. The Chapter began by answering what were the motivations behind the EU's involvement in migration regulation. Next, it looked at how this process took place. It was acknowledged that before the Treaty of Amsterdam, cooperation in this area was mostly intergovernmental. In fact, the entry into force of the Treaty of Amsterdam in 1999, together with the Tampere European Council Conclusions in the same year, constitutes the starting point of my period of research. The years 1999–2009 have been divided into two different parts: Tampere and the Hague. Both parts have been devoted to considering the legislative changes that the involvement of the EU has brought up until 2009. Special attention has been paid to the ongoing clash between the positions of the Commission and Parliament, on the one hand, and some Member States and the Council on the other, with the Court playing an independent role with its rulings and the European Council varying its position along the years. These tensions seem to persist and the Stockholm Programme is not completely clear about which path will be followed by the Common Immigration policy. However, the renewed reference to the Tampere dogma of giving third-country nationals comparable treatment to that of EU citizens, anticipates the necessity of a generous and open policy in the area. Finally, the procedural changes brought by

135 *Ibid.*, p. 60.

Lisbon increase the influence of the Parliament, Court and Commission, which have traditionally been actors with a less restrictive view than the Council, as was evaluated in Chapter 1.

Chapter 3 concludes this second Section by looking at the historical developments which led to the adoption of the Long-term Residence Directive.

Chapter 3

The Adoption of the Long-Term Residence Directive

1. *Introduction*

The previous Chapter set the general framework for the more specific analysis of Directive 2003/109 to which I will devote Sections III and IV. Some of the issues already discussed will arise again throughout the following pages. For example, the dichotomy between the Commission and Parliament, on the one hand, and the Council and certain Member States on the other. Or the tensions between treating third-country nationals in an unequal way with European citizens, on the one hand, and granting them similar rights to those of European citizens on the other hand.

Council Directive 2003/109/EC concerning the status of third-country nationals who are long-term residents was adopted on 25 November 2003. The Directive has as its legal basis Article 63(3) and 63(4) of the EC Treaty, which has been renumbered as Article 79(2)(b) of the TFEU. While acknowledging the positive contributions of the Directive in some aspects,[1] some commentators have described it as inadequate and unsatisfactory.[2]

In the next two Sections, I will discuss those criticisms. However, in this Chapter, I intend to consider the importance of the Directive and the process for its adoption. Obviously, this also raises the question why the Directive was adopted to begin with. In order to do that, I will first mention the historical antecedents of the Directive. I will then briefly look at the negotiations for its adoption, paying special attention to the introduction of the integration conditions. As will be seen later, these integration conditions will constitute the

---

1 For instance, before the adoption of the Directive, third-country nationals could only move to another EU country for three months. For a complete overview of the situation of third-country nationals before the adoption of the Directive see H. Staples (1999), *The Legal Status of Third-country Nationals Resident in the European Union*, Kluwer Law International: The Hague.

2 S. Peers, (2004), "Implementing Equality? The Directive on Long-term Resident Third Country Nationals", *European Law Review*, Vol. 29(4), p. 437–460, at 437; L. Halleskov (2005), "The Long-term Residents Directive: A Fulfilment of the Tampere Objective of Near Equality?" *European Journal of Migration and Law*, Vol.7 (2), pp. 181–201, at 201.

main part of my analysis in the next Chapters. I will follow by giving an overall picture of the Directive itself. I will end by introducing what I will cover in the subsequent Sections and the reasons why I have chosen to analyse certain Articles of the Directive in more depth.

Thus, the questions for this Chapter are the following:

1. Why was it important to adopt a Directive on long-term resident third-country nationals? Was it really necessary to adopt a measure on this issue?
2. What are the historical legislative antecedents with regard to long-term residents in Europe?
3. What was the process for adopting the Directive? How did the integration conditions enter the negotiations?
4. What are the main features of the Directive? What are the elements that I will analyse in more depth in the following Chapters and what is the rationale for selecting them?

These questions have already been raised by other scholars whose work and contributions will be acknowledged in the following pages. It is however key to deal with them here as they provide an indispensable background to understanding the following Chapters.

2. *The Importance of Adopting a Directive on Long-Term Residents*

Why was it important to legislate on third-country nationals with a long period of residence in Europe? Was it really necessary to draft a Directive on this issue? Why was it essential to have a new special EC residence status?[3] According to some estimates, in January 2006, the number of third-country nationals residing in the EU was 18.5 million, which constituted 3.8 per cent of the total population (493 million).[4] This number would have grown to 20 million by 1 January 2009.[5] Thus, the large number of people in this category

---

[3] K. Groenendijk (2007), "The Long-Term Residents Directive, Denizenship and Integration", in A. Baldaccini, E. Guild and H. Toner (eds.), *Whose Freedom, Security and Justice? EU Immigration and Asylum Law and Policy*, Hart Publishing: Oxford, pp. 429–450, at 429.

[4] European Commission, Third Annual Report on Migration and Integration, COM (2007) 512 final, Brussels 11.9.2007, at 3. This estimate includes Bulgaria and Romania as EU Member States.

[5] K. Vasileva (2010), "Statistics in Focus", Eurostat, 45/2010, p. 1.

merited a European instrument dealing with them.[6] Despite the fact that the Tampere Conclusions called upon Member States to facilitate the acquisition of their respective nationalities by long-term residents living in their territory,[7] this has proven difficult to achieve. First, there are States outside the EU which do not accept renunciation of citizenship. This, combined with the fact that some Member States do not recognise multiple nationality except in very limited cases,[8] deprives numerous third-country nationals of the possibility to become naturalised. Second, there has been a new trend in Europe of tightening naturalisation requirements. The Netherlands is a good example: the 2003 amendment to the Act on Dutch Nationality introduced the requirement to pass a four-hour written test in both language (speaking, reading and writing) and general knowledge of Dutch society, in order to obtain citizenship. Following this change, the number of applications for naturalisation fell dramatically.[9] This trend of tightening naturalisation requirements can also be seen in other countries such as Denmark,[10] the UK[11] and France,[12] among others. Finally, many third-country nationals may legitimately be unwilling to lose their former nationality for numerous reasons. In that sense, more bilateral agreements on double nationality seem necessary as dual citizenship can

---

[6] According to data from Eurostat, there were 501.225 long-term residence permits granted in the 24 Member States bound by the Directive in 2008 and 521.907 in 2009. See this information *at* http://epp.eurostat.ec.europa.eu/portal/page/portal/population/data/database

[7] Tampere European Council Conclusions, paragraph 21.

[8] Among them we can mention Austria, Denmark, Germany and the Netherlands. H. Waldrauch (2006), "Acquisition of Nationality", in R. Bauböck, E. Ersbøll, K. Groenendijk and H. Waldrauch (eds.), *Acquisition and Loss of Nationality. Policies and Trends in 15 European Countries*, Amsterdam University Press: Amsterdam, extensive online version of Chapter 3, *at* http://www.imiscoe.org/natac/, at 40–41.

[9] K. Groenendijk (2004), "Legal Concepts of Integration in EU Migration Law", *European Journal of Migration and Law*, Vol. 6, pp. 111–126, at 112. See also R. van Oers (2008), "From Liberal to Restrictive Citizenship Policies: the Case of the Netherlands", *International Journal on Multicultural Societies (IJMS*), Vol. 10 pp. 40–59, at 49.

[10] S. Adamo (2008) "Northern Exposure: The New Danish Model of Citizenship Test", *International Journal on Multicultural Societies (IJMS)*, Vol. 10, pp. 10–28.

[11] B. Ryan (2009), "The Integration Agenda in British Migration Law", in K. Groenendijk, S. Carrera and E. Guild (eds.), *Illiberal Liberal States: Immigration, Citizenship and Integration in the EU*, Ashgate: Surrey, pp. 277–298.

[12] S. Carrera (2009), "Nationality, Immigration and 'the Republican Integration' in France", in K. Groenendijk, S. Carrera and E. Guild (eds.), *Illiberal Liberal States: Immigration, Citizenship and Integration in the EU*, Ashgate: Surrey, pp. 315–335, especially at 318–322.

be seen as an "integrative mechanism for managing the increasing transnational mobility of people".[13]

Groenendijk mentions some other reasons which made the adoption of a Directive imperative. First, Union law had focused exclusively on extending residence rights for European citizens and their dependants. Third-country nationals seemed to be invisible.[14] By so doing, Union law tended "to reinforce the idea that unequal treatment of EU citizens and third-country nationals is justified",[15] regardless of the fact that third-country nationals formed an integral part of Europe's societies and contributed to their development.[16] The fact that third-country nationals are a fundamental part of the EU links with another idea expressed by Groenendijk which is that not only will most third-country nationals residing in the Union remain there in the future, but there will also be more arriving in the coming years for a variety of reasons, including Europe's own labour needs.[17] The European Commission constantly emphasises in its reports the crucial role that immigration will play in the future EU's economic performance, especially since the population is gradually ageing and declining in Europe.[18] Finally, in the words of Groenendijk and Guild:

> With regard to EU citizens secure residence status and equal treatment ever since the establishment of the Community have been considered essential conditions for integration in the host society. Why would this be different for settled immigrants from non-EU countries?[19]

---

13 S. Pratt (2006), "Immigration, Integration and Citizenship: Latest Developments and the EU's Role" in S. Carrera (ed.), *The Nexus between Immigration, Integration and Citizenship in the EU*, CHALLENGE Collective Conference Volume, Centre for European Policy Studies, CEPS: Brussels, pp. 10–13, at 11.

14 T. Kostakopoulou (2002), "Long-term Resident Third-Country Nationals in the European Union: Normative Expectations and Institutional openings", *Journal of Ethnic and Migration Studies*, Vol. 28(3), pp. 443–462, at 443.

15 K. Groenendijk (2001), "Security of Residence and Access to Free Movement for Settled Third-Country Nationals under Community law", in E. Guild and C. Harlow (eds.), *Implementing Amsterdam, Immigration and Asylum rights in EC Law*, Hart Publishing: Oxford/Portland, pp. 225–240, at 225.

16 T. Kostakopoulou (2002), "Long-term Resident Third-Country Nationals in the European Union: Normative Expectations and Institutional openings", *Journal of Ethnic and Migration Studies*, Vol. 28(3), pp. 443–462, at 444.

17 K. Groenendijk (2001), "Security of Residence and Access to Free Movement for Settled Third-Country Nationals under Community law", in E. Guild and C. Harlow (eds.), *Implementing Amsterdam, Immigration and Asylum rights in EC Law*, Hart Publishing: Oxford/Portland, pp. 225–240, at 225–26.

18 See Chapter 2 above.

19 K. Groenendijk and E. Guild (2001), "Converging Criteria: Creating an Area of Security of Residence for Europe's Third Country Nationals", *European Journal of Migration and Law*, Vol. 3, pp. 37–59, at 40.

The importance of adopting a European provision dealing with the status of third-country nationals who had been residing in the Union for a long period was clear. In fact, there had already been some initiatives on this issue before the adoption of the Amsterdam Treaty. The next point briefly analyses those proposals.

3. *The Historical Antecedents*

There are several historical antecedents to the adoption of the Directive. In 1976 there was a Resolution by the Council of Ministers recognising the need to grant third-country nationals equal treatment in several areas. This was followed by proposals by NGOs in the mid-1980s and by a Recommendation adopted by the Parliamentary Assembly of the Council of Europe in 1988.[20] Two more precise antecedents can be found in the 1990s. The first one dates back to March 1996 when the Council adopted, on a proposal by the French Presidency, its Resolution on the status of third-country nationals residing on a long-term basis in the territory of the Member States.[21] The second antecedent is the 1997 Commission proposal for a Convention on the admission of third-country nationals.[22] The European Parliament approved the Commission's

[20] K. Groenendijk (2006), "The Legal Integration of Potential Citizens: Denizens in the EU in the Final Years before the Implementation of the 2003 Directive on Long-Term Resident Third Country Nationals" in R. Bauböck, E. Ersbøll, K. Groenendijk and H. Waldrauch (eds.), *Acquisition and Loss of Nationality. Policies and Trends in 15 European Countries*, Amsterdam University Press: Amsterdam, online version of Chapter 10, *at* http://www.imiscoe.org/natac/, pp. 385–410.

[21] Council Resolution of 4 March 1996 on the status of third-country nationals residing on a long-term basis in the territory of the Member States, OJ 1996 C 80/2. See on this K. Groenendijk and E. Guild (2001), "Converging Criteria: Creating an Area of Security of Residence for Europe's Third Country Nationals", *European Journal of Migration and Law*, Vol. 3, pp. 37–59, at 49; D. Kostakopoulou (2002), "'Integrating' Non-EU Migrants in the European Union: Ambivalent Legacies and Mutating Paradigms", *Columbia Journal of European Law*, Vol. 8(2), 181–201, at 188–192; S. Guèvremont, (2009), *Vers un Traitement Équitable des Étrangers Extracommunautaires en Séjour Régulier. Examen des Directives sur le Regroupement Familial et sur les Résidents de Longue Durée,* Wöhrmann Print Service: Zutphen, pp 307–318.

[22] Commission proposal for a Convention on the admission of third-country nationals, 30 July 1997, OJ 1997 C 337/9. See on this S. Peers (1999), "Raising Minimum Standards or Racing to the Bottom? The Commission's Proposed Migration Convention", in E. Guild (ed.), *The Legal Framework and Social Consequences of Free Movement of Persons in the European Union*, Kluwer Law International: The Hague.

proposal, subject to certain amendments, in 1999.[23] The invariable dichotomy in the approach to immigration management between the Commission, backed most of the time by the European Parliament,[24] and the Council and some Member States was present in these two proposals. On the one hand, the Council's motivation for adopting some kind of measure was that the integration of long-term residents provided them with more security, stability and social peace, in both their daily life and work, in the different Member States.[25] On the other hand, the Commission's position was that the integration of long-term residents was "an imperative dictated by the democratic and humanitarian tradition of the Member States".[26] In fact, the Commission's approach was "to take the existing rules of Community law on free movement of persons...as a model for the rights of certain categories of third country nationals and make exceptions...where necessary".[27] This was in contradiction to the Council's position. Accordingly, whereas the Council Resolution stated that long-term residence status should be granted after a minimum of ten years, the Commission's proposal reduced that period to five years' residence if a permit for a further five years had already been granted. The Commission in any case, as Boelaert rightly mentions, "regarded this Convention as an opportunity to provide input for a debate on immigration questions prior to the entry into force of the Amsterdam Treaty".[28]

---

[23] Legislative resolution embodying Parliament's opinion on the proposal for a Council Act establishing the Convention on rules for the admission of third-country nationals to the Member States (COM (97)0387 – C4-0681/97 – 97/0227(CNS)), OJ 1999 C150/196.

[24] It is notable that in 1990 the European Parliament proposed extension of the scope of application of Regulation 1612/68 to second-generation immigrants, refugees and stales persons. K. Hailbronner (1995), "Third-country Nationals and EC Law" in A. Rosas and E. Antola (eds.), *A citizens' Europe. In Search of a New Order*, Sage Publications: London/Thousand Oaks/New Delhi, pp. 182–206, at 196. For a concise analysis of the positions of the Commission and the Parliament with regard to long-term residents in the 1980s and early 1990s see T. Kostakopoulou (2002), "Long-term Resident Third-Country Nationals in the European Union: Normative Expectations and Institutional openings", *Journal of Ethnic and Migration Studies*, Vol. 28(3), pp. 443–462, at 446–448.

[25] Preamble to the Resolution of 4 March 1996.

[26] Commission proposal for a Convention on the admission of third-country nationals, p. 5.

[27] K. Groenendijk (2001), "Security of Residence and Access to Free Movement for Settled Third-Country Nationals under Community law" in E. Guild and C. Harlow (eds.), *Implementing Amsterdam, Immigration and Asylum rights in EC Law*, Hart Publishing: Oxford/Portland, pp. 225–240, at 231.

[28] S. Boelaert-Suominen (2005), "Non-EU Nationals and Council Directive 2003/109/EC on the Status of Third-country Nationals who are Long-term Residents: Five Paces Forward and Possibly Three Paces Back", *Common Market Law Review*, 42(4), pp. 1011–1052, at 1018.

The Commission's intention was successful. Since 1997 there were several proposals by NGOs concerning the status of third-country nationals.[29] In addition, there was a suggestion by a law practitioners' association.[30] Moreover, there was another proposal by a group of senior officials from seven Member States and Switzerland in 1999, as well as a Recommendation by the Committee of Ministers of the Council of Europe.[31] In the case of the Council of Europe, there were already previous instruments which dealt with the status of third-country nationals with long residence.[32] Finally, the Migration Policy Group also contributed to the debate.[33]

The whole setting changed with the adoption of the Amsterdam Treaty and with the agreement of the Tampere European Council Conclusions, which advocated further integration of third-country nationals within the Union, with rights and obligations comparable to those of EU citizens.[34] As Groenendijk points out:

> [T]he highest political body of the Union publicly recognised that the European Union has become an area of immigration and that long-term immigrants, irrespective of their nationality, should not be treated as second class citizens, but are entitled to equal treatment, secure residence rights and the option of full citizenship.[35]

---

[29] See on this S. Guèvremont, (2009), Vers un Traitement Équitable des Étrangers Extracommunautaires en Séjour Régulier. Examen des Directives sur le Regroupement Familial et sur les Résidents de Longue Durée, Wöhrmann Print Service: Zutphen, pp. 255–307.

[30] Immigration Law Practitioners' Association (ILPA) and S. Peers (2000), "The Amsterdam Proposals. The ILPA/MPG Proposed Directives on Immigration and Asylum", ILPA and Migration Policy Group: London/Brussels, at 141–160.

[31] See on this K. Groenendijk and E. Guild (2001), "Converging Criteria: Creating an Area of Security of Residence for Europe's Third Country Nationals", *European Journal of Migration and Law*, Vol. 3, pp. 37–59, at 50. See also on the Council of Europe's Recommendation and on other instruments by the Council of Europe K. Groenendijk (1999), "Long-Term Immigrants and the Council of Europe", *European Journal of Migration and Law*, Vol. 1, pp. 275–292.

[32] See on these instruments, K. Groenendijk (1999), *ibid.*

[33] J. Niessen (2000), *The Management and Managers of Immigration*, Migration Policy Group: Brussels, p. 20.

[34] Presidency Conclusions of the Tampere European Council 15 and 16 October 1999, paragraphs 18 and 21. See Chapter 2 above.

[35] K. Groenendijk (2001), "Security of Residence and Access to Free Movement for Settled Third-Country Nationals under Community law" in E. Guild and C. Harlow (eds.), *Implementing Amsterdam, Immigration and Asylum rights in EC Law*, Hart Publishing: Oxford/Portland, pp. 225–240, at 234.

In line with the Tampere mandate, the Commission announced in a Communication in 2000 that it would propose legislation concerning the status of long-term residents.[36] The Commission declared that the proposal would include measures regarding not only protection against expulsion or other rights, but also the possibility to reside in another Member State, which was considered as "an important factor of mobility within the labour market of the Union".[37] The Commission went as far as to propose for the future a kind of civic citizenship which would be inspired by the Charter of Fundamental Rights and based on the EC Treaty.[38] This idea was supported by the European Parliament.[39] However, this initiative was later abandoned by the Commission in its following Communications.

It is in this context that the adoption of the Directive must be understood. A common framework for the regulation of the status of long-term resident third-country nationals was needed: Directive 2003/109 was designed to fill that vacuum.

4. *The Process of its Adoption*

The Commission followed the guidance it had received from the European Council at Tampere and tabled a proposal for a Directive in 2001.[40] The Council reached a political agreement in June 2003.[41] As Halleskov mentions, the same dichotomy between the position of the Commission and the Council can be found in the negotiations. Whereas the Commission's proposal departed from the existing rules on free movement of workers, the Council's final text was founded on the existing national provisions in the Member States, some of which, especially Austria and Germany, tried "to retain their national

---

36 European Commission, Communication on a Community Immigration Policy, COM (2000) 757 final, p.10.

37 *Ibid.*, p. 10.

38 *Ibid.*, p. 22.

39 European Parliament Resolution on the Communication from the Commission on Immigration, Integration and Employment, OJ 2004 C92E/390, paragraph 33.

40 Proposal for a Council Directive concerning the status of third-country nationals who are long-term residents, COM (2001) 127 final, OJ 2001 C 240/79. See on the proposal J. Handoll (2003), "The Status of Third-Country Nationals Residing on a Long-term Basis", in P. de Bruycker (ed.), *The Emergence of a European Immigration Policy*, Bruylant: Bruxelles, pp. 269–362, at 328–348.

41 For a historical overview of the Council negotiations see S. Peers and N. Rogers (2006) (eds.), *EU Immigration and Asylum Law: Text and Commentary*, Martinus Nijhoff: Leiden/Boston, at 623–28.

prerogatives on key issues and to restrict the rights of long-term residents as much as possible."[42] In that process of Europeanisation of the immigration rules there was, however, a fundamental change as the Commission and the CJEU will have a say in the future, as will be seen in the following two Sections.

Thus, the Council watered down the Commission's proposal and limited some of its most important suggestions.[43] However, the most remarkable addition by the Council to the Commission's proposal was the introduction of Article 5(2) allowing for integration conditions. Integration is an elusive concept whose meaning is difficult to determine.[44] Groenendijk has highlighted three perspectives on the relationship between law and integration. The first one considers that secure residence status and equal treatment are tools for integration. The second puts forward the idea that secure residence status should be the remuneration for already completed integration. A third one argues that lack of integration or the supposed unfitness to integrate would suffice to refuse admission to the country.[45]

For our purposes, the first two perspectives (secure residence as a tool for integration versus secure residence as the remuneration for an already completed integration) are central to the analysis of the Directive.[46] The first two perspectives are present in the Directive, which makes their scrutiny very relevant since they are at odds with each other. The views of the Commission and of some of the Member States in the Council were different on this issue. Whereas the Commission interpreted integration in light of the first perspective, the Council introduced Articles 5(2) and 15(3) which are in line with the second perspective on integration.

In its proposal, the Commission was willing to secure the genuine integration of third-country nationals.[47] Moreover, this integration was recognised as a two-way process to which both the immigrants and the host society contributed. In that sense, the Commission considered that equality in different areas

---

[42] L. Halleskov (2005), "The Long-Term Residents Directive: A Fulfilment of the Tampere Objective of Near-Equality?" *European Journal of Migration and Law,* Vol. 7, pp. 181–201, at 183–184.

[43] *Ibid.*, at 183.

[44] S. Carrera (2005), "Integration as a Process of Inclusion for Migrants? The case of Long-term Residents in the EU", CEPS Working Document, No. 219/March 2005.

[45] K. Groenendijk (2004), "Legal Concepts of Integration in EU Migration Law", *European Journal of Migration and Law*, Vol. 6, pp. 111–126, at 113.

[46] The third one is more relevant in the context of Directive 2003/86 on the right to family reunification. See Chapter 7 below.

[47] Proposal for a Council Directive concerning the status of third-country nationals who are long-term residents, COM (2001) 127 final, OJ 2001 C 240/79, at 3.

such as conditions of work, access to services and civic and political rights promoted integration.[48] That is why the Commission inserted two Recitals into its proposal which are in line with the first perspective on the relationship between integration and law: equal treatment and a secure residence status enhance integration. Recital 5 of the proposal, which was kept as Recital 4 in the final Directive adopted, read as follows:

> The integration of third-country nationals who are long-term residents in the Member States is a key element in promoting economic and social cohesion, a fundamental objective of the Community...[49]

In turn, Recital 10 of the proposal, which was maintained as Recital 12 in the final Directive, established:

> In order to constitute a genuine instrument for the integration of long-term residents into the society in which they live, long-term resident status should ensure equality of treatment with citizens of the Member State in a wide range of economic and social matters.[50]

Hence, the proposal was in line with the way in which integration had been usually understood in the EU: more rights and security of residence will enhance integration. Or in other words, integration is facilitated by equality of treatment. Thus, in this perspective, integration is intrinsically related to non-discrimination.[51]

Nevertheless, the Council introduced two Articles which are in line with the second meaning identified by Groenendijk. Article 5(2) especially, but also Article 15(3), of the final Directive state that granting a long-term residence permit, with the rights and security of residence that come with it, is a prize for integration that has already been completed. That is why some Member States might be using integration in order to deny a long-term residence permit to certain third-country nationals. The validity and limits of this use will be thoroughly analysed in Chapters 7 and 9.

This second perspective was introduced into the Directive on an initiative from certain Member States, notably Austria, Germany and the Netherlands.[52]

---

[48] *Ibid.*, p. 7.

[49] *Ibid.*, p. 27.

[50] *Ibid.*, p. 27. The final version of the Council only added the words "under the relevant conditions defined by this Directive". See Recital 12 of the final Directive.

[51] K.S. Ziegler (2005), "Integrating Integration?", *European Journal of Migration and Law*, Vol. 7, pp. 119–122, at 119.

[52] K. Groenendijk (2004), "Legal Concepts of Integration in EU Migration Law", *European Journal of Migration and Law*, Vol. 6, pp. 111–126, at 122–123.

The negotiations have been explained in great detail by Carrera.[53] It is interesting to mention that it was not only the Commission that opposed the introduction of the integration conditions, but also some other Member States, such as France, Sweden and Belgium.[54] The introduction of the integration requirements represented a new feature which tried to shift the meaning and scope of the Directive. According to this new meaning, the third-country national would have to show integration before acquiring the rights and the security of residence that the long-term resident status entails. In that way some Member States were trying "to keep as much sovereignty as possible" when deciding who would be granted the long-term residence permit.[55] Accordingly, integration could become "a process of excluding the 'others' who fail to pass the 'integration test'" rather than a process of inclusion.[56] Integration is transformed into the test by which someone may shift from the category of "them" into the category of "us".[57]

It will obviously be up to the Court to uphold this interpretation or not, especially in light of the general scope and objective of the Directive which is to grant those third-country nationals who have resided for a period of five years in a Member State long-term residence status. In any case, this addition exposes important characteristics of the vision that some Member States have about third-country nationals. As Carrera points out:

> The increasing restrictions it gathered as it moved towards a final compromise reveal relevant features of the attitudes of some Member States towards the 'Other' and her/his acquisition of secure residence and mobility rights.[58]

The rationale for the introduction of this requirement was running contrary to the logic, also explicitly mentioned in the Directive, that after a period of time of lawful residence…the third-country national is "becoming more like 'one of us' and less like 'one of them'".[59] Some Member States in the Council

---

[53] S. Carrera (2009), *In Search of the Perfect Citizen? The Intersection between Integration, Immigration and Nationality in the EU*, Martinus Nijhoff: Leiden/Boston, at 175–183.

[54] *Ibid.*, at 133.

[55] *Ibid.*, at 136.

[56] S. Carrera (2005), "'Integration' as a Process of Inclusion for Migrants? The Case of Long-Term Residents in the EU", Centre for European Policy Studies, CEPS: Brussels, Working Document No. 219/March 2005, at 1.

[57] *Ibid.*, p. 18.

[58] S. Carrera (2009), *In Search of the Perfect Citizen? The Intersection between Integration, Immigration and Nationality in the EU*, Martinus Nijhoff: Leiden/Boston, at 173.

[59] J. Handoll (2003), "The Status of Third-Country Nationals Residing on a Long-term Basis", in P. de Bruycker (ed.), *The Emergence of a European Immigration Policy*, Bruylant: Brussels, pp. 269–362, at 270.

felt that those third-country nationals would have to demonstrate their integration before acquiring the status. The CJEU and the Commission will have the final word on this issue.

5. *The Main Elements of the Adopted Directive*

This part provides a quick overview of the main elements of the final version adopted. The Directive is divided into four Chapters. The subject matter of the Directive is established in the first Chapter in Article 1. According to that Article, the Directive determines:

> the terms for conferring and withdrawing long-term resident status granted by a Member State in relation to third-country nationals legally residing in its territory, and the rights pertaining thereto.

Second, the Directive also lays down:

> the terms of residence in Member States other than the one which conferred long-term status on them for third-country nationals enjoying that status.

The objectives of the Directive are more complicated, however, than the subject matter and, in my opinion, may be divided into three groups:

Integration of the third-country nationals
This objective is mentioned consistently in the Commission's proposal and in the preamble to the adopted Directive, specifically in Recitals 4 and 12, already mentioned above.

Granting of rights and obligations comparable to those of EU citizens
This aim is mentioned both in the Commission's proposal and in the preamble as a prerequisite to the above-mentioned objective. This is expressed in Recital 12 of the preamble, already analysed, and it is also in line with the Tampere Conclusions previously discussed.

The establishment of a common immigration policy
This aspiration goes hand in hand with the establishment of an area of freedom, security and justice. This also enhances the attainment of the internal market. Recital 18 of the Directive provides that:

> Establishing the conditions subject to which the right to reside in another Member State may be acquired by third-country nationals who are long-term residents should contribute to the effective attainment of an internal market as an area in which the free movement of persons is ensured.

In order to assess the achievement of this objective, special attention should be paid to the level of policy convergence which has been attained with this Directive.[60]

These different objectives will be assessed in the following two Sections of the book, when I will scrutinise the implementation of some provisions by Member States.

Coming back to the analysis of the Directive, it can be seen how Article 3 excludes some third-country nationals from its scope, which will be analysed in Chapter 4, whereas Article 3(3) provides that it applies without prejudice to more favourable provisions of bilateral and multilateral agreements.

Chapter II sets out the rules for obtaining the long-term residence permit in a Member State. The Directive applies to third-country nationals who have been residing regularly and continuously within the territory of a Member State for five years "immediately prior to the submission of the relevant application" (Article 4). Article 5 deals with the conditions for acquiring this status (sickness insurance, stable and regular resources and integration conditions). The implementation of these integration conditions are a central element as will be seen in Chapter 7 of this book. Article 6 provides Member States with the possibility to refuse granting the status on grounds of public policy or public security. Article 7 lays down the procedure required in order to apply for a long-term residence permit. Article 8 establishes the important principle that a long-term residence permit will be permanent unless it is lost in accordance with Article 9. Article 9 establishes the withdrawal or loss of this status under certain circumstances (fraudulent acquisition, adoption of an expulsion measure or absence for more than 12 consecutive months), whereas Article 10 provides for the obligation to ensure the possibility to mount a legal challenge in such cases and the obligation for the Member State concerned to give reasons for any decision rejecting an application or withdrawing that status.

Article 11 is one of the key provisions as it enumerates some rights which long-term residents enjoy on an equal footing with nationals, as well as certain limitations to that enjoyment. Notably, long-term residents enjoy equal treatment with nationals as regards access to employment and self-employed activity, education and vocational training, recognition of professional diplomas,

---

[60] By policy convergence I refer "not only to the degree of harmonisation or level of 'Europeanisation' based on the number of legal instruments that have been adopted at the EU level, but also to the discretion left to member states in the application of a wide range of provisions incorporated in the EU laws." T. Balzacq and S. Carrera (2005), *Migration, Borders and Asylum. Trends and Vulnerabilities in EU Policy*, Centre For European Policy Studies, CEPS: Brussels, at 2.

certificates and other qualifications, social security, social assistance and social protection, tax benefits, access to procedures for obtaining housing, freedom of association and affiliation and membership of an organisation representing workers or employers and free access to the entire territory. These rights are subject to certain limitations, also included in Article 11.[61] It can be affirmed that Article 11 offers a quite comprehensive list of rights in which only certain political rights (for example, the right to vote and stand as a candidate in municipal elections) might be missing. The Commission's proposal was more comprehensive[62] but any limitation on these rights will be subject to the scrutiny by the Commission and the CJEU.

Article 12 deals with the expulsion of long-term residents and Chapter 5 of this book will be devoted to its analysis.

Article 13 establishes that Member States are free to issue their own permanent residence permits in accordance with national law. Those national residence permits might be easier to obtain but they do not confer the right of residence in other Member States as provided in the next Chapter of the Directive.

In fact, Chapter III sets up the possibilities, conditions and limitations for residence in other Member States. Chapter 6 of the book will provide an in-depth examination of these provisions.

Finally, Chapter IV contains some final provisions regarding entry into force, transposition and the obligation for the Commission to produce reports on the application of the Directive as well as proposing amendments if necessary.

6. *The Key Provisions in the Directive*

In the following two Sections of this work, which include respectively Chapters 4 to 6, and 7 to 9, I will deal with four Articles in the Directive: Articles 3(2) (e), 12 and 14 in Section III and Article 5(2) in Section IV. These are, in my opinion, the most important ones from the perspective of a third-country national for the reasons explained below.

Article 3(2) (e) sets out that third-country nationals whose "residence permit has been formally limited" may not be able to obtain long-term residence

[61] See on this L. Halleskov, (2005), "The Long-term Residents Directive: A Fulfilment of the Tampere Objective of Near Equality?", *European Journal of Migration and Law*, Vol.7(2), pp. 181–201.

[62] See Proposal for a Council Directive concerning the status of third-country nationals who are long-term residents, COM (2001) 127 final, OJ 2001 C 240/79, Article 12.

status. Hence, this Article touches upon the first fundamental question that has to be asked when dealing with this legal instrument: which third-country nationals are eligible for obtaining this status? The interpretation of this provision is central in order to analyse the subsequent provisions. In other words, if a third-country national is not eligible for this status, there is no need to look at the rest of the elements.

Article 5(2) establishes that "Member States may require third-country nationals to comply with integration conditions, in accordance with national law". Therefore, this Article deals with the next fundamental question for a third-country national: what are the conditions that I have to fulfil in order to be eligible for the status? Article 5(2) is key because most Member States have introduced some integration conditions which might be difficult to fulfil and hence might deprive many eligible third-country nationals of the possibility to obtain a more secure status. The centrality of this provision and the importance of the analysis of the integration conditions, which go beyond a purely legal perspective, mean that I will devote Section IV, Chapters 7, 8 and 9 to its scrutiny.

Article 12 deals with the possibility to expel a long-term resident. This is also very significant for a third-country national. The question here is: once I have obtained the long-term residence permit, what is my security of residence? In other words, may I be expelled for committing a minor offence or do I have enhanced protection?

Finally, Articles 14, 15 and Chapter III of the Directive establish more broadly the possibility to reside in other Member States. This is also essential and, in fact, it has already been mentioned that one of the objectives of the Directive is to establish the conditions for residing in other Member States. Here the question is: once I have obtained the long-term residence permit, is it possible for me to reside in other Member States in the Union?

There is another Article which I could have included in my analysis because of its relevance and importance. That is Article 11 on the rights that third-country nationals obtain once they acquire long-term residence status, and which have been mentioned above. However, it is impossible to deal with it in this work because its length would require several chapters to explain the implementation of the various rights included within it.[63]

[63] See on Article 11 L. Halleskov (2005), "The Long-term Residents Directive: A Fulfilment of the Tampere Objective of Near Equality?" *European Journal of Migration and Law*, Vol.7(2), pp. 181–201; M. Bell (2007), "Civic Citizenship and Migrant Integration", *European Public Law*, Vol. 13(2), pp. 311–333, at 321–326.

Hence, I intend to touch upon various related matters in each of the following Chapters 4 to 6 and Chapters 7 to 9. The questions that I will answer in Sections III and IV are the following:

1. What advantages may third-country nationals obtain from the Directive?
2. What are the limitations to those advantages? Were those limitations present in the Commission's proposal? Are there any similar limitations for European citizens? What have been the main criticisms to those limitations by academics?
3. How are Member States implementing the Directive? Are there any changes with regard to the situation before the adoption of the Directive? Are those changes positive or negative for third-country nationals?
4. How could these Articles be interpreted by the CJEU? Are there any parallels that could be drawn from its previous case law on Turkish citizens, European citizens or from its interpretation of other immigration Directives?

These questions, therefore, look at how Member States have implemented the Directive, paying special attention to my four case studies (Spain, Italy, Sweden and Latvia) but also mentioning the problems present in its transposition in other countries. These questions then look at the way in which primarily the Court of Justice as well as the national Courts, but also the Commission, could interpret some of the provisions. The answers to these various questions will provide a clearer picture of whether the EU is constructing a "Legal Other" through the implementation and interpretation of the Long-term Residence Directive, or whether the long-term residence Directive has the potential to become a subsidiary form of EU citizenship which escapes direct control by Member States. That is the central question of this book as was explained in Chapter 1.

7. *Conclusion*

This second Chapter of Section II has provided the background to the adoption of the Long-term Residence Directive. First of all, it was seen that there were various reasons which made it advisable to adopt common legislation in the area. In fact, this Chapter showed how the idea of giving more rights and security of residence, to third-country nationals who have had their homes for a long time in the EU, was an old one for different European institutions, as well as for other stakeholders such as NGOs. However, an analysis of the negotiations illustrated that even if the three institutions agreed on adopting a measure, the usual divergence in their positions was still present.

The introduction of Article 5(2) allowing Member States the possibility to introduce integration conditions has a special significance for our investigation. This provision will be analysed at length in Chapters 7, 8 and 9. Finally, the Chapter provided an overview of the main elements of the Directive, in addition to a more in-depth explanation for the rationale in choosing to consider in more detail certain Articles in the next two Sections. In fact, I have introduced the questions that will be answered in the following Chapters which will allow the reader to see whether the EU is in the process of constructing a new "Legal Other", or whether, on the contrary, the status of third-country nationals is getting closer to that of EU citizens through a long-term residence status with the potential to become a subsidiary form of EU citizenship which escapes direct control by Member States.

Section III

The Content of the Long-Term Residence Directive

Chapter 4

Scope of the Directive: Article 3

1. *Introduction*

In this Section of the book, I will consider the content of the Long-term Residence Directive and investigate the implementation and possible interpretation of some of its provisions, notably Articles 3, 12 and 14.

In this Chapter, I will examine Article 3, which defines the scope of the Directive. I will follow the same structure in the next two Chapters. First, I will highlight the main provisions of this Article. I will then consider the limitations, and compare them with the Commission's proposal. I will pay particular attention to the clause by which long-term residence may not be granted to those third-country nationals whose "residence permit has been formally limited". In this regard, I will review the criticism that other authors have expressed with reference to this limitation. I will also briefly indicate whether or not those limitations are applicable to European citizens. The main bulk of my analysis will be to see how some Member States are interpreting this provision and how they are implementing it in their national legal orders. As in the next two Chapters, I will pay special attention to my four case studies. Nevertheless, I will also try to identify important problems in two other Member States, Austria and Cyprus, which will assist me in my analysis of possible interpretation by the CJEU, as well as by national courts. The Commission could also take into consideration any possible problems in the implementation of this provision in some Member States. The situation before the adoption of the Directive will also be examined to see to what extent the position of the third-country national has changed. Once I have analysed Article 3, it will then be possible to see how the CJEU could interpret it, particularly in light of its previous case law on Turkish citizens.[1] I will consider particular issues which have been the subject of interpretation by the CJEU in the context of the Turkey Agreement. It will then be possible to draw some

---

[1] See on this R. Gutmann (1999), *Die Assoziationsfreizügigkeit türkischer Staatsangehöriger: Ihre Entdeckung und ihr Inhalt*, Nomos Verlagsgesellschaft: Baden-Baden.

conclusions as to whether the Court could interpret in the same way some of the questions raised in relation to the implementation of Article 3.[2]

Thus, the questions for this Chapter are as follows:

1. Which third-country nationals may acquire long-term residence status? What does the Directive say with regard to its scope?
2. What are the limitations in the Directive? Were those limitations present in the Commission's proposal? What have been the main criticisms of those limitations? Are there any similar limitations applicable in any way to European citizens?
3. How are Member States implementing the Directive? Are there any changes with regard to the situation before the adoption of the Directive?
4. How could the CJEU interpret this Article? Are there any parallelisms that could be drawn from its previous case law on the Turkey Agreement?

2. *The Scope of the Directive*

I will investigate here which third-country nationals may acquire long-term residence status. Article 3 deals with the scope of the Directive. According to Article 3(1), the "Directive applies to third-country nationals residing legally in the territory of a Member State". Hence, the first important consideration is that the Directive does not apply to those third-country nationals who are irregularly present in the EU. Irregular migrants constitute an insignificant proportion of the total population of the EU.[3] However, the approach to dealing with their situation is mostly restrictive and has as its main purpose the expelling of undocumented migrants, especially since the recent adoption of the so-called Returns Directive.[4] Consequently, the third-country nationals in

[2] See for a very brief analysis of some of the issues discussed in this Chapter: D. Acosta (2011), "Directive 2003/109 on Long-term Residence for Third-Country Nationals: Possible Future Interpretation by the European Court of Justice" in C. Murphy and P. Green (eds.), *Law and Outsiders: Norms, Processes and Othering in the 21st Century*, Hart: Oxford, pp. 143–165, at 145–149.

[3] See on this Chapter 1 above.

[4] Directive 2008/115/EC of the European Parliament and of the Council of 16 December 2008 on common standards and procedures in Member States for returning illegally staying third-country nationals, OJ 2008 L 348/98. For an analysis of the Directive see A Baldaccini (2009), "The Return and Removal of Irregular Migrants under EU Law: An Analysis of the Returns Directive", *European Journal of Migration and Law* 11, pp. 1–17. See also D. Acosta (2009), "The Good, the Bad and the Ugly in EU Migration Law: Is the European Parliament Becoming Bad and Ugly (The Adoption of Directive 2008/115: The Returns Directive)", *European Journal of Migration and Law*, Vol. 11(1), pp. 19–39.

this situation of administrative irregularity may only be within the scope of the Directive if they benefit from a regularisation of their situation, at an individual or collective level.[5] Once they have regularised their situation they will have the opportunity to acquire a long-term residence permit.[6]

Article 3 of the Directive has to be read together with Article 4(1). This Article provides that: "Member States shall grant long-term resident status to third-country nationals who have resided legally and continuously within its territory for five years immediately prior to the submission of the relevant application". It is central to emphasise that the Directive demands five years of lawful residence and not five years holding a residence permit. Thus, those periods in which a third-country national did not have a residence permit, for example, because of an administrative delay, will count towards the five-year total.[7] Moreover, many authors have understood that Article 4(1) has direct effect.[8] I agree with this interpretation as Article 4(1) confers on third-country nationals a right which is enforceable by them in the national courts of a Member State and which the latter must protect.

Finally, Article 3(3) provides that the Directive shall apply without prejudice to more favourable provisions of bilateral or multilateral agreements. I will not deal with this subject further.[9]

3. *Limitations*

Here I intend to examine the limitations in order to answer three main questions: were they present in the Commission's proposal? Are there similar ones applicable to European citizens? And what have been the main criticisms by other scholars?

Article 3(2) establishes the limitations to the general rule stated above. It defines the third-country nationals to whom the Directive does not apply.

---

[5] See on regularisations Chapter 1 above.

[6] S. Peers (2004), "Implementing Equality? The Directive on Long Term Resident Third Country Nationals", *European Law Review*, Vol. 29(4), pp. 437–460, at 444.

[7] *Ibid.*, p. 445.

[8] *Ibid.*, p. 443; K. Groenendijk (2007), "The Long-Term Residents Directive, Denizenship and Integration", in A. Baldaccini, E. Guild and H. Toner (eds.), *Whose Freedom, Security and Justice? EU Immigration and Asylum Law and Policy*, Hart Publishing: Oxford, pp. 429–450, at 439.

[9] See on Article 3(3) of Directive 2003/109, S. Boelaert-Suominen (2005), "Non-EU Nationals and Council Directive 2003/109/EC on the Status of Third-country Nationals who are Long-term Residents: Five Paces Forward and Possibly Three Paces Back", *Common Market Law Review*, Vol. 42(4), pp. 1011–1052, at 1035–1048.

The Commission, when it first suggested it, had in mind a horizontal instrument which would define the scope of the proposal in broad terms.[10] However, the Commission also understood that, based on the temporary nature of their residence, certain categories of third-country nationals should be excluded as they did not intend to settle in the Member State in which they currently resided. Following that rationale, the Commission realised that refugees and doctoral students would be included within the scope of the Directive. However, the Council rejected both categories, and the list of third-country nationals who cannot apply for a long-term residence permit was completed as follows in Article 3(2):

a. Those who reside in order to pursue studies or vocational training;
b. Those who are authorised to reside in a Member State on the basis of temporary protection or are awaiting a decision on their status;
c. Those who are authorised to reside in a Member State on the basis of a subsidiary form of protection or are awaiting the outcome of such an application;
d. Those who are refugees or have applied for recognition as refugees;
e. Those who reside solely on temporary grounds such as au pairs or seasonal workers, or as workers posted by a service provider for the purposes of cross-border provision of services, or as cross-border providers of services;
f. Those who enjoy diplomatic status;
g. Those whose residence permit has been formally limited.

Hence, the final version included two important modifications to the one originally proposed by the Commission: the above-mentioned exclusion of doctoral students and refugees,[11] and the inclusion of a clause regarding those whose residence permit had been formally limited. I will focus on the second limitation[12] as its importance rests on the fact that on many occasions Member States do not grant third-country nationals an unlimited residence permit.

---

[10] Proposal for a Council Directive concerning the status of third-country nationals who are long-term residents, COM (2001) 127 final, OJ 2001 C 240/79, p. 12.

[11] The European Commission made a proposal in 2007 to extend the scope of Directive 2003/109 to beneficiaries of international protection. That proposal had not been approved by 1 December 2010. See Proposal for a Council Directive Amending Directive 2003/109/EC to Extend its Scope to Beneficiaries of International Protection, COM (2007) 298 final, Brussels, 6.6.2007. See on this Chapter 1 above.

[12] On the exclusion of refugees see L. Halleskov (2005), "The Long-term Residents Directive: A Fulfilment of the Tampere Objective of near Equality?" *European Journal of Migration and Law*, Vol.7 (2), pp. 181–201, at 184–85.

On the contrary, they are usually limited by economic activity, by time, or by both.[13] Apparently, this sentence was added following a proposal from Belgium, without any further justification.[14] Scholars lamented this exclusion from the scope of the Directive of a potentially large number of third-country nationals. Guild, for instance, argued that this could make "a mockery of the Tampere Council Meeting's statement of intention."[15] In turn, Peers signalled that the definition of "limited" would be an issue of Union law and not of national law. Moreover, he argued:

> In light of the purpose of the Directive, the exception can only apply to persons whose residence permit cannot in principle be extended under the relevant applicable rules at all, or for more than a certain period (totalling less than five years).[16]

It is, in any case, regrettable that such an ambiguity was inserted into the Directive.[17] Furthermore, there is nothing similar for European citizens. According to Article 16 of Directive 2004/38, Union citizens acquire a right of permanent residence when they have lived regularly and continuously in the territory of another Member State and, hence, there is no similar limitation to Article 3(2) of Directive 2003/109.

4. *Implementation*

Here, I examine how Member States are implementing the Directive. In particular, I investigate the way in which they are implementing the clause "where their residence permit has been formally limited" in their national legislations.

---

[13] C. Adam and A. Devillard (2008), *Comparative Study of the Laws in the 27 EU Member States for Legal Migration*, European Parliament Study, Policy Department C: Citizens' Rights and Constitutional Affairs: Brussels, at 76–77.

[14] L. Halleskov (2005), "The Long-term Residents Directive: A Fulfilment of the Tampere Objective of Near Equality?" *European Journal of Migration and Law*, Vol.7 (2), pp. 181–201, at 184–85.

[15] E. Guild (2004), *The Legal Elements of European Identity: EU citizenship and Migration Law*, Kluwer Law International, European Law Library: The Hague, at 225.

[16] S. Peers (2004), "Implementing Equality? The Directive on Long Term Resident Third Country Nationals", *European Law Review* 29(4), pp. 437–460, at 448–49.

[17] Ireland, which is not bound by this Directive, seems to have followed this line of thought in its 2010 Immigration, Residence and Protection Bill not yet adopted by 1 December 2010. Section 46(5) (f) states that a period of residence shall not be reckonable for the purposes of obtaining long-term residence when "it is a period where the foreign national's residence permission was non-renewable or otherwise expressly subject to a condition that the period not be reckonable for purposes of this section".

I will not present an exhaustive analysis of how all 24 Member States are implementing this aspect. Instead, I will consider some important problems that have arisen in some Member States, notably Austria and Cyprus, as their implementation may not be in line with the Directive. Next, I will explore in more depth its transposition in my four case studies. I will also briefly mention the general situation within the EU before its adoption. I will then be able to see in the next part how the CJEU might interpret this provision in light of its previous jurisprudence, and how the Commission could react to its implementation in some Member States. There seem to be two fundamental problems which could arise in the interpretation of Article 3.

4.1. *Exclusion of Categories of Third-country Nationals*

The first problem would be to see to what extent the list presented is exhaustive. This is the case according to, for example, Peers.[18] However, there is the risk that some Member States might classify the status of some groups of third-country nationals as temporary. That would *a priori* exclude those groups from the possibility of obtaining the permit. This might be the case in ***Austria***. There are different types of residence titles according to the Austrian Settlement and Residence Act, two of which are of interest for our subject: 1) "Settlement permit", for a non-temporary limited settlement in the Federal territory for a specific purpose with the possibility of obtaining a residence title "long-term resident's EC residence permit"; and 2) "Residence Permit", "for a non-permanent limited residence in the Federal territory for a specific purpose with the possibility of obtaining a settlement permit afterwards, unless otherwise provided for by this Federal law".[19]

There are, therefore, two different permits. The first makes it possible to obtain the long-term residence permit. The second, on the contrary, presupposes the possibility of obtaining the first permit, unless otherwise provided by the Austrian Settlement and Residence Act. This distinction is very relevant, as according to Article 2(3) of the same Act: "The legal residence of an alien by virtue of a residence permit is not considered as settlement". As has been seen, it is only with a settlement permit, and not with a residence permit, that a third-country national can acquire long-term residence status. Hence, a question immediately arises: which categories of third-country nationals are granted a residence permit and not a settlement permit? The answer to that

[18] S. Peers (2004), "Implementing Equality? The Directive on Long Term Resident Third Country Nationals" *European Law Review* 29(4), pp. 437–460, at 446.

[19] Article 8 Austrian Settlement and Residence Act.

question can be found in Articles 58 to 67 in which the categories of third-country nationals who are granted a residence permit are described. I will briefly take two of those categories as an example: social service workers and artists.

The former comes under Article 66. Article 66(1) describes the prerequisites that someone has to possess in order to be admitted as a social service worker. In turn, Article 66(2) provides that the "resident permit shall be issued for a period of validity not exceeding one year; renewal is not permitted." Consequently, this category of workers would not create problems with regard to the scope of the Directive due to the fact that they are clearly excluded, as their residence permit cannot be extended for longer than a year.

The latter category, artists, is different. Their status is enshrined in Article 61, which describes the conditions that they have to fulfil in order to be granted a residence permit as artists. A disparity with the previous provision on social service workers is that there is no similar clause stating that their residence permit cannot be extended beyond one year. Consequently, what would be the case if an artist who has been legally and continuously residing for five years in Austrian territory wishes to obtain the long-term residence permit? Certainly, he could always apply for a change of status, which would be subject to the quota requirement,[20] but could the Austrian authorities deny him an EC long-term residence permit on the basis that he was residing in Austria with a residence and not a settlement permit? I will return to this question in the next part where I will see how the CJEU has in the past dealt with a similar issue with regard to Turkish workers.

4.2. *Exclusion of Third-country Nationals who have resided in a Member State for Five Years with Different Renewed Residence Permits*

This case is different from the one above. Here I am not describing categories of third-country nationals excluded *a priori* from the possibility of obtaining a long-term residence permit because of their performance of a particular profession. The issue here is to see what happens with those third-country nationals who reside in the EU with temporary limited permits which are, nonetheless, renewed, producing the result that the non-European citizen resides for five years in the Member State and is eligible to obtain long-term residence status. A similar situation has already occurred in ***Cyprus***.

The facts are the following: In 2000, Mrs Cresencia Cabotaje, a citizen from the Philippines, arrived regularly in Cyprus in order to work as a

[20] Article 12 Austrian Settlement and Residence Act.

domestic worker. She first had a three months' residence and employment permit, which was then extended to four years. Before her permit expired, she was granted a further non-renewable permit for two more years. Later, when she had completed five years of continuous and legal residence, she applied for a long-term residence permit, on the basis of Article 4(1) of Directive 2003/109. Nevertheless, her application was rejected due to the fact that she did not come within the scope of the Directive, as her residence permit had been limited in time.

The matter arrived at the Supreme Court, which is the highest court in the Republic of Cyprus and against whose rulings there is no judicial remedy under Cypriot law.[21] The Court began by acknowledging that the Directive had direct effect as of 23 January 2006, regardless of the fact that Cyprus had not implemented it by that date.[22] Nevertheless, the Court understood that based on Article 3(2) (e), the third-country national did not have the right to a long-term residence permit.[23] The Court argued that a third-country national with a limited residence permit could not have expectations to "put down roots in the country", in the sense of Recital 6 of the Directive. The Court said that the residence permit had been granted to work for a specific employer and that, moreover, the applicant had accepted, by going to Cyprus to work in very specific employment, that the temporary restriction was an inseparable condition of her permit. Hence, according to the Court, not to grant a long-term residence permit was in line with the Directive, even if the third-country national had already resided legally and continuously in the country for five years. It is notable that the Court included another argument in defence of its position, which cannot be found in any of the Articles of the Directive. The Court said that the immigration policy of the Republic of Cyprus should take into account various factors, such as the degree of the possibility of accepting and assimilating third-country nationals, due to the Republic's position, small size and population. This would be, according to the Court, a legitimate parameter of interpretation within the framework of the Directive.

This decision by the Supreme Court of Cyprus raises some questions. First, to what extent the Court of last instance had to send a preliminary question to

---

21 *Cresencia Cabotaje Motilla v Republic of Cyprus through the Interior Minister and the Chief Immigration Officer*, Supreme Court Case No. 673/2006 (21 January 2008).

22 The Directive was later implemented by Article 18Z (2) of the Aliens and Immigration Law Cap 105, as amended by Law 8(1)/2007. Trimikliniotis has pointed out that whereas Directive 2003/109 reads "persons whose residence permit has been formally limited" the Cypriot implementing legislations states "persons whose residence permit has been formally limited *as to its duration*". See N. Trimikliniotis (2010), "Country Report: Cyprus", EUDO Citizenship Observatory, January 2010, Revised April 2010, p. 17.

23 The Decision was taken by a majority of nine judges with four others dissenting. *Ibid.*, at 17.

the CJEU on the matter?[24] Second, what would have been the interpretation of this case had it arrived at the CJEU, especially in light of its previous jurisprudence with regard to Turkish workers? Third, is it possible for a country to take into consideration other, in the words of the Court, "legitimate parameters" in order not to grant a long-term residence permit? I will not deal with the first question here as it is not within the scope of this work.[25] I will return to questions two and three in the next part, following my analysis of the implementation of the Directive in my four case studies.

4.3. *Implementation in Italy, Spain, Sweden and Latvia*

The implementation of this provision in my four case studies has not posed many problems when compared with Cyprus and Austria.

Italy

This provision was implemented correctly. According to Article 9 of the Single Text on Immigration,[26] those third-country nationals who have resided regularly for five years in Italy may apply for a long-term residence permit. Article 9(3) excludes certain third-country nationals from the possibility of obtaining it in line with Article 3(2) of the Directive.

Spain

This provision was implemented correctly. According to Article 32(2) of the Aliens Law,[27] those third-country nationals who have resided continuously for five years in Spain have the right to obtain long-term residence status.

---

[24] This has been criticised by some authors. See N. Kyriakou (2010), "National Judges and Supranational Laws on the Effective Application of the EC Law and the ECHR: The Case of Cyprus", June 10 2010, p. 19, *at* SSRN: http://ssrn.com/abstract=1623560 (accessed 1 December 2010).

[25] See on this Case 283/81, *CILFIT Srl v Ministero della Sanità*, [1982] ECR 3415. See also J. Steiner and L. Woods (2009), *EU Law*, Oxford University Press: Oxford, at 239–246.

[26] The Directive was implemented in Italy by the Decreto legislativo 8 gennaio 2007, n.3 Attuazione della direttiva 2003/109/CE relativa allo status di cittadini di Paesi terzi soggiornanti di lungo periodo, which amended the Decreto legislativo 25 luglio 1998, n. 286, Testo unico delle disposizioni concernenti la disciplina dell'immigrazione e norme sulla condizione dello straniero. The Single Text on Immigration was then modified by Legge 15 luglio 2009, n. 94, Disposizioni in materia di sicurezza pubblica.

[27] The Directive has been implemented in Spain by the Aliens Law: Ley Orgánica 2/2009, de 11 de diciembre, de reforma de la Ley Orgánica 4/2000, de 11 de enero, sobre derechos y libertades de los extranjeros en España y su integración social, BOE 12 diciembre de 2009. A Regulation developing this Law had not been adopted by 1 December 2010. See on this Law: D. Acosta (2010), "La Nueva Ley de Inmigración en España. Un Primer Análisis de sus Aspectos Liberales y Restrictivos" in J. Roy and R. Domínguez (eds.), *España, la Unión*

There is no mention of third-country nationals with a formally limited residence permit.

Sweden

There is a slight problem with the implementation of this provision. According to Chapter 5a section 1 of the Aliens Act,[28] a long-term residence permit "shall be granted if the applicant has spent at least five years in Sweden without interruption and during this time has had, and at the time of the application has a permanent residence permit". This need to have a permanent residence permit during the five years would seem to present a problem. However, there are no categories of immigrants residing legally and continuously in the country for five years without having received a permanent residence permit. This principle is nonetheless contrary to the Directive and should be amended. As in the case of Spain, there is no mention of a formally limited residence permit.

Latvia

There are no particular issues with regard to implementation. The Long-term Residence Law[29] provides in its first Article the possibility of obtaining the permit after five years of regular residence. Non-citizens in Latvia are treated as long-term residents under Directive 2003/109.[30]

The implementation by these four Member States show that there is consensus by a majority that has correctly understood the provisions in this Article, in clear contrast with the cases of Cyprus and Austria mentioned

Europea y la Integración Latinoamericana, Florida European Union Centre/Jean Monnet Chair: Miami, pp. 51–61. For an analysis of the Spanish immigration legislation prior to the adoption of the last modification see C. Gortázar (2002), "Spain: Two Immigration Acts at the End of the Millennium. The Organic Law on the Rights and Liberties of Aliens in Spain and their Social Integration: Organic Law 4/2000 of January 11 Modified by Organic Law 8/2000 of December 22", *European Journal of Migration and Law*, Vol. 4(1), pp. 1–21; E. Relaño Pastor (2004), "¿Sancionar al Inmigrante o Proteger las Fronteras?: Un Análisis Críticos de la Ley de Extranjería 14/2003, de 20 de noviembre, y la Política de Inmigración Común de la Unión Europea", *Diario La Ley*, AÑO XXV. Número 6017, jueves, 13 de mayo de 2004, pp. 1–8.

28 The Directive was implemented in Sweden by the Aliens Act (2005:716) Issued: 29 September 2005, with amendments: up to and including Swedish Code of Statutes 2009:16. It entered into force: 31 March 2006.

29 In Latvia the Directive was implemented by Law "Long-term resident status of the European Community in Latvia" which was enacted on 21 July 2006 and by the Immigration Law in force since 1 May 2003, with its amendments up to 22 April 2010.

30 K. Kruma (2009), "Checks and Balances in Latvian Nationality Policies: National Agendas and International Frameworks", in R. Bauböck, B. Perchinig and W. Sievers (eds.) (2009), *Citizenship Policies in the New Europe*, Amsterdam University Press: Amsterdam, pp. 67–96, at 73.

above. Sweden should however redraft its legislation in order to not breach the Directive.

To conclude, I will briefly refer to the general situation in the Member States before the adoption of the Directive. It seems, according to the study by Groenendijk, Guild and Barzilay, that some Member States discriminate against some third-country nationals in order to exclude them from the scope of their national long-term residence permits, depending on the residence or employment status that they had before applying for it.[31] Suffice it to say here, that once those concepts have been worded in the Directive, it is clear that Member States cannot continue any discriminatory practice, as they are subject to the decisions of the CJEU, and the implementation of the Directive will be monitored by the European Commission.

5. *Possible Interpretation by the CJEU*

In this part I intend to answer two questions. First, I will see how the CJEU has interpreted similar issues in the Turkey Agreement. Second, I will investigate whether I can establish some parallelism between the previous case law on that agreement and Article 3 of the Directive.

In the previous pages I individualised three controversies with regard to the interpretation of Article 3:

1. Is it possible under the terms of the Directive to exclude *a priori* certain categories of third-country nationals, for example artists, from the scope of the Directive?
2. What would be the situation if someone with consecutive limited and non-renewable permits fulfilled the requirement of five years' continuous and legal residence? Would it be possible to deny that person a long-term residence permit? Does the fact that the person agreed to enter a Member State in order to work for a specific employer on a temporary basis allow the Member State not to grant a long-term residence permit?
3. What tools can be used to interpret the Directive?

The Court of Justice has already faced similar situations which might help to answer these questions. In particular, there are a number of judgments regarding the situation of Turkish workers under Decision 1/80[32] which I shall

[31] K. Groenendijk, E. Guild and R. Barzilay (2000), *Study on the Legal Status of Third-Country Nationals who are Long-Term Residents in a Member State of the European Union*, Centre for Migration Law, Radboud University of Nijmegen, Nijmegen: The Netherlands, p. 100.

[32] Decision No 1/80 of the Association Council.

use in order to give a possible response to the previous issues. For our purposes, the most relevant Article in Decision 1/80 is 6(1), which is worded as follows:

> 1. Subject to Article 7 on free access to employment for members of his family, a Turkish worker duly registered as belonging to the labour force of a Member State:
>   - shall be entitled in that Member State, after one year's legal employment, to the renewal of his permit to work for the same employer, if a job is available;
>   - shall be entitled in that Member State, after three years of legal employment and subject to the priority given to workers of Member States of the Community, to respond to another offer of employment, with an employer of his choice, made under normal conditions and registered with the employment services of that State, for the same occupation;
>   - shall enjoy free access in that Member State to any paid employment of his choice, after four years of legal employment.

There is constant case law regarding Article 6 and Decision No 1/80 in general and some important steps that the Court has always followed in order to support its case law:

Direct effect

The Court has, time after time, argued that Article 6(1) of Decision 1/80 has direct effect and, thus, Turkish nationals who satisfy its provisos may rely directly on the rights given to them.[33] It could certainly be the case that Article 4(1) of Directive 2003/109 also has direct effect.[34] Indeed this was conceded by the Cyprus Supreme Court. This was also recognised in an instruction from 2009 by the Spanish Ministry of Labour and Immigration. Spain had not implemented the Directive by that time but the Ministry admitted that a third-country national could directly rely on it in order to obtain the long-term residence permit.[35]

First entry into a Member State

The Court has consistently held that Decision No 1/80 does not encroach upon the competence that Member States retain in order to regulate the first entry

[33] See Case C-192/89, *S.Z. Sevince v Staatssecretaris van Justitie* [1990] ECR I-03461.

[34] K. Groenendijk (2007), "The Long-Term Residents Directive, Denizenship and Integration", in A. Baldaccini, E. Guild and H. Toner (eds.), *Whose Freedom, Security and Justice? EU Immigration and Asylum Law and Policy*, Hart Publishing: Oxford, pp. 429–450, at 439; S. Peers (2004), "Implementing Equality? The Directive on Long Term Resident Third Country Nationals" *European Law Review*, Vol. 29(4), pp. 437–460, at 443.

[35] Instrucción DGI/SGJR/04/2009, Spanish Ministry of Labour and Immigration.

into its territory of a Turkish national, as well as the provisos under which he may take up his first employment and the conditions under which he works during his first year of residence.[36] However, once that first year ends, Member States lose these prerogatives whereas, at the same time, Turkish nationals obtain some rights as workers already integrated into the labour force of the particular Member State. When Turkish workers have a stable and secure position in the labour force, they obtain these rights regardless of the reason for which their first residence permit was originally granted.[37]

This rationale is also applicable to Directive 2003/109. In fact, the Directive remains silent as to a possible right of entry into the territory. However, once a third-country national has been legally resident in a Member State for a period of five years, he obtains certain rights. The third-country national will be able to acquire long-term residence status, regardless of the reasons for his first entry, unless he is included within one of the categories of Article 3.

Integration of Turkish workers

The Court has also always stated that, according to its third Recital in the preamble, Decision No 1/80 seeks to improve the treatment to be given in the social field to workers and members of their families in relation to the arrangements introduced by Decision No 2/76.[38] This is further emphasised by the fact that Article 6(1) of Decision No 1/80 is considered to be a system of gradual integration of Turkish workers into the host State's labour force, whose scope cannot be unilaterally modified by the Member States.[39]

This seems to be also the case with Directive 2003/109. According to the preamble, "the integration of third-country nationals who are long-term

---

[36] See for example Case C-237/91, *Kazim Kus v Landeshauptstadt Wiesbaden* [1992] ECR I-06781, paragraph 25; Case C-98/96, *Kasim Ertanir v Land Hessen* [1997] ECR I-05179, paragraph 23. However, Member States are precluded by Article 13 of Decision No 1/80 from introducing, as from the date on which Decision No 1/80 entered into force in each Member State, "any new restrictions on the exercise of the free movement of workers, including those relating to the substantive and/or procedural conditions governing the first admission to the territory of that Member State of Turkish nationals intending to exercise that freedom". See Case C-92/07, *European Commission v Kingdom of the Netherlands*, 29 April 2010, [2010], paragraph 49.

[37] Case C-237/91 *Kus*, paragraph 23; Case C-355/93, *Hayriye Eroglu v Land Baden-Württemberg* [1994] ECR I-05113, paragraph 22. See also K. Groenendijk, E. Guild and R. Barzilay (2000), *Study on the Legal Status of Third-Country Nationals who are Long-Term Residents in a Member State of the European Union*, Centre for Migration Law, Radboud University of Nijmegen: Nijmegen, The Netherlands, at 100–101.

[38] *Ibid.*, paragraph 20.

[39] Case C-1/97, *Mehmet Birden v Stadtgemeinde Bremen* [1998] ECR I-07747, paragraph 37.

residents in the Member States is a key element in promoting economic and social cohesion…"[40] Moreover, Recital 12 provides that:

> In order to constitute a genuine instrument for the integration of long-term residents into society in which they live, long-term residents should enjoy equality of treatment with citizens of the Member State in a wide range of economic and social matters, under the relevant conditions defined by this Directive.[41]

Consequently, it seems that the same logic is valid here. I will return to this question when I will deal with the concept of integration in Section IV of the book.

Effectiveness
The Court has constantly mentioned the importance of an interpretation which would not deprive Decision No 1/80 of its practical effect.[42] That would be the case for instance, if Member States were allowed to unilaterally adopt measures with the effect of preventing certain Turkish workers from enjoying the rights derived from Article 6(1).[43] This is a principle of interpretation which is certainly well-founded in the case of Directive 2003/109.

With these premises in mind, it is now possible to undertake a review of the case law and see what parallelisms the Court could establish in order to apply the same principles of interpretation to Article 3 of Directive 2003/109. In order to do that I will attempt to answer the three questions that I posed above regarding different issues that have already arisen with regard to the Directive by following a simple structure. I will first look at how the Court has interpreted Article 6 of Decision No 1/80 in similar cases and then at the possible application of that interpretation to the Directive.

5.1. *Exclusion of Certain Categories of Third-country Nationals from the Scope of Directive 2003/109*

The fundamental questions here are:

Is it possible to exclude *a priori* certain categories of Turkish workers from the scope of Decision No 1/80? Consequently, is it possible to exclude some categories of third-country nationals from the scope of Directive 2003/109?

---

[40] Recital 4 of the preamble of Directive 2003/109.

[41] Recital 12 of the preamble of Directive 2003/109.

[42] Case C-98/96, *Kasim Ertanir v Land Hessen* [1997] ECR I-05175, paragraph 32; Case C-36/96 *Faik Günaydin v Freistaat Bayern* [1997] ECR I-05143, paragraph 38.

[43] Case C-98/96 *Ertanir*, paragraph 31.

In the case *Kasim Ertanir v Land Hessen*[44] the Court had an opportunity to look at a similar situation to the one it could encounter when interpreting Article 3 of the Long-term Residence Directive. Mr Ertanir was a chef specialising in Turkish cuisine who was allowed to enter Germany under a work and residence permit, which only allowed him to reside there for a period of three years, performing a specific job for a specific employer. After a first period of residence in Germany in 1991, he went back to Turkey. He later re-entered Germany on 14 April 1992. He was issued several residence permits which always bore a remark to the effect that the permit would expire at the end of his employment as a chef in the restaurant which engaged him. On 13 April 1995, he applied to have his residence permit extended for a further two years. However, his application was rejected on the basis that under German law specialist chefs could only work in the country for a maximum period of three years. It was also added that, under a 1995 decree issued by the German authorities, Decision No 1/80 did not apply to specialist chefs.

The German court asked the CJEU three questions. The important one here is the third one: Is it possible for a Member State to create rights of residence that do not confer from the outset the benefit of Article 6(1) of Decision No 1/80? In other words, is it possible to exclude entire categories such as specialist chefs, or artists or others?

The Court followed the same four steps mentioned previously in order to give a negative answer to the question. It first recalled that Article 6(1) has direct effect.[45] It went on by calling to mind that Member States are free to decide on the first entry of a Turkish national and can establish the conditions under which he works for up to one year.[46] Its argument continued by explaining that Member States could not adapt as they pleased the rules governing Turkish workers who were already integrated into their labour force. That would certainly, the Court went on, deprive Decision No 1/80 of any practical effect.[47] Finally, the Court pointed out that such "legislation would undermine the gradual integration of Turkish workers".[48] Consequently, the Court answered in the negative the question whether it was possible to exclude at the outset whole categories of workers, such as specialist chefs, from the rights conferred in Article 6(1).[49]

---

[44] Case C-98/96, *Kasim Ertanir v Land Hessen* [1997] ECR I-05179.

[45] *Ibid.*, paragraph 24.

[46] *Ibid.*, paragraph 30.

[47] *Ibid.*, paragraph 32.

[48] *Ibid.*, paragraph 35.

[49] *Ibid.*, paragraph 37.

It is very probable that the same logic applies to Directive 2003/109. First of all, the Court would probably establish that Article 4(1) has direct effect. It could certainly reiterate that Member States are free to decide which third-country nationals enter their territory (with the exception of some categories such as family members). The third point would also be valid here, as Member States are not allowed to interpret the terms of the Directive in a manner contrary to the principle of effectiveness. Finally, it is clear that the Directive is an instrument of the utmost importance for the integration of third-country nationals. The above-mentioned discussion leads me to conclude that the Austrian implementation of the Directive, analysed previously, would be incompatible with the Directive. Hence, Member States could not exclude at the outset from the scope of Directive certain categories of workers such as artists. Moreover, if for whatever reason, Austria renewed the residence permit of a social service worker year by year, arriving at a residence period of five years, that person would also be entitled to the long-term residence permit.

5.2. *Non-renewable Residence Permits*

The question here is to see the following:

What would be the situation if someone with consecutive limited and non-renewable permits fulfilled the requirement of five years' continuous and legal residence? Does the fact that that person entered a Member State in order to work for a specific employer on a temporary basis allow a Member State not to grant the long-term residence permit? How did the CJEU react in similar cases when interpreting Decision No 1/80?

Here there are two interesting questions that were raised in the case in Cyprus. The first looks at the possibility of denying a long-term residence permit to someone who has legally resided in a Member State for a period of five years with consecutive residence permits which were, in principle, non-renewable. The second explores to what extent the fact that the worker willingly entered the EU in order to perform a job for a specific employer on a temporary basis gives the Member State the right not to grant the permit, as the third-country national knew before-hand that the stay in the EU was going to be provisional. The CJEU addressed these two questions in the following case.

Mr Günaydin was a Turkish national who entered Germany in 1976 and studied German and engineering until 1986. In 1986 he was taken on by Siemens in order to pursue a training course of several years' duration, at the end of which he would be transferred to Turkey to manage a subsidiary of that company. Mr Günaydin always understood that the residence and employment permits he was granted had the purpose of preparing for his subsequent return to Turkey in order to work for the same company in his country of origin. Indeed, the temporary residence permit, extended several times, always bore the remark that it would lapse upon his ceasing to be employed in Germany. The various work permits only allowed him to work for the same company. On 15 February 1990, Mr Günaydin applied for a permanent residence permit. The application was rejected, based on the fact that he could not rely either on a claim to an unrestricted residence permit or the principle of the protection of legitimate expectations. It was argued that his work was limited to participation in a training programme of a temporary nature and therefore he could not be considered to have been duly registered as belonging to the labour force, within the meaning of Article 6(1) of Decision No 1/80. Consequently, two questions were addressed to the CJEU: By the first one, the Court had to answer whether Mr Günaydin could be considered to be part of the labour force within the meaning of Article 6(1) of Decision No 1/80, taking into account that he had been authorised to pursue paid employment of a temporary nature and for the purpose of preparing for work with a subsidiary company in Turkey. By the second question, the Court was asked to explain whether, in case the answer to the first question was positive, that would not constitute an abuse of law as Mr Günaydin had declared his intention to return to Turkey.

The Court, in its answer to the first question, pursued once again the same reasoning as in *Ertanir* analysed above. First, it was recalled that Article 6(1) had direct effect.[50] Second, Member States were free to decide on the first entry of a Turkish national and could establish the conditions under which he worked for up to one year.[51] Third, the Court went on, that did not allow Member States "to modify unilaterally the scope of the system of gradual integration of Turkish workers in the host State's labour force".[52] Fourth, that was the case as the effect of that interpretation "would be to render Decision No 1/80 meaningless and deprive it of any practical effect".[53] As a consequence, the Court concluded that it could not be argued that Mr Günaydin's residence and work permits were merely temporary as that could deprive Turkish workers of rights which they had acquired regardless of the reason why the right to enter, work or reside had been initially granted.[54] Mr Günaydin was then entitled to rely on Article 6(1) of Decision No 1/80. This same reasoning was also

[50] Case C-36/96, *Günaydin*, paragraph 24.
[51] *Ibid.*, paragraph 36.
[52] *Ibid.*, paragraph 37.
[53] *Ibid.*, paragraph 38.
[54] *Ibid.*, paragraphs 48 to 52.

applied to a similar question in *Ertanir* explained above,[55] as well as in *Birden*, analysed below.

Mr Birden was a Turkish national who was permitted to enter Germany in 1990, where he married a German national in 1992. He was granted a residence permit as well as an unconditional work permit. Mr Birden could not find a job and started to receive social assistance. Later he initiated a contract of employment as a semi-skilled worker for a Cultural Centre. That contract was established for a year, from 1 January 1994 to 31 December 1994 and it was consequently renewed for another year. On 10 June 1995, Mr Birden's marriage came to an end and on 15 August 1995 the German authorities refused to extend his residence permit. The explanation by the German authorities was that he was divorced and that, for the purposes of Article 6(1) of Decision No 1/80, he was not duly registered as belonging to the labour force as his contracts had been temporary. Contrary to that rationale, the Court stated that:

> the fact that the employment contracts offered to the person concerned by the public authorities were only temporary has no relevance for the purposes of interpreting Article 6(1) of Decision No 1/80, in so far as the activity pursued by him in the host Member State satisfies the conditions laid down by that provision.[56]

Hence, the answer to the question seems clear: the temporary nature of the contract does not impede Turkish workers from relying on Decision No 1/80. However, what would happen if a third-country national of one of the categories explicitly mentioned in Article 3(2)(e) of Directive 2003/109, such as an au pair, regularly resided for five years in a Member State? Would that person have the right to obtain a long-term residence permit? A similar situation arose on the interpretation of Decision No 1/80 in the case *Payir*.[57] The facts are the following: Ms Payir, a young Turkish woman, was granted leave to enter the UK in April 2000, valid until April 2002, subject to the condition that she only worked as an au pair. In April 2002, she applied for leave to remain in the UK, in reliance upon Decision No 1/80, as she had been engaged by the same employer for more than one year and she wished to go on working for that same employer. However, her application was refused. The matter was referred to the Court, which had to answer whether someone who had entered a Member State as an au pair could rely on Decision No 1/80.

---

[55] Case C-98/96, *Ertanir*, paragraphs 53–62.

[56] Case C-1/97, *Birden*, paragraph 39.

[57] Case C-294/06, *Ezgi Payir, Burhan Akyuz and Birol Ozturk v Secretary of State for the Home Department* [2008] ECR I-00203.

Member States opposed this rationale as they said it would have serious consequences for them as they would no longer be free to determine the conditions of entry for Turkish national into their territories. The Court followed its usual steps of interpretation by referring to the direct effect of Article 6(1),[58] the competence of Member States to regulate first entry of third-country nationals,[59] the need not to deprive Decision No 1/80 of its effectiveness[60] and the integration of Turkish workers.[61] The Court then concluded that:

> Consequently...the reasons for which leave to enter was granted to the Turkish national concerned...cannot in themselves prevent the person concerned from being able to rely on Article 6(1) of Decision No. 1/80. The same applies to statements of intention made by those nationals to the effect that they do not wish to remain in the host Member State for more than two years...and to temporal limitations attaching to their leave to remain.[62]

Thus, it may be said that if a Member State admits a third-country national for a temporary purpose as defined under Article 3(2)(e), for example, to work as an au pair, but eventually extends the residence permit for more than five years, that Member State can no longer claim that the residence permit was for a temporary purpose. Any other interpretation would deprive Directive 2003/109 of its effectiveness as it would give Member States a free hand to exclude whole categories of third-country nationals from its scope.

Consequently, it can be concluded that there is consistent case law in the direction of considering that the temporary nature of a contract does not impede Turkish workers from relying on Decision No 1/80 if the employment lasts for the period required in Article 6(1). In fact, the Court has also established that when that period is not attained, the Turkish citizen does not have the right to rely on Article 6 of Decision No 1/80.[63] It is very probable that the CJEU will follow this same underlying principle when it interprets Article 3 of Directive 2003/109. It seems fair to assume that the Court will decide in a case such as the one of Mrs Cabotaje in Cyprus in favour of the applicant. If a third-country national like Mrs Cabotaje has resided regularly and continuously for a period of five years in a Member State, the temporary nature of her residence

---

58 *Ibid.*, paragraph 42.

59 *Ibid.*, paragraph 36.

60 *Ibid.*, paragraph 43.

61 *Ibid.*, paragraph 37.

62 *Ibid.*, paragraph 44.

63 See Case C-230/03, *Mehmet Sedef v Freie und Hansestadt Hamburg* [2006] ECR I-00157. Nonetheless, in this case the Court made a broad interpretation of the exceptions provided in Article 6(2) of Decision No 1/80 and the Turkish citizen was finally allowed to rely on Article 6(1).

permits cannot impede the third-country national from relying on Article 4(1) of the Directive in order to obtain a long-term residence permit, provided she fulfils the other conditions.

In October 2010 the CJEU received a reference for a preliminary ruling from the Dutch Supreme Administrative Court (*Raad van State*).[64] The issue concerns an imam, who had been regularly residing for a period of six years in the Netherlands. However, according to Dutch immigration law, the residence of religious ministers is always temporary. Hence, the CJEU will have the chance to interpret this provision in line with its previous jurisprudence on Turkish workers in order not to deprive the Directive of its effectiveness.

What about the second question? Would it constitute an abuse of rights by the third-country national if he knew that his residence permit was limited? The Court answered that the position of Mr Günaydin did not constitute an abuse of rights. The Court understood that Mr Günaydin could first have thought about returning to Turkey and then changed his mind. In such circumstances, the Court went on, it was for the national authorities to demonstrate that the Turkish citizen made the statement that he wished to leave the host Member State after a certain period, in order to obtain a permit on false premises. Therefore, the Court concluded that this does not constitute an abuse of rights.[65]

In *Ertanir* the Court reinforced the judgment just mentioned and established some important standards which could certainly be applicable to third-country nationals in the situation of Mrs Cabotaje in the Cyprus case:

> Moreover, the fact that the worker was notified upon being issued with his permit to enter the host Member State that his residence and his employment were subject to the observance of certain conditions regarding duration and substance does not affect that interpretation.[66]

The interpretation to which the Court is referring is to understand that Mr Ertanir was entitled to rely on Article 6(1) of Decision No 1/80. In order to support that reasoning the Court went on by stating:

> Accordingly, the interpretation of the concept in question does not depend on subjective circumstances, such as the awareness on the part of the person concerned of the existence of restrictions, of such a kind as to deprive him of rights acquired under Decision No 1/80, to which the national authorities have made subject his residence and/or his work in the host Member State.[67]

---

64 Reference for a preliminary ruling from the Raad Van State (Netherlands) lodged on 20 October 2010 – Staatssecretaris van Justitie v M. Singh (Case C-502/10).

65 Case C-36/96, *Günaydin*, paragraphs 58 to 60.

66 Case C-98/96, *Ertanir*, paragraph 58.

67 *Ibid.*, paragraph 61.

Thus, it seems fair to conclude that this logic could be applicable to Directive 2003/109. In the previous case of the worker in Cyprus, the Supreme Court of Cyprus should have referred this question to the CJEU, which would probably have followed the same rationale it adopted in these two cases. The European Commission could also launch an infringement proceeding against Cyprus since it seems that the Supreme Court's interpretation is being followed which has left thousands of migrant workers outside of the scope of the implementing legislation.[68]

5.3. *Tools to Interpret the Directive*

The key question here is: What tools can be used to interpret the Directive?

To conclude this set of questions, I will scrutinise the validity of taking into consideration other factors underlying immigration, such as the possibility of Cyprus accepting and assimilating third-country nationals, which constituted, or so the Supreme Court of Cyprus argued, a legitimate parameter within the framework of the Directive. This is a question of a different kind from the ones posed previously but it is worth analysing as national courts play a central role in interpreting the Directive. The same question arose in the recent *Metock* ruling by the CJEU.[69] This case concerned the situation of Mr Metock and other third-country nationals who were irregularly present in Ireland but had married European citizens residing there. The first question that the Court addressed was whether it was possible to have the requirement of prior lawful residence in a Member State before moving to a second Member State as a family member of a European citizen. Several governments argued that "in a context typified by strong pressure of migration, it is necessary to control immigration at the external borders of the Community…", as "an interpretation of Directive 2004/38 prohibiting a host Member State from requiring prior lawful residence in another Member State would undermine the ability of the Member States to control immigration at their external frontiers".[70] The Irish government also understood "that that interpretation would have serious consequences for the Member States by bringing about a great increase in the number of persons able to benefit from a right of residence in the Community".[71]

---

[68] N. Trimikliniotis (2010), "Country Report: Cyprus", EUDO Citizenship Observatory, January 2010, Revised April 2010, p. 18.

[69] Case C-127/08, *Blaise Baheten Metock and Others v Minister for Justice, Equality and Law Reform,* [2008] ECR I-06241. See above Chapter 2 above.

[70] *Ibid.*, paragraph 71.

[71] *Ibid.*, paragraph 72.

The Court replied following a three-step logic in light of the text of the Directive:

First, it argued that not all third-country nationals had a right of entry into a Member State, but only those who were certain family members of a European citizen who had exercised the possibility of residing in a second Member State.[72] Accordingly, the Court could argue in the case of Cyprus that not all third-country nationals have the possibility of obtaining long-term residence status, but only those who have lived regularly and continuously for a five-year period in the country.

Second, the Court stated that Member States could still refuse entry on grounds of public policy, public security or public health.[73] Consequently, it could be argued in the case of Cyprus that, in accordance with Article 6 of Directive 2003/109, the authorities always keep the prerogative not to grant long-term residence status on grounds of public policy or public security.

Finally, the Court explained that Member States always had the possibility of terminating any right in cases of abuse of rights or fraud, such as in a marriage of convenience.[74] Again, in the case of Cyprus, it could be said that Cypriot authorities would always have the chance to withdraw long-term residence status in cases of fraudulent acquisition, according to Article 9(1) (a) of Directive 2003/109.

The Supreme Court of Cyprus was wrong in its interpretation of the Directive. It cannot be inferred from any Article in the Directive that the possibility of accepting and assimilating third-country nationals due to the characteristics of a country constitutes a legitimate parameter within the framework of the Directive. Member States keep their prerogatives, limited in certain cases such a family reunion, to accept or not the first admission of a third-country national. However, as Peers has argued, "the definition of limited residence permits is an issue of Community law".[75] Thus, and following on Peers' argument, Member States can only exclude those third-country nationals whose residence permit cannot be renewed at all, "or for more than a certain period (totalling less than five years)."[76] Thus, whenever a third-country national has resided regularly and continuously for a period of five years in a Member State, he obtains the right to a long-term residence permit, regardless of the limitations present on his residence permit. Hence, only those

---

[72] *Ibid.*, paragraph 73.

[73] *Ibid.*, paragraph 74.

[74] *Ibid.*, paragraph 75.

[75] S. Peers (2004), "Implementing Equality? The Directive on Long Term Resident Third Country Nationals" *European Law Review*, Vol. 29(4), at 448–449.

[76] *Ibid.*, p. 449.

third-country nationals whose residence permit cannot be renewed at all and who reside for less than five years in a Member State may be excluded from the scope of the Directive. Once a third-country national completes five years of legal and continuous residence he cannot be excluded from the scope of the Directive, as that would render the Directive meaningless.

6. *Conclusion*

This first part of the analysis of Directive 2003/109 has examined Article 3. This Article is important because of the introduction of the exclusion from the scope of the Directive of those third-country nationals whose residence permit had been formally limited. This clause was severely criticised as it could impede the granting of a more secure status to many third-country nationals. I have attempted to see how the CJEU would interpret this provision in light of its previous case law on Turkish citizens. The CJEU has always tried to give the same interpretation to analogous provisions of Decision No 1/80 with those on the free movement of EU citizens.[77] That is why it is almost certain that it will also apply the same interpretation tools it used with regard to EU citizens and Turkish workers when faced with cases regarding Directive 2003/109. In that regard, the principle of effectiveness and the fact that the preamble to the Directive makes reference to the Tampere Conclusions seem to presuppose an interpretation in line with its previous case law.[78] The Court would also certainly contribute to the coherence of Union law. As Groenendijk argues:

> The AG Leger in his opinion in *Cetinkaya* case explicitly argued that the Court when interpreting Decision 1/80 should take into consideration developments of Community law, such as the introduction of citizenship of the Union, the conclusions of the European Council in Tampere in 1999 on the integration of third-country nationals in their country of residence and Directive 2003/109 on long-term resident TCN. This argument works both ways. When interpreting the latter Directive, the Court will not forget its own case law on Decision 1/80.[79]

[77] E. Guild (2001), *Immigration Law in the European Community,* Kluwer Law International: The Hague, especially at pp. 121–171.

[78] K. Groenendijk (2006), "Family Reunification as a Right under Community Law", *European Journal of Migration and Law,* Vol. 8 (2), pp. 215–230, at 226.

[79] K. Groenendijk (2006), "Citizens and Third Country Nationals: Differential Treatment or Discrimination?", in J.Y. Carlier, E. Guild & B. Coulie (eds.), *The Future of Free Movement of Persons in the EU,* Collection du Centre des Droits de L'Homme de l'Université Catholique de Louvain, Bruylant, Brussels, pp. 79–101, at 94.

An interpretation in line with its previous case law would certainly help in the integration of third-country nationals. Those third-country nationals who reside regularly and continuously in Member States for a period of five years would be within the scope of the Directive regardless of the limits in their residence permit. This interpretation would bring legal certainty to the situation of those third-country nationals present in Europe.

Finally, the European Commission could launch infringement proceedings against those Member States, such as Cyprus, which are not correctly implementing this provision.

Chapter 5

Protection Against Expulsion: Article 12

1. *Introduction*

Security of residence is certainly one of the central aspects of the Directive and of the integration of third-country nationals. In the absence of that security there is "no incentive for the society to invest in the individual or for the individual to seek to become part of the society".[1] If the immigrant fears that he could be expelled, "that fear will reinforce the orientation towards the country of origin".[2] The relevance of a secured status is hence evident. Thus, in this Chapter I will now turn to the examination of the protection against expulsion for long-term residents under the Directive.

The two fundamental questions in this Chapter are the following: (i) on what grounds may a third-country national long-term resident be expelled? (ii) What are the factors that have to be taken into account before expelling that third-country national?

In order to answer these questions I will first look at Article 12, which provides for the possibility of expelling status-holders under certain circumstances, and I will investigate the limitations to that possibility of expulsion under the Directive. Here, the limitations will be positive for the long-term resident as they will restrict the prospect of expulsion. As this is different from the other Chapters, where the limitations always put a ceiling on the rights that third-country nationals would otherwise have, the structure of this Chapter has been slightly altered. Consequently, after analysing Article 12 of the Directive, I will scrutinise how the Commission's proposal was worded and how Directive 2004/38 differs from Directive 2003/109 with regard to the expulsion of European citizens. I will also refer to Directive 64/221 as most of the case law on EU citizens is based on this Directive, which was repealed

---

[1] E. Guild (2004), "Citizens, Immigrants, Terrorists and Others", in A. Ward and S. Peers (eds.), *The European Charter of Fundamental Rights, Politics, Law and Policy*, Hart: Oxford, pp. 231–47, at 236.

[2] K. Groenendijk (2001), "Long-Term Immigrants and the Council of Europe", in E. Guild and P. Minderhoud (eds.), *Security of Residence and Expulsion. Protection of Aliens in Europe*, Kluwer Law International: The Hague/London, pp. 7–22, at 8.

by Directive 2004/38 as of 30 April 2006.[3] This will also allow me to briefly signal the main criticisms by other academics to these divergences. By analysing these differences it will be possible to subsequently explore how the CJEU could interpret the similar, but slightly divergent, provisions under both Directives. In this respect, it will be central to pay special attention to the Court's prior case law on Turkish citizens. Before analysing possible interpretation by the Court, I will briefly consider the implementation of the Directive in my four case studies. I will not look at other countries, as according to my research, it seems that there are no serious problems with the implementation of these provisions. Furthermore, the most important part in this Chapter, as I have mentioned above, is to see the possible interpretation by the CJEU of these slightly differing provisions. I will end with some conclusions and closing thoughts and will also add some recommendations that could be used by the Commission.[4]

Thus, the questions for this Chapter are as follows:

1. On what grounds may Member States take a decision to expel a long-term resident? What are the limitations to that prerogative in the Directive?
2. Are those limitations different from the ones worded in the Commission's proposal? Are those limitations different from the ones being applied to European citizens according to Directive 2004/38 or the earlier Directive 64/221? What have been the main criticisms by other academics?
3. How are Member States implementing the Directive? Are there any changes with regard to the situation before its adoption?
4. What could be the interpretation of this Article by the CJEU? Are there any parallels that could be drawn from its previous case law on European or Turkish citizens?

2. *Expulsion*

Here I will describe under what circumstances Member States may take a decision to expel a long-term resident and what the limitations to that

[3] Council Directive 64/221/EEC of 25 February 1964 on the co-ordination of special measures concerning the movement and residence of foreign nationals which are justified on grounds of public policy, public security or public health, Official Journal 056, 04.04.1964, P.0850–0857.

[4] See for a very brief analysis of some of the issues discussed in this Chapter: D. Acosta (2011), "Directive 2003/109 on Long-term Residence for Third-Country Nationals: Possible Future Interpretation by the European Court of Justice" in C. Murphy and P. Green (eds.), *Law and Outsiders: Norms, Processes and Othering in the 21st Century*, Hart: Oxford, pp. 143–165, at 161–164.

prerogative are. The Directive's preamble in its Recital 16 states the important principle that "long-term residents should enjoy reinforced protection against expulsion". That protection is based, the same Recital says, "on the criteria determined by the decisions of the European Court of Human Rights". Consequently, the underlying principle is clear: long-term residents should only be expelled in very specific circumstances and after taking into account various factors. Thus, expulsion is an exceptional measure.

According to Article 12 (1) of the Directive, "Member States may take a decision to expel a long-term resident solely where he/she constitutes an actual and sufficiently serious threat to public policy or public security". Hence, this Article is exhaustive and under no other circumstances may a long-term resident be expelled. The word "solely" impedes Member States from taking any other considerations into account.

This is further limited by Articles 12(2) and 12(3) which establish the constraints against the possibility of expelling a long-term resident. According to Article 12(2), the decision to expel a long-term resident "shall not be founded on economic considerations". In turn, Article 12(3) lays down the factors that have to be taken into consideration before adopting such a decision:

a. The duration of the residence of the long-term resident in the Member State.
b. The age of the long-term resident.
c. The consequences for the long-term resident and the family members.
d. The links that the long-term resident has with the country of residence or the absence of those links with the country of origin.

These circumstances are based on the decisions of the European Court of Human Rights (ECtHR) relating to Article 8 of the European Convention of Human Rights and Fundamental Freedoms (ECHR) on the right to respect for private and family life.[5] Consequently, when interpreting them, the CJEU

---

5 For a concise account of the case law regarding Article 8 on the right to respect for private and family life, but also on Article 3 on the prohibition on torture, see D. Thym (2008), "Respect for Private and Family Life under Article 8 ECHR in Immigration Cases: a Human Right to Regularize Illegal Stay?", *International and Comparative Law Quarterly*, Vol. 57(1), pp. 87–112; P. van Dijk (2001), "Protection of 'Integrated' Aliens Against Expulsion under the European Convention on Human Rights", in E. Guild and P. Minderhoud (eds.), *Security of Residence and Expulsion: Protection of Aliens in Europe*, Kluwer Law International: The Hague, pp. 23–40; N. Blake QC and R. Husain (2003), *Immigration, Asylum and Human Rights*, Oxford University Press: Oxford, at 165–198; F. Jacobs, R.White and C.Ovey (2010), *The European Convention on Human Rights*, Oxford University Press: Oxford, fifth edition; A. Mowbray (2007), *Cases and Materials on the European Convention on Human Rights*, Oxford University Press: Oxford, second edition. See also Case C-60/00, *Mary Carpenter v Secretary of State for the Home Department*, [2002] ECR I-6279.

will always refer to the case law by the ECtHR.[6] In fact, Article 6(3) TEU provides that fundamental rights as guaranteed by the ECHR constitute general principles of Union law. Moreover, the Charter of Fundamental Rights of the EU also includes Article 7, which is devoted to the respect for private and family life.[7]

As will be seen below, these circumstances are slightly dissimilar from the circumstances that have to be taken into account when expelling a European citizen. The CJEU will have to interpret whether there are any differences between long-term residents and European citizens based on that slightly divergent wording in both Directives.

3. *Comparison with the Commission's Proposal and Directive 2004/38*

Here I intend to look at the Commission's proposal and Directive 2004/38, as well as making reference to Directive 64/221, which has been repealed, in order to answer three questions: Was the Commission's proposal worded in a different way? Is Directive 2004/38 more generous for European citizens with regard to their security of residence in another Member State? What have been the main criticisms by scholars?

The Commission's proposal was more generous than the final Directive adopted, as it was inspired by existing Union law on free movement of European citizens.[8] However, by and large, the wording of both Directive 2003/109 and Directive 2004/38 is identical. The final text adopted omitted some prerequisites that appeared in the proposal and which are also in Directive 2004/38. The importance of these omissions will be analysed later when I consider the way in which the Court could interpret these provisions for long-term residents. The key features which were omitted from the final version are the following:

First, in the proposal, Member States could only take a decision to expel a long-term resident based on his "personal conduct", when the threat affected

---

6 See especially Üner v. the Netherlands [GC], no. 46410/99, 18 October 2006 and *Berrehab v. The Netherlands,* no. 10730/84, 21 June 1988, Series A. 126/177.

7 Article 6(1) of the TEU (as amended by Lisbon) refers to the Charter of Fundamental Rights by stating: "The Union recognises the rights, freedoms and principles set out in the Charter of Fundamental Rights...which shall have the same legal value as the Treaties".

8 S. Peers and N. Rogers (eds.) (2006), *EU Immigration and Asylum Law: Text and Commentary*, Martinus Nijhoff Publishers: Leiden, at 622. See Article 13 of the European Commission proposal for a Council Directive concerning the status of third-country nationals who are long-term residents, COM (2001) 127 final, Brussels, 13.3.2001.

a "fundamental interest of society".[9] These two requirements are present for EU citizens in Article 27(2) of Directive 2004/38. The first requirement was also present in Article 3(1) of Directive 64/221. However, the second one arose from the interpretation of the CJEU as will be seen below.

Secondly, according to the Commission's proposal, personal conduct was not considered a sufficiently serious threat when Member States did not "take severe enforcement measures against its own nationals who commit the same type of offence".[10] As before, this was omitted from the final version. However, this applies to EU citizens as it has been upheld by the CJEU on several occasions, as will be seen below.[11]

Finally, the definitive version erased the requirement that criminal convictions could not automatically "warrant an expulsion decision".[12] This is also applicable to EU citizens according to the CJEU case law also analysed below. In fact, Article 3(2) of Directive 64/221 established that "previous criminal convictions shall not in themselves constitute grounds" for expelling someone.

In addition, in the Commission's version, the challenges to expulsion decisions had a suspensory effect and emergency expulsion proceedings against long-term residents were forbidden.[13] These factors are also set out in Article 28 of Directive 2004/38, which also provides that before taking an expulsion decision on grounds of public policy or public security, the host Member State shall take account of a number of considerations, such as how long the individual concerned has resided on its territory, his/her age, state of health, family and economic situation, social and cultural integration into the host Member State and the extent of his/her links with the country of origin. A comparative analysis of this provision with Article 12 of Directive 2003/109 highlights two differences. First, the list in Directive 2004/38 is not exhaustive whereas the list in Directive 2003/109 is. Second, when expelling a European citizen Member States have to take his health into consideration. This is not provided in Directive 2003/109. As is the case for long-term residents, European citizens cannot be expelled on economic grounds.[14]

---

9 Article 13(1) of the European Commission proposal.

10 *Ibid.*, Article 13(2).

11 This requirement was not present either in Directive 64/221.

12 *Ibid.*, Article 13(3).

13 *Ibid.*, Article 13 (5) and (7). It is interesting to note that collective expulsions of foreigners are forbidden by Art 4 of Protocol 4 to the ECHR. This Protocol has not been signed by Greece and it has not been ratified by the UK. The rest of the EU members have ratified it.

14 Article 27 (1) of Directive 2004/38. This was also present in Article 2(2) of Directive 64/221. It is interesting to note however that the European Commission forgot to mention this in its 2009 Communication on the implementation of Directive 2004/38. See Commission

Moreover, in the European citizen's Directive, extra protection is granted to those who have the right of permanent residence after five years[15] and to those who have resided in the host Member State for the previous ten years or who are minors. This last group can only be expelled on imperative grounds of public security.[16] This differs from the Long-term Residence Directive where there is no such additional protection for these groups.

All these differences have prompted academics to criticise expulsion and its limitations under the Directive as inadequate. For example, Peers has argued that the Tampere principles have been "further disregarded as regards protection against expulsion".[17] Nonetheless, the degree of the importance of the differences in the wording of both Directives will be analysed below as future interpretation by the CJEU might mitigate its relevance, as happened for Turkish citizens.

4. *Implementation*

The purpose of this part is to answer two questions: How are Member States implementing the Directive? And, are there any changes with regard to the situation before its adoption?

The objective here is not to present a concise analysis of how all 24 Member States are implementing this provision. I will limit myself instead to briefly looking at how my case studies are transposing it in their national legal orders to see if they are correctly implementing these provisions. I will follow by giving some examples of how the factors that have to be taken into account before expelling a long-term resident still allow for the expulsion of some third-country nationals who might have a very strong link with the respective Member State. I will end by seeing what the situation was before the adoption of the Directive, and what changes it has brought for long-term residents.

The implementation of this provision in my four case studies does not pose severe problems although there are some inclusions required that the Commission might be willing to point out:

Communication, On Guidance for Better Transposition and Application of Directive 2004/38/EC on the Right of Citizens of the Union and their Family Members to Move and Reside Freely within the Territory of the Member States, COM (2009) 313 final, 2.7.2009.

15 These persons can only be expelled on serious grounds of public policy or public security. See Art 28 (2) of Directive 2004/38.

16 See Art 28(3) (a) and (b) of Directive 2004/38. See on Article 28 Case C-145/09 of 23 November 2010, *Land Baden-Württemberg v Panagiotis Tsakouridis*, [2010].

17 S. Peers (2004), "Implementing Equality? The Directive on Long-term Resident Third Country Nationals", *European Law Review*, Vol. 29(4), pp. 437–460, at 452.

Spain

According to Article 57(5) (b) of the Immigration Law, long-term residents in Spain can only be expelled if they commit a very serious offence (under Article 54(1)) or a less serious one when it is committed twice in one year. Spain has not transposed the clause that states that the status-holder has to be "an actual and sufficient serious threat to public policy or public security". In that sense, the implementation is incomplete. Before taking that decision, Spain has to consider the following factors: the duration of the residence and the links created in Spain, the age, the consequences for the long-term resident and for the family members and the links with the country to which the status-holder is going to be expelled. This seems to be in line with Article 12(3) of the Directive. However, Spain has not transposed Article 12(2), which provides that a decision to expel a long-term resident cannot be founded on economic considerations. This provision is however capable of having direct effect.

According to Article 54(1), read together with Article 57(5), a long-term resident might be expelled if he becomes involved in an activity which is contrary to the public order or if he participates in activities which are contrary to the external security of the State or which can be detrimental to Spanish relations with other countries. This last case does not fit within the definition of Article 12(1) of the Directive, which does not include the possibility for expelling someone when his activities damage the external relations of a Member State. Hence, this is probably not in line with the Directive. The rest of the cases do not pose any particular problems.

Italy

According to Article 9(10) of the Single Text on Immigration, an expulsion decision may be adopted against a status-holder national in the following cases:

a. Where there are serious reasons endangering the public order or safety of the State;
b. Pursuant to section 3, paragraph 1, of law decree no. 144/2005, converted into Law 31 July 2005, no. 155 (law concerning the fight against terrorism);
c. Where the foreigner falls within one of the categories listed either under article 1 of law no. 1453/1956 (prevention measures against dangerous persons for safety and public morality) or under article 1 of law no. 575/1965 (law concerning the fight against the mafia).

According to Article 9(11), before adopting an expulsion measure, Italy has to take into account the age of the person concerned, the length of the stay in Italy, the consequences of the expulsion for the person concerned and the members of his family and the existence of family and social ties with Italy and the absence of those ties with the country of origin. These provisions seem to be in line with the Directive. However, Italy has not expressly implemented Article 12(2), which provides that an expulsion decision shall not be founded on economic considerations. Furthermore, the requirement of Article 12(1) that the status-holder has to be "an actual and sufficiently serious threat" is not clearly transposed either. In that sense, the implementation is incomplete and the Commission could point that out.

Sweden

In Sweden, a long-term resident may be expelled, according to Chapter 8 Section 8 of the Aliens Act (2005:716), if he "is convicted of an offence that is punishable by imprisonment". A long-term resident "may also be expelled if a court sets aside a suspended sentence or probation that has been imposed on an alien and imposes another penalty".

In order to be expelled, though, the third-country national has to be sentenced to a more severe penalty than a fine and has to either "be assumed that he or she will be guilty of continued criminal activity", or to have committed a very serious offence "in view of the resulting damage, danger or violation of private or public interests". According to Chapter 8 Section 12, a third-country national who has been residing in Sweden for five years, which will be the case for any long-term resident, can only be expelled "when there are exceptional grounds". Here the requirement that the long-term resident has to constitute "an actual and sufficiently serious threat" is lacking. In order to be in line with the Directive, Sweden should probably include this clarification.

According to Chapter 8 Section 11 of the Aliens Act (2005:716), when a court considers whether a third-country national should be expelled under Section 8, it must take into account the alien's ties to Swedish society. The court has to pay particular attention to the following factors:

1. The third-country national's personal circumstances;
2. Whether the third-country national has any child in Sweden and, if so, the child's need for contact with him or her;
3. The family situation in other respects; and
4. The length of the residence in Sweden.

Here it can be seen that Sweden has not correctly implemented the Directive unless it is understood that included in the third-country national's personal circumstances are age and the consequences of the absence of links with the country of origin. Article 12(2) of the Directive, which makes reference to the impossibility of adopting an expulsion decision based on economic grounds, has not been explicitly transposed but it seems that, according to the

Swedish Migration Board, there are no expulsion decisions taken on those grounds.

Latvia

In Latvia, a long-term resident may be expelled, according to Article 12(6) of the Law on the status of EU permanent residence, only if he constitutes a threat to "public order or public security". However, Latvia has not implemented the four factors that have to be taken into consideration before expelling a status-holder. Nevertheless, the national courts will, in practice, take these factors into consideration. Thus, the Commission should pay special attention to this poor implementation of Article 12(3).

I will now very briefly look at how the limitations in the Directive work in practice. As has been seen, Member States have to take into consideration a number of factors before expelling a long-term resident. However, a quick glance at these factors show that some long-term residents may still be expelled even when they have very strong links with the respective Member State:

Duration of the residence: In some EU Member States, a third-country national with long-term residence status can be expelled even after many years of residence in that country, in some cases even more than 20 years.[18]

The age of the person concerned: here, as in the previous case, in some EU Member States, minors can be the subject of an expulsion measure.[19]

The consequences for the person concerned and family members: there is extensive jurisprudence from the ECtHR on this.[20]

The links with the country of residence or the absence of links with the country of origin: a clear link with the country of residence is to have been born there. Yet, some European Member States allow for the expulsion of long-term residents born in their territory.[21]

---

[18] A long-term resident can be expelled after many years of residence, among others, in the following countries: France, Austria, Finland, Slovenia, Estonia and Greece. It is also possible in the three countries which do not apply the Directive: UK, Ireland and Denmark. See J. Niessen, T. Huddleston and L. Citron (2007) (in cooperation with A. Geddes and D. Jacobs), *Migrant Integration Policy Index*, British Council and Migration Policy Group: Brussels. See www.integrationindex.eu

[19] Among them, Austria, Italy, Slovenia, Finland. Once again, this also applies to the UK, Denmark and Ireland. *Ibid.*

[20] E. Guild (2004), *The Legal elements of European Identity: EU citizenship and Migration Law*, Kluwer Law International, European Law Library: The Hague, at 137–146.

[21] This list includes Italy, Finland, France, Slovakia, Greece or Estonia among others. This applies to Ireland and Denmark as well. See J. Niessen, T. Huddleston and L. Citron (2007) (in cooperation with A. Geddes and D. Jacobs), *Migrant Integration Policy Index*, British Council and Migration Policy Group: Brussels. See www.integrationindex.eu

A final question is relevant in this part of my analysis. It is important to see what the situation was before and to what extent the Directive has improved it or not. In a study in 1998, some academics questioned the suitability of having vague concepts, such as public order or public security, in the law of the different Member States. They argued that this gave administrative authorities wide discretion.[22] This has changed with the Directive.

Before its adoption, all Member States had expulsion based on grounds of public order or public security. In some countries, such as Germany, it was even possible to expel someone on general preventive grounds.[23] This is certainly not possible now considering the wording of the Directive. In other countries, such as Belgium, Finland or Sweden, the grounds were interpreted in a similar way to those for European citizens.[24] This will probably be the case with the Directive if the CJEU follows its previous rationale, as will be seen below.

Regarding my case studies, it seems that prior to the adoption of the Directive they all had quite similar provisions to the present ones. Italy[25] had two grounds for expulsion which have been now increased to three as has been acknowledged above. Spain[26] had almost identical stipulations, whereas the case in Sweden[27] was the same as now. Latvia also had a similar protection with its national permanent residence permit.[28]

The importance of having a Directive in which the factors that have to be taken into consideration before expelling a long-term resident are enumerated is evident. These concepts do certainly have an EU law meaning.[29] Consequently, they will have to be interpreted now in light of the well-established principles of EU law, such as effectiveness and proportionality, as will be seen in Chapter 9 with regard to integration conditions. Member States are also obviously subject to the control of the Community institutions (Commission and CJEU) in this area.

---

22 K. Groenendijk, E. Guild and H. Dogan, (1998), *Security of Residence of Long-Term Migrants: A Comparative Study of Law and Practice in European Countries,* Council of Europe, Strasbourg, p. 105.

23 K. Groenendijk, E. Guild and R. Barzilay (2000), *Study on The Legal Status of Third-Country Nationals who are Long-Term Residents in a Member State of the European Union,* Centre for Migration Law, Radboud University of Nijmegen, Nijmegen: The Netherlands, at 104.

24 *Ibid.,* p. 104.

25 *Ibid.,* pp. 61–64.

26 *Ibid.,* p. 82.

27 *Ibid.,* p. 85.

28 See Articles 23 and 36 of the Immigration Law, in force since 1 May 2003, with its amendments up to 26 February 2009.

29 See below Chapter 9.

5. *Possible Interpretation by the CJEU*

In this point, I intend to answer three questions: How is the CJEU interpreting the limitations to the possibility of expelling a European citizen? How is it interpreting the possibility of expelling Turkish citizens? Would it be possible to apply the same rationale to the expulsion of long-term residents? I will start by looking at the case law dealing with EU citizens and then move on to the one dealing with Turkish citizens.

5.1. *European Citizens*

Regarding European citizens, there is some case law on the exact meaning of some of the requirements, seen above, that have to be taken into account:

Personal conduct
This requirement, which was worded in Article 3(1) of Directive 64/221, was first interpreted in *Bonsignore v Köln.*[30] In this case, an Italian national faced deportation as a measure of a general preventive nature.[31] The Court said that:

> Measures adopted on grounds of public policy and for the maintenance of public security against the nationals of member states of the Community cannot be justified on grounds extraneous to the individual case... (and) only the personal conduct of those affected by the measures is to be regarded as determinative.[32]

As has been seen, the final version of Directive 2003/109 erased the requirement present in the Commission's proposal to take into consideration the personal conduct of the long-term resident third-country national. However, it was established for European citizens in Article 27(2) of Directive 2004/38. The Court will have to interpret this difference in wording as will be seen below.

Genuine and sufficiently serious threat affecting one of the fundamental interests of society
The need to take into consideration that the threat has to affect one of the fundamental interests of society when expelling a European citizen is established in Article 27(2). However, this requirement was not worded in Directive 64/221. In fact, it was first defined by the CJEU in *Bouchereau.*[33]

[30] Case 67/74, *Carmelo Angelo Bosignore v. Oberstadtdirektor der Stadt Köln* [1975] ECR 00297.
[31] N. Foster (2006) *Foster on EU Law*, Oxford University Press: Oxford, p. 371.
[32] Case 67/74, *Bosignore* [1975] ECR 00297, paragraph 6.
[33] Case 30/77, *Régina v Pierre Bouchereau*, [1977] ECR 1999.

A French citizen had been convicted several times in the UK for drug possession.[34] The Court decided that:

> In so far as it may justify certain restrictions on the free movement of persons subject to Community Law, recourse by a national authority to the concept of public policy presupposes, in any event, the existence ... of a genuine and sufficiently serious threat affecting one of the fundamental interests of society.[35]

Thus, the Court was drawing the boundaries of the concept of public policy. In that sense, it was reinforcing its previous judgment in *van Duyn* where it had already stated that the concept of public policy had to be interpreted strictly when it was used as a justification for derogating from the fundamental principle of freedom of movement for workers.[36] For our purposes, the important point to be emphasised is that the final version of Directive 2003/109 erased this requirement for long-term resident third-country nationals. Consequently, the Court will have to pronounce on this divergent wording.

Severe enforcement measures against its own nationals

When expelling a European citizen, personal conduct cannot be considered a sufficiently serious threat when Member States do not take severe enforcement measures against its own nationals who commit the same type of offence. This requirement was not included in Directive 64/221 and it is not worded in Directive 2004/38 either. Its application comes from the case law of the CJEU. In fact, it was first mentioned in *Adoui and Cornaille,*[37] which concerned two French prostitutes in Belgium. The Court declared that:

> [C]onduct may not be considered as being of a sufficiently serious nature to justify restrictions on the admission to or residence within the territory of a Member State of a national of another Member State in a case where the former Member State does not adopt, with respect to the same conduct on the part of its own nationals repressive measures or other genuine and effective measures intended to combat such conduct.[38]

Once more, this requirement does not appear in the final version of Directive 2003/109 but it is expected that the CJEU would also apply it to long-term residents by analogy.

---

[34] N. Foster (2006), *Foster on EU Law,* Oxford University Press: Oxford, p. 371.

[35] Case 30/77, *Bouchereau* [1977] ECR 1999, paragraph 35.

[36] Case 41/74, *Yvonne van Duyn v Home Office*, 4 December 1974, [1974] ECR 1337, paragraph 18.

[37] Cases 115, 116/81, *Rezguia Adoui and Dominique Cornuaille v Belgian State* [1982] ECR 01665.

[38] *Ibid.*, paragraph 8.

Criminal convictions cannot automatically warrant an expulsion decision
A similar requirement establishing that "previous criminal convictions shall not in themselves constitute grounds for taking such measures" comes in Article 27(2) of Directive 2004/38. It was also worded in Article 3(2) of Directive 64/221. However, the CJEU went a step further by establishing that present criminal convictions cannot automatically warrant an expulsion decision. This was established by the Court in *Calfa*.[39] Donatella Calfa was an Italian tourist in Greece who was found guilty of an offence of possession of drugs and sentenced to three months' imprisonment and, by way of an additional penalty, to expulsion for life from Greek territory. The Court found that EC law precludes national legislation which requires the automatic expulsion following a criminal conviction without taking into account the danger which the person represents for the requirements of public policy or the personal conduct of the offender.[40] As in the previous cases, this provision was erased in the final version of Directive 2003/109 although once again the Court could apply it to long-term residents by analogy.

Consequently, a question arises: how are these differences in the wording between the two Directives to be interpreted? The question is difficult but there are some elements which might help in framing an answer. Some academics have compared the rights of Turkish nationals under the Turkey agreement with the rights of EU citizens. Guild arrives at the conclusion that the interference with the rights of Turkish nationals "should not be subject to a lower level of protection than in respect of Community nationals in the absence of a clear indication by the legislator that that is the intention".[41] She goes on by pointing out that if the legislator is consistent in its approach, the Court is permitted and indeed required to have a consistent interpretation as well.[42] The Court had the possibility of pronouncing on this in the case of *Nazli*,[43] and in a number of other cases following *Nazli* related to Turkish nationals.

5.2. *Turkish Citizens*

Regarding Turkish citizens there is also some case law which has to be taken into consideration. The first relevant case to mention is *Nazli*.

---

39 Case C-348/96, *Criminal proceedings against Donatella Calfa*, 19 January 1999, [1999] ECR I-11. For an analysis of this case see C. Gortázar Rotaeche and F. Basabe LLoréns (1999), "Comments on the 'Donatella Calfa' Case (C-348/96 of 19 January 1999)", *European Journal of Migration and Law*, Vol. 1, pp. 357–364.

40 *Ibid.*, paragraphs 27–29.

41 E. Guild (2001), *Immigration Law in the European Community*, Kluwer Law International: The Hague, p. 163.

42 *Ibid.*, p. 169.

43 Case C-340/97 *Nazli v Stadt Nürnberg*, [2000] ECR I-00957.

Mr Nazli was a Turkish national who entered Germany in 1978 and worked there from 1979. In 1992, he was implicated in a case of drug trafficking. He was detained and sentenced to a term of imprisonment of 21 months for being an accomplice to the trafficking of 1,500 grams of heroin. The national court suspended the entire sentence as Mr Nazli had played a minor role in the commission of the offence, was well integrated and was feeling genuine remorse. Mr Nazli found another job and went on working. However, when he requested the extension of his residence permit almost three years later, it was denied on the basis that he had committed an offence under the law on narcotics. Accordingly, he received an expulsion order. The question of the validity of his expulsion came up as it was founded exclusively on general preventive grounds directed at deterring other third-country nationals from committing similar offences. It has already been analysed how expulsion on general preventive grounds is not possible for EU nationals. The CJEU thus faced a similar case with the difference being that the person concerned was a Turkish national. The CJEU arrived, however, at a similar conclusion and ruled that the scope of a public policy exception for the expulsion of a Turkish national has to be determined with reference to the interpretation given to that exception for EU nationals.[44] The Court followed two steps of analysis in order to arrive at this conclusion:

The objective of Decision No 1/80

The CJEU first examined the objective of Decision No 1/80 for Turkish nationals by looking at its preamble and provisions, in order to see the approach of the legislator.[45] The Court concluded that Turkish nationals had to be treated, as far as possible, as EU citizens.[46]

The examination of Directive 2003/109 could certainly prompt a similar conclusion. This is clear from the wording of Recital 2, which makes reference to the Tampere Conclusions and recalls that the legal status of third-country nationals has to be approximated to that of Member States' nationals. Moreover, Recital 16 provides that, "long-term residents should enjoy reinforced protection against expulsion". Accordingly, the CJEU could conclude that long-term residents have to be treated, as far as possible, as European citizens.

The formulation of the terms in both pieces of legislation

The CJEU used as a further justification for its approach the fact that the formulation of the terms for Turkish citizens in Decision No 1/80 and the one

[44] *Ibid.*, paragraph 56.

[45] *Ibid.*, paragraphs 53–54.

[46] *Ibid.*, paragraph 55.

provided for EU citizens under the Treaty are almost identical.[47] In fact, Article 14(1) of Decision No 1/80 provides that "the provisions of this section shall be applied subject to limitations justified on grounds of public policy, public security or public health". The Court then recalled its case law on the subject with regard to European citizens, and it mentioned *Bouchereau, Calfa and Bonsignore,* which have been analysed above, and applied the same principles of interpretation present in those rulings to Decision No 1/80.

The CJEU dealt with a number of other cases regarding security of residence of Turkish nationals. Its conclusions were always in line with *Nazli*. This is clear, for example, in *Cetinkaya*.[48] Mr Cetinkaya was a Turkish national born in Germany in 1979. Between 1995 and 1999 he worked for short periods for a number of different employers. However, also during those years (between 1996 and 2000), he was sentenced several times mostly for trafficking of narcotics. Consequently, he was arrested in 2000 and detained in a juvenile centre until he was released in 2001 after following a drug detoxification course. Once he had completed a new detoxification course in 2002, the remainder of his sentence was suspended. In 2002 Mr Cetinkaya resumed his secondary education and continued attending detoxification courses. However, in 2000, Mr Cetinkaya had been notified of his expulsion from Germany. After several actions against that order the matter arrived at the Administrative Court of Stuttgart, which decided to refer some questions to the CJEU. The relevant question for our purposes is the following:

> Is Article 14(1) of Decision No 1/80 to be interpreted as meaning that a change in the circumstances of the person or persons concerned which has come about after the most recent administrative decision and which no longer allows a limitation under Article 14 of Decision No 1/80 must be taken into account in judicial proceedings?[49]

The answer that the CJEU gave to this question is certainly relevant as it points out once again that Turkish nationals have to be treated, as far as possible, as European citizens with regard to security of residence. In fact, the Court, after recalling its previous ruling in *Nazli*, made reference to its judgment in *Orfanopoulos and Oliveri*,[50] which were cases dealing with the expulsion of a Greek and an Italian from Germany. The Court had already established in *Orfanopoulos and Oliveri* the following:

---

[47] *Ibid.*, paragraph 56.

[48] Case C-467/02, *Inan Cetinkaya v Land Baden-Württemberg*, [2004] ECR I-10895.

[49] *Ibid.*, paragraph 17.

[50] Joined Cases C-482/01 and C-493/01, *Orfanopoulos and Oliveri v Land Baden-Württemberg*, [2004] ECR I-0000.

> Article 3 of Directive 64/221 precludes a national practice whereby the national courts may not take into consideration, in reviewing the lawfulness of the expulsion of a national of another Member State, factual matters which occurred after the final decision of the competent authorities which may point to the cessation or the substantial diminution of the present threat which the conduct of the person concerned constitutes to the requirements of public policy.[51]

After recalling this judgment the Court applied the same principle to *Cetinkaya* and laid down that when expelling a Turkish national account has to be taken of factual matters which occurred after the final decision by the authorities.[52]

Over the years the Court has systematically referred to *Nazli*, as well as to other cases relating to European citizens, in order to apply the same principles used for European citizens to the interpretation of Article 14 of Decision No 1/80. This has been the case, for example, in *Aydinli,*[53] *Dogan,*[54] *Derin*[55] or *Polat.*[56] In addition, the CJEU has sometimes referred to its case law on Turkish citizens in order to interpret cases dealing with European citizens. This was the case, for example, in *Orfanopoulos and Oliveri* mentioned above, where the Court referred to *Nazli.*[57]

The terms in Directive 2004/38 and 2003/109 are also almost identical, as has been explained above. Thus, the Court could certainly follow its approach with regard to Turkish citizens and apply it to long-term residents. In fact, as Guild points out when referring to *Nazli*:

> This judgment is a most welcome development in Community law regarding security of residence. The assimilation of protection of residence for certain third-country nationals…to the level enjoyed by Community nationals where this is possible and appropriate…diminishes the differential in rights between migrant Community nationals and third-country nationals in a State. It also simplifies the job of both the administration and the courts of the Member States as there is only one test to be applied in respect of Community law, no matter whether it derives directly from the EC Treaty or from some other source such as a third country agreement.[58]

---

[51] *Ibid.*, paragraph 82.

[52] Case C-467/02, *Cetinkaya*, paragraph 48.

[53] Case C-373/03, *Ceyhun Aydinli v Land Baden-Württemberg*, [2005] ECR I-06181.

[54] Case C-383/03, *Ergül Dogan v Sicherheitsdirektion für das Bundesland Vorarlberg*, [2005] Page I-06237.

[55] Case C-325/05, *Ismail Derin v Landkreis Darmstadt-Dieburg*, [2007] ECR I-06495.

[56] Case C-349/06, *Murat Polat v Stadt Rüsselsheim*, [2007] ECR I-08167.

[57] Joined Cases C-482/01 and C-493/01, *Orfanopoulos and Oliveri*, paragraphs 50 and 68.

[58] E. Guild (2001), "Security of Residence and Expulsion of Foreigners: European Community Law" in E.Guild and P. Minderhoud (eds.), *Security of Residence and Expulsion: Protection of Aliens in Europe*, Kluwer Law International: The Hague/London/Boston, pp. 59–80, at 79.

Hence, one may conclude, the Court should take a consistent approach when interpreting the concepts of public policy and public security for long-term residents, with its jurisprudence for EU citizens on the issue of security of residence. Moreover, the Court has already taken that position when interpreting the concept of public policy for Tunisian workers, under the Euro-Mediterranean agreement, in line with its previous case law on European citizens and Turkish workers.[59]

Groenendijk also mentions the principle of proportionality in order to further stress the idea that long-term residents will have to be treated in a similar fashion to European citizens when facing expulsion.[60] This will certainly be in line with the Tampere principles mentioned in Recital 2 of the preamble and will also be consistent with the idea of giving long-term residents a "reinforced protection against expulsion" as declared in Recital 16.

6. *Conclusion*

This part of my analysis has looked at one of the most important provisions in the Directive. As has been mentioned, security of residence constitutes a key element in the integration of third-country nationals who obtain the status of long-term residents.

A first reading of Article 12, comparing it with Directive 2004/38, is disappointing. The reasons for this are that many of the elements that have to be taken into account when expelling a European citizen are not present in the final version of the Directive, as the Council erased those provisions from the Commission's proposal. That is why many academics regretted those differences in wording and expressed their disenchantment.

Nevertheless, with this in-depth comparison between the provisions in both Directives, as well as a review of the case law of the CJEU, I have tried to show that the Directive brings many improvements with regard to the security of residence of long-term residents. There are two reasons to see this Directive as a positive step in this area. First, as has been shown, there are certain elements that Member States cannot take into consideration any longer when expelling a long-term resident, such as economic considerations. This was not the case before in every single Member State and thus the Directive is an improvement.

---

[59] Case C-97/05, *Mohamed Gattoussi v Stadt Rüsselsheim*, [2006] ECR I-11917, paragraph 41.

[60] K. Groenendijk (2006) "Citizens and Third-Country Nationals: Differential Treatment or Discrimination?" in J.Y. Carlier, E. Guild & B. Coulie (eds.), *The Future of Free Movement of Persons in the EU*, Bruylant: Brussels, Collection du Centre des Droits de L'Homme de l'Université Catholique de Louvain, pp. 79–101, at 91–93.

Second, there is a convincing case for arguing that the CJEU will probably interpret the possibility of expelling a long-term resident with the same principles applied to European citizens. The Court's previous case law with regard to Turkish citizens, and especially its decision on *Nazli,* goes clearly in the direction of contributing to the coherence of Union law. Moreover, if national officials implementing the law had to apply different sets of rules, this would lead to discrimination and there would be many situations in which the rules could be wrongly interpreted.

The European Commission also has to be vigilant and may make use of infringement procedures. The analysis of my four case studies has illustrated that Member States seem to have correctly implemented the Directive to a large extent. There are however some elements in which the transposition does not seem correct or complete, which the Commission will have to pinpoint in order for them to accurately implement these elements.

To conclude, if the Court follows its previous line of reasoning applied to cases with regard to Turkish citizens, and if Member States implement correctly the provisions in the Directive with the advice from the Commission, it can be stated that the security of residence of status-holders has certainly been improved and has reached a level comparable to that of European citizens as the Tampere Conclusions envisaged. This will no doubt facilitate the integration of third-country nationals.

Chapter 6

Residence in the Other Member States: Article 14

1. *Introduction*

In this Chapter I will now turn to the analysis of the free movement possibilities that long-term residents have to reside in another Member State. As in the previous Chapter where I analysed security of residence, the possibility to reside in another Member State enhances the integration of third-country nationals in the EU.[1] The Commission was well aware of this when it produced its proposal for a Directive.[2] That is why the limitations to residence in another Member State are a critical aspect of the Directive.

I will first look at the provisions in the Directive in Chapter III, especially Article 14. I will then consider its limitations, analysing whether those limitations were present in the Commission's proposal and paying special attention to criticisms by scholars. As usual, I will also compare the Directive with the provisions of Directive 2004/38, which are applicable to European citizens who move to another Member State. Next, I will look at how Member States are implementing some of the limitations in the Directive, notably the possibility for Member States to apply national procedures regarding the requirements that status-holders have to fulfil in order to exercise an economic activity in a second Member State, and the option to apply integration measures in that second Member State. Special attention will be

---

1 See on this S. Iglesias Sánchez (2009), "Free Movement as a Precondition for Integration of Third Country Nationals in the European Union", in K. Groenendijk, S. Carrera and E. Guild (eds.), *Illiberal Liberal States: Immigration, Citizenship and Integration in the EU*, Ashgate: Surrey, pp. 205–220; See also T. Hoogenboom (1992), "Integration into Society and Free Movement of Non-EC Nationals", *European Journal of International Law*, Vol. 3, pp. 36–52.

2 In that proposal it was stated that: "The Commission considers that full integration also entails the right for long-term residents to reside in other Member States and that the time has come to implement Article 63(4) of the EC Treaty. A genuine area of freedom, security and justice, a fundamental objective of the European Union, is unthinkable without a degree of mobility for third-country nationals residing there legally, and particularly for those residing on a long-term basis". See European Commission, Proposal for a Council Directive Concerning the Status of Third-Country Nationals who are Long-Term Residents, COM (2001) 127 final, OJ 2001 C 240/79, p. 8.

paid to these national procedures as they are critical to this part of my analysis. It will not be possible here to compare the current situation to the one before the adoption of the Directive, as free movement possibilities were very limited for long-term residents prior to its implementation.[3] In fact, those third-country nationals who regularly resided in one Member State, and who were willing to move to another one, had to go through the same administrative procedures as if they were coming from a country outside the EU.[4] Finally, I will evaluate how the CJEU could interpret some of the provisions present in this Chapter and what the Commission could say about its implementation. I will end with some concluding remarks.

Hence, the questions for this Chapter are the following:

1. What are the possibilities for a status-holder to move to reside in another Member State?
2. What are the limitations in the Directive to that possibility to reside in another Member State? Were those limitations present in the Commission's proposal? What have been the main criticisms to those limitations by academics? Are there any similar limitations applicable to European citizens?
3. How are Member States implementing the Directive in their national legal orders? What are the usual national procedures that have to be fulfilled in order to exercise an economic activity in a Member State?
4. How could the CJEU interpret some of the provisions present in Chapter III? What could the Commission mention about its implementation?

2. *The Possibility to Reside in another Member State*

Here I will investigate what are the provisions in the Directive regarding the possibility for a long-term resident to reside in another Member State. Chapter III of the Directive is entitled "Residence in the other Member States". This is certainly a very important part of the Directive. In fact, according to

---

[3] There was for example one Decision relating to travel facilities for school pupils from third countries under the Maastricht Treaty, 94/795/JHA: Council Decision of 30 November 1994 on a joint action adopted by the Council on the basis of Article K.3.2.b of the Treaty on European Union concerning travel facilities for school pupils from third countries resident in a Member State, OJ 1994 L 327. See on this J. Handoll (2003), "The Status of Third-Country Nationals Residing on a Long-term Basis", in P. de Bruycker (ed.), *The Emergence of a European Immigration Policy*, Brylant: Brussels, pp. 269–362, at 309.

[4] S. Iglesias Sánchez (2009), "Free Movement of Third Country Nationals in the European Union? Main Features, Deficiencies and Challenges of the New Mobility Rights in the Area of Freedom, Security and Justice", *European Law Journal*, Vol. 15(6), pp. 791–805.

Article 1(b), one of the two subject matters of the Directive is to determine "the terms of residence in Member States other than the one which conferred long-term status on them for third-country nationals enjoying that status". Therefore, the legislator considered residence in another Member State as one of the two most important goals to achieve. This idea is further reinforced by Recital 18 which establishes that the possibility to reside in another Member State "should contribute to the effective attainment of an internal market as an area in which the free movement of persons is ensured. It could also constitute a major factor of mobility, notably on the Union's employment market".[5]

Article 14 provides that a long-term resident shall acquire the right to reside in another Member State, for a period exceeding three months if he fulfils certain conditions.[6] This is obviously a great advancement as, before the adoption of the Directive, the possibility to reside in another Member State did not exist and third-country nationals had to follow the national provisions in order to be granted entry into another Member State for a period longer than three months. According to the Directive, the status-holder can obtain residence in another Member State on three grounds:

a. to exercise an economic activity in an employed or self-employed capacity;
b. to pursue studies or vocational training; or
c. for other purposes.

Here I am mainly interested in the possibility to reside in another Member State to exercise an economic activity in an employed or self-employed capacity. In that sense, Article 14(3) read together with Article 21(2) obliges the second Member State to allow the status-holder from another Member State

[5] It is interesting to mention that, according to Article 18 of Council Directive 2009/50 on Highly skilled workers, "after eighteen months of legal residence in the first Member State as an EU Blue Card Holder, the person concerned and his family members may move to a Member State other than the first Member State for the purpose of highly qualified employment under the conditions set out in this Article". This is certainly a big departure from the Long-term Residence Directive, as highly skilled third-country nationals only have to reside for one and a half years and not for five years in order to be able to move to another Member State for the purposes of highly qualified employment. See Council Directive 2009/50/EC of 25 May 2009 on the conditions of entry and residence of third-country nationals for the purposes of highly qualified employment, OJ 2009 L 155/17.

[6] The Directive does not concern the conditions for the admission of third-country nationals to another Member State for a period of less than three months. This situation is covered by the Regulation (EC) No 562/2006 of the European Parliament and of the Council establishing a Community Code on the rules governing the movement of persons across borders (Schengen Borders Code), 15 March 2006, OJ 2006 L 105/1.

[7] See the wording of this Article below in this Chapter.

to have free access to employment after he has been employed in that second Member State for a period of 12 months.[7] Long-term residents enjoy equal treatment when they initially begin an employment or self-employment activity in another Member State provided that the second Member State does not apply any of the various limitations,[8] to which I will now refer.

3. *Limitations*

Here I intend to look at the limitations to answer three questions: Were those limitations present in the Commission's proposal? Do European citizens face any similar impediments to their free movement? What have scholars censured with regard to these limits?

The limitations to the general principle of the possibility to reside in another Member State are scattered throughout Chapter III of the Directive. I will divide them between employment-related limitations and admission-related ones:

3.1. *Employment-related Limitations*

There are various employment-related limitations:

Labour market test

First, Member States may examine the situation of their labour market (Article 14(3)).[9] According to this Article, Member States may, after examining the situation of their labour market, apply their national procedures regarding the requirements for filling a vacancy or for exercising such activities. The precise meaning and possible interpretation of this provision will be further analysed below because of its importance, as it seems that it may include the possibility for the Member State to require a work permit.[10]

---

[8] S. Peers (2004), "Implementing Equality? The Directive on Long Term Resident Third Country Nationals", *European Law Review*, Vol. 29(4), pp. 437–60, at 454.

[9] Article 14(3) reads as follows: "In cases of an economic activity in an employed or self-employed capacity referred to in paragraph 2(a), Member States may examine the situation of their labour market and apply their national procedures regarding the requirements for respectively, filling a vacancy, or for exercising such activities".

[10] K. Groenendijk (2007), "The Long-Term Residents Directive, Denizenship and Integration", in A. Baldaccini, E. Guild and H. Toner (eds.), *Whose Freedom, Security and Justice? EU Immigration and Asylum Law and Policy*, Hart Publishing: Oxford, pp. 429–450, at 447.

Preference for Union citizens or other third-country nationals
Second, they may give preference to Union citizens or to other third-country nationals who reside legally and receive unemployment benefits in the Member State concerned (Article 14(3) second indent).[11]

Quotas
Third, they may limit the total number of persons entitled to be granted a right of residence, whether they are moving to work, study or for other purposes, provided that such limitations are already in place at the time of adoption of the Directive (Article 14(4)).[12]

First year restriction
Fourth, during the first year, Member States may restrict access to employment in activities different from those for which the status-holder was granted an employment permit (Article 21(2)).[13] This will be further analysed below.

Students and inactive long-term residents
Fifth, Member States may decide whether or not status-holders who move in order to pursue studies or for other purposes have the right to work (Article 21(2) second indent).

3.2. *Admission-related Limitations*

Member States may once again require the same conditions that were imposed in order to obtain a long-term residence permit in the first

[11] This exception comes from the Community preference principle. This principle was endorsed in a non-binding Council resolution in 1994: "Member States will consider requests for admission to their territories for the purpose of employment only where vacancies in a Member State cannot be filled by national and Community manpower or by non-Community manpower lawfully resident on a permanent basis in that Member State and already forming part of the Member State's regular labour market". Council Resolution of 20 June 1994 on Limitations of Admission of Third-country Nationals to the Territory of the Member States for Employment, OJ 1996 C 274/3.

[12] The situation with regard to highly skilled workers is similar. Although there are no quotas, Member States may determine their volume of admission for third-country nationals entering their territory for the purposes of highly qualified employment. See Articles 6 and 18(7) of Council Directive 2009/50.

[13] Article 21(2) reads as follows: "Member States may provide that the persons referred to in Article 14(2)(a) shall have restricted access to employed activities different than those for which they have been granted their residence permit under the conditions set by national legislation for a period not exceeding 12 months".

Member State: stable and regular resources, sickness insurance and integration measures (Article 15).[14] With regard to integration, Member States cannot require any integration if the status-holder previously had to comply with integration conditions in order to be granted the long-term residence permit. Nonetheless, the status-holders can always be required to attend language courses (Article 15(2) (3)).[15]

None of these limitations were present in the Commission's proposal.[16] Moreover, the Commission had added an important Article that was completely left out of the final Directive. Article 16 (2) provided that long-term residents would retain their status as workers in some cases: when they were incapacitated for work as a result of illness or accident,[17] when they were unemployed but entitled to unemployment benefits (as long as such entitlement subsisted) or when they embarked on vocational training related to their previous occupational activity (unless they were in a state of involuntary unemployment). These grounds were, although reduced, very similar to the ones for European citizens under Directive 2004/38.[18]

In fact, and turning now to European citizens, a comparison can be drawn between this Directive and Directive 2004/38. Freedom of movement and residence is clearly one of the most important features of European citizenship.[19] In addition, free movement of persons constitutes one of the four fundamental freedoms of the internal market.[20] EU citizens can, in principle, move freely and reside in any other EU country subject to certain limitations on grounds of public policy, public security or public health. For our purposes here it is central to mention that the two most important limitations which are optional in the Long-term Residence Directive, the possibility to examine the situation of the labour market and integration measures, are not applicable to European citizens.

Moreover, it seems that long-term residents residing in another Member State do not have a period in which to seek a job, other than the three months

---

14 See on these conditions in the first Member State Chapter 7 below.

15 In clear contrast, highly skilled workers do not have to fulfil any integration measures when they move to reside in another Member State for the purpose of highly qualified employment. Article 18 of Directive 2009/50.

16 See Arts 15–21 of the proposal.

17 Turkish citizens do not have this right either. The Court decided a case of a Turkish worker who became permanently incapacitated as a result of an accident. It interpreted that Article 6(2) of Decision No 1/80 did not grant him a right of residence in such a case. See Case C-434/93, *Ahmet Bozkurt v Staatssecretaris van Justitie* [1995] ECR I-01475.

18 Art 7 (3) of Directive 2004/38.

19 Art 20 TFEU.

20 Recital 2 of Directive 2004/38.

in which they can be in another Member State at the beginning without applying for a residence permit. In fact, Member States may withdraw a residence permit when the conditions in Articles 14 to 16 are no longer met.[21] This is completely different from the situation for European citizens[22] whose status is contained in Article 14(4)(b) of Directive 2004/38. It is stated that they cannot be expelled if they "can provide evidence that they are continuing to seek employment and that they have a genuine chance of being engaged". This comes as a result of the well established CJEU jurisprudence in the matter, which grants a minimum period of six months as a job seeker.[23]

All this prompts Iglesias to make a distinction between free movement rights, which "are directly endowed by the Treaty to nationals of the Member States" and mobility rights, which "are only granted by secondary law, and in a very limited way".[24]

Other scholars have referred to the limitations provided in this Chapter of the Directive as one of its major weaknesses. Kocharov, for instance, argues that the fact that there is no mutual recognition of residence permits is the main flaw.[25] And Skordas considers that the Directive increases the possibility of "fragmentation of the European labour market in national segments" as it only provides a " 'marginal' mobility between two Member States".[26] Groenendijk deems the possibility to allow a labour market test and the application of national procedures, for example, a work permit, in order to be employed or self employed in the second Member State as one of the two main Achilles'

---

21 See Art 15(1) read together with Art 22(1) (b) of the long-term residence Directive.

22 It is interesting to note that, according to Article 13 of Council Directive 2009/50 on highly skilled workers, highly skilled workers have the right to look for a job for a period of three months in the event of unemployment. This will give this group of third-country nationals a better chance in case of unemployment. However it is, in any case, a very limited right and probably not sufficient, even for a highly skilled worker, to find another equivalent job. See Directive 2009/50/EC of 25 May 2009 on the conditions of entry and residence of third-country nationals for the purposes of highly qualified employment, OJ 2009 L 155/17. See on this Directive E. Guild (2007), *EU Policy on Labour Migration. A First look at the Commission's Blue Card Initiative*, CEPS Policy Brief No. 145, Centre for European Policy Studies: Brussels, at 6.

23 Case C-292/89 *R. v. Immigration Appeal Tribunal ex p. Antonissen* [1991] ECR I-745. See also Article 7 (3) (c) of Directive 2004/38.

24 S. Iglesias Sánchez (2009), "Free Movement of Third Country Nationals in the European Union? Main Features, Deficiencies and Challenges of the New Mobility Rights in the Area of Freedom, Security and Justice", *European Law Journal*, Vol. 15(6), pp. 791–805.

25 A. Kocharov (2008), "What Intra-Community Mobility for Third Country Workers?" *European Law Review*, Vol. 33(6), pp. 912–26, at 918.

26 A. Skordas (2006), "Immigration and the Market: The Long Term Residence Directive", *Columbia Journal of European Law*, Vol. 13, pp. 201–229, at 203.

heels of the Directive, the other one being the possibility to ask for integration conditions.[27] For Boelaert, the main problem is that the Directive does not expressly address the question of whether status-holders have the right to move to a second Member State. In her view, this is only answered in an indirect manner and it falls short of one of the main purposes of the Directive.[28]

Nevertheless, as Kocharov rightly points out, these conditions are all optional. Hence any Member State could abstain from their application and grant free access from the very first day. She argues, however, that this is not a very likely scenario.[29] Is that true? How are Member States implementing the Directive? Are they making use of all the exceptions? This will be the next point to be analysed.

4. *Implementation*

In this section I intend to look at how Member States are implementing two important limitations in the Directive: the possibility to apply national procedures and the option to impose integration measures. As has been mentioned above, both limitations are optional and their importance is crucial for those status-holders who would like to reside in another Member State. With regard to the first one, it has been said by some authors that a labour market test weakens equality. This is because a status-holder can apparently be refused entry in order to work even if he is offered a job, for reasons of the situation in the labour market.[30] He can also be denied that authorisation if he wishes to exercise an economic activity in a self-employed capacity even if he has the appropriate funds. I will see below if this is the correct interpretation of this provision. With reference to integration, it has been argued that it segments the Union's labour market as it makes the intra-Community mobility of long-term residents more difficult, which in the end has as a consequence the stay of long-term residents in the first Member State.[31] Moreover, the imposition of

---

27 K. Groenendijk (2007), "The Long-Term Residents Directive, Denizenship and Integration", in A. Baldaccini, E. Guild and H. Toner (eds.), *Whose Freedom, Security and Justice? EU Immigration and Asylum Law and Policy*, Hart Publishing: Oxford, pp. 429–450, at 442.

28 S. Boelaert-Suominen (2005), "Non-EU Nationals and Council Directive 2003/109/EC on the Status of Third-country Nationals who are Long-term Residents: Five Paces Forward and Possibly Three Paces Back", *Common Market Law Review*, Vol. 42(4), pp. 1011–1052, at 1029–30.

29 A. Kocharov (2008), "What Intra-Community Mobility for Third Country Workers?" *European Law Review*, Vol. 33(6), pp. 912–26, at 919.

30 *Ibid.*, at 923. This seems to be the situation in Germany, as will be seen below.

31 A. Skordas (2006), "Immigration and the Market: The Long Term Residence Directive", *Columbia Journal of European Law*, Vol. 13, pp. 201–229, at 222.

integration conditions in the second Member State questions the value of the long-term residence status in the first Member State. In fact, it undermines the assumption under which a status holder in one Member State should be considered to be integrated into the EU as a whole. Obtaining the long-term residence permit itself should indeed be sufficient proof of integration.

These two provisions certainly reduce the prospects of contributing to the attainment of an internal market in which free movement of persons is ensured as established in Recital 18 of the Directive. The way in which Member States have transposed these optional provisions is thus of utmost importance.

Before analysing the implementation of these two provisions, I will briefly explain the procedure for applying for a permit in order to exercise an economic activity in the EU. Member States usually differentiate between residence permits, which have a wider scope, and work permits.[32] Most Member States require third-country nationals to acquire a work permit.[33] The granting of such a permit is usually discretionary and takes into consideration the situation in the labour market. However, most Member States have rules which exempt certain groups from the requirement to obtain a work permit.[34]

With regard to admission for self-employed activities, there are some Member States that require a work permit and others that only require a residence permit. Here the main criterion for granting such a permit is the self-establishment project (resources, added value for the economy etc.).[35]

Hence, it is now relevant to see the situation in my four case studies, as well as in other Member States, which may be in breach of the Directive. There are two important problems that I would like to identify at this stage: First, the practice in some Member States of asking for a work permit even after the status-holder has worked in that second Member State for one year. Second, the application of integration conditions instead of integration measures. I will look later at the possibility to apply national procedures in

---

[32] Ecotec Research and Consulting (2000), *Admission of Third Country Nationals for Paid Employment or Self-Employed Activity*, Ecotec: Brussels. There is a proposal at EU level to unify both the residence and the work permit. See Proposal for a Council Directive on a Single Application Procedure for a Single Permit for Third-country Nationals to Reside and Work in the Territory of a Member State and on a Common Set of Rights for Third-country Workers Legally Residing in a Member State, COM (2007) 638 final, Brussels, 23.10.2007. This Directive had not been adopted as of 1 December 2010.

[33] This is not the case with the points based system in the UK, for example. See on this H. Wray (2009), "The Points Based System: A Blunt Instrument? *Immigration, Asylum and Nationality Law*, Vol. 23(3), pp. 231–251.

[34] Ecotec Research and Consulting (2000), *Admission of Third Country Nationals for Paid Employment or Self-Employed Activity*, Ecotec: Brussels, p. 12.

[35] *Ibid.*, p. 21.

order to allow a status holder to exercise an economic activity in a second Member State.

Work permit after one year

As has already been mentioned, it seems that Member States may ask the status-holder from another Member State to apply for a work permit for the first entry into the second Member State. The precise meaning of this provision will be scrutinised below. ***Germany*** is a good example to mention here. It follows from Section 38a (3) of the German Residence Act that status-holders coming from another Member State may only take up employment if they fulfil one of the following conditions: they comply with the criteria of Section 19 (highly qualified migrants); they comply with the criteria of Section 20 (researchers); or they comply with the criteria of Section 18 (all other labour migrants). The general rule under this last Section 18(2) is that the federal employment agency has to grant approval.[36] The third-country national will always be required to have a concrete employment offer in Germany (see Section 18(5)). Apparently, a situation could arise in which the federal employment agency would not grant approval, even if the status-holder had a job offer. That is inferred from the numerous tests that have to be satisfied before granting that approval.[37] I will see below whether the possibility not to grant a residence and work permit to a status-holder could be in breach of the Directive.

The situation is different where a status-holder has worked for one year in a second Member State. As Groenendijk points out,[38] once the status-holder has worked for one year, he obtains free access to the labour market except for jobs that entail even occasional involvement in the exercise of public authority[39] and the jobs reserved for national, EU or EEA citizens.[40] Nevertheless, there are some Member States which require yet another work permit when changing jobs after the first year. This is in breach of the Directive, as will be seen below in the case of Italy.

---

36 A. Wiesbrock (2010), *Legal Migration to the European Union*, Martinus Nijhoff: Leiden, p. 399.

37 *Ibid.*, p. 414.

38 K. Groenendijk (2005), "Access of Third-Country Nationals to Employment under the New EC Migration Law", in F. Julien-Laferrière, H. Labayle and O. Edström (eds.), *The European Immigration and Asylum Policy: Critical Assessment Five Years After the Amsterdam Treaty*, Brussels: Bruylant, pp. 141–174, at 157–160.

39 Article 11(1) (a) of Directive 2003/109.

40 Article 11(3) (a) of Directive 2003/109.

Integration measures
As has been already analysed, Member States may require a status-holder coming from another Member State to comply with integration measures, if he was not required to fulfil any integration conditions in order to obtain the long-term residence permit in the first Member State. However, in ***France***, for example, long-term residents coming from another Member State have to sign an integration contract, even if they complied with integration conditions when they obtained the long-term residence permit in the first Member State.[41] That integration contract obliges them to undertake courses in civic formation, language (in case they do not have a sufficient level of French) and a session on information of life in France. The contract is signed for one year and it can be extended for an additional year under certain circumstances.[42] Non-compliance with the integration contract can be taken into account in order to not renew the residence permit.[43] The signature of an integration contract for those long-term residents who complied with integration conditions when they obtained the long-term residence permit in the first Member State is forbidden by the Directive. Hence, as these long-term residents coming from another Member State are asked to follow the same integration courses as any third-country national entering for the first time into the country, France is in breach of the Directive.
The situation with regard to my four case studies is as follows:

Sweden
In Sweden, long-term residents coming from another Member State have a right to reside in Sweden. According to the Aliens Ordinance, a long-term resident from another Member State coming into Sweden is exempt from the work permit requirement.[44] Hence long-term residents acquire free access to employment in Sweden from the first day.

In Sweden long-term residents coming from another Member State do not have to comply with any integration measure. This is consistent with the fact that a third-country national applying for the long-term residence permit in Sweden does not have to fulfil any integration conditions.

Sweden has, therefore, implemented the Directive in a favourable way for long-term residents coming from another Member State. These long-term residents will have the possibility to obtain a job in order to reside in Sweden without any further requirements.

[41] Article L 311-9 and L. 313-4-1 of the CESEDA.
[42] Article R. 311-27 of the CESEDA.
[43] See Chapter 7 below.
[44] Chapter 5 Section 1 of the Aliens Ordinance (2006:97).

Italy

Long-term residents coming from another Member State can ask to reside in Italy in order to work,[45] pursuant to Article 5(3) bis of the immigration Law. This Article establishes that the residence permit for work purposes (*contratto di soggiorno per lavoro*) is provided once there is an employment contract, which is defined in Article 5 bis. It can be inferred that the status-holder requires a work permit in order to pursue an economic activity in Italy. Moreover, Article 36 (bis) of the implementing regulation establishes that in order to change employment there is the need to sign a new residence permit for work purposes. This is in breach of the Directive as, according to Article 21(2) of the Directive, long-term residents coming from another Member State cannot have imposed on them any restriction on access to employment activities after 12 months, as seen above.

In Italy long-term residents coming from another Member State do not have to comply with any integration measures. However, if the long-term resident coming from another Member State would like to acquire a long-term residence permit in Italy after five years, he would have to pass a test in Italian according to the new text following the 2009 reform.[46] The 2009 reform also sets up an integration contract to be signed when the third-country national requests a residence permit. From the reading of the new Article 4 bis it is not entirely clear whether long-term residents coming from another Member State should also sign it. This is probably the case as this Article provides that a long-term resident cannot be expelled if he does not fulfil the conditions signed in the integration contract. Hence, it can only be a long-term resident coming from another Member State. This might be clarified in the implementing regulation.

Spain

In Spain the 2009 reform to the 2000 immigration Law brought important modifications and finally implemented the Directive.[47] On the one hand,

---

[45] Article 9 bis (1) of the Italian immigration law.

[46] Article 9 (2) bis of the Italian immigration law.

[47] The Directive had not been implemented in due time. However, there was an Instruction that ordered to the administrative authorities to directly apply Directive 2003/109 to status-holders coming from another Member State. That Instruction recognised the direct effect of Article 14. Instrucción DGI/SGRJ/04/2008 of the Ministry of Labour and Social Affairs. See on this S. Iglesias Sánchez (2008), "La Aplicación Directa de la Directiva 2003/109/CE a los Nacionales de Terceros Estados que Acrediten Ser Titulares del Estatuto de los Residentes de Larga Duración en otros Estados Miembros de la UE", *Revista de Derecho Migratorio y Extranjería*, Vol. 19, pp. 81–98.

Article 32(3) provides that long-term residents from another Member State can enter the country in order to pursue an economic activity in an employed or self-employed capacity, under the conditions to be established in the Regulation not yet adopted by 1 December 2010. There is no mention of a work permit, although that might be adopted in the Regulation. This is relevant as the CJEU found that Spain had not implemented the Directive as there were no provisions in this area.[48] On the other hand, Spain does not impose any integration requirements. This is consistent with the fact that Spain does not require any integration conditions in order to obtain a long-term residence permit.

Latvia

In Latvia, status-holders coming from another Member State are required to have an employment permit during the first year, but they obtain free access to the employment market after then.[49]

With regard to integration, status-holders are not required to pass a language examination in Latvian. However, in order to perform certain professions it is required to have adequate knowledge of Latvian, which varies according to the profession.[50] This could be in breach of the Directive, depending on the profession for which knowledge of Latvian is required and the level demanded. It could run contrary to general principles of Union law, such as proportionality.[51]

With these cases considered, it is important to now turn to the possible interpretation of these clauses by the CJEU and the Commission.

5. *Possible Interpretation by the CJEU*

In the previous pages I have identified two important problems with regard to the possibility for status-holders to move to reside in another Member State. The first one is the possibility to apply national procedures regarding the requirements for exercising an economic activity. The second one is the likelihood of imposing integration measures when the status-holder from another Member State enters to reside in the second Member State. In the following pages, I intend to see what the limits are to these limitations. In other words,

---

48 Case C-59/07 *Commission v Spain*, 15 November 2007, [2007] ECR I-00161, paragraph 18.

49 Article 15 of Law "Long-term resident status of the European Community in Latvia" read together with Articles 9 and 23(6) of the Immigration Law.

50 See for the list of professions Annex to Cabinet Regulations 7 July 2009.

51 See Chapter 9 below.

I will see what the European Commission could say about the implementation of these requirements and whether Member States may have misunderstood them. I will also see whether the CJEU could shed some light on their interpretation.

5.1. *The Possibility to Apply National Procedures*

The first difficulty is the possibility to apply national procedures which would apparently grant an employment permit to those status-holders willing to reside in another Member State. As has been seen above, Article 14(3) provides that Member States may "examine the situation of their labour market and apply their national procedures regarding the requirements for, respectively, filling a vacancy, or for exercising such activities". This is certainly something which could impede the mobility of long-term residents to other Member States. Is there any room for interpretation here? What is the precise meaning of this provision?

There are two possible interpretations. The first one believes that those Member States that have used this possibility to require a long-term resident coming from another Member State to apply for an employment permit could perhaps do so. According to Brinkmann:

> This provision means that third-country nationals have no right of free movement to the same extent as Union citizens enjoy they only have a right of movement if they have a valid job offer and are admitted by the second Member State.[52]

As will be seen below, some authors do not agree with this interpretation. Something that is clear though is that the situation is different once a Member State has granted an employment permit to a long-term resident coming from another Member State. In that case, after one year, the long-term resident is entitled to work in any employment activity even if it is different from the one for which he was granted the residence permit. Hence he has free access to employment after a maximum period of one year. Consequently, those Member States which require a new employment permit in order to continue an economic activity or to change the job sector after the first year, such as Italy, are in breach of the Directive. The European Commission could, consequently, launch infringement proceedings.

As I have just mentioned, there is a second interpretation of Article 14(3) by some authors who do not agree with the one just mentioned. Guild, for instance, argues that:

---

[52] G. Brinkmann (2004), "The Immigration and Asylum Agenda", *European Law Journal* 10(2), pp. 182–199, at 192.

> It would be contrary to the meaning of the directive if this provision were to be interpreted as meaning that States are entitled to continue to apply their national requirements on work permits as this would render pointless the "right" of free movement for paid employment which the directive purports to grant qualifying third country nationals. It seems that the right of Member States is to apply their existing procedures regarding access to the labour market but not their requirements. The only requirements which can be applied under the directive as regards labour market access for qualifying third country nationals are those set out in the directive itself.[53]

Guild argues that this interpretation is consistent with the CJEU's interpretation of Article 6(3) of Decision No 1/80 of the EEC Turkey Association Agreement which allows Member States to apply their national procedures regarding the continued employment of Turkish workers. To support her argument, Guild mentions the case of *Kus*.[54] The facts are the following: Mr Kus was a Turkish national who entered Germany in 1980 to marry a German national and did so in 1981. However, Mr Kus divorced in 1983 and in 1984 the Mayor of Landeshauptstadt Wiesbaden refused to renew his residence permit. The German Court referred the question to the CJEU to see if there was any advantageous solution for Mr Kus under Article 6 of Decision No 1/80. I have mentioned this Article in the Chapter 4 above. The important point here was to interpret Article 6(3) of Decision No 1/80, which is worded as follows: "The procedures for applying paragraphs 1 and 2 shall be those established under national rules". The CJEU had, consequently, to answer in this case what was the meaning of Article 6(3). The precise question was:

> [D]o the rules governing the effects on rights of residence of the decisions of the EEC-Turkey Association Council concerning rights of employment fall within the implementing provisions which under Article 6(3) of that decision are to be adopted by the Member States on their own responsibility, without being bound by Community law?[55]

As Guild rightly points out, "it was argued that this meant that the right to continued employment could not be directly effective as it was meditated by national procedures".[56] However, the CJEU arrived at a different conclusion. In order to do that it followed the steps outlined below:

---

[53] E. Guild (2004), *The Legal elements of European Identity: EU citizenship and Migration Law*, Kluwer Law Internacional, European Law Library: The Hague, p. 231.

[54] Case C-237/91, *Kazim Kus v Landeshauptstadt Wiesbaden*, 16 December 1992, ECR [1992] I-06781.

[55] *Ibid.*, paragraph 7.

[56] E. Guild (2004), *The Legal elements of European Identity: EU citizenship and Migration Law*, Kluwer Law International, European Law Library: The Hague, p. 231.

Direct effect

The CJEU began by acknowledging that, as it had already stated in *Sevince*,[57] Article 6(1) of Decision No 1/80 has direct effect. Hence, it is important to see whether Article 14(1) also has direct effect. On the one hand, some authors claim that Article 14(1) has direct effect.[58] Moreover, some Member States, such as Spain, have recognised the direct applicability of the Directive because of the legislator's failure to act.[59] Also in Spain, a national Court recognised the direct effect of Article 14 in a case brought by a Colombian woman who held a long-term residence permit in Germany and was willing to reside in Spain in a self-employed capacity. Spain had not yet implemented the Directive but the Court nevertheless recognised her possibility to rely on Article 14 of the Directive before that national court.[60] On the other hand, some authors do not agree with this interpretation. Kocharov, for instance, mentions that:

> The so-called "right" to move under the LTR Directive is conditional on being admitted by the second Member State. Combining optional conditions enables Member States to re-define in national law who and on what terms can move. The multitude of optional conditions potentially result in such a wide array of rules applicable across the 24 Member States, that it is difficult to envisage how an individual would be able to rely upon the Directive in court to establish an EC law right of residence, let alone work, in another Member State.[61]

The importance of whether or not Article 14 has direct effect is evident and it is very probable that the CJEU will argue that Article 14 is capable of having direct effect. I base this reasoning on the Spanish case mentioned above and also on the ruling by the CJEU in *Baumbast*. In *Baumbast* the Court established that even if Article 18 EC[62] was subject to limitations and conditions,

---

[57] Case C-192/89, *Sevince*, ECR [1990] I-3461.

[58] S. Peers (2004), "Implementing Equality? The Directive on Long-term Resident Third Country Nationals", *European Law Review*, Vol. 29(4), p. 437–460, at 443.

[59] Instrucción DGI/SGJR/04/2009, Spanish Ministry of Labour and Immigration. See on this S. Iglesias Sánchez (2008), "La Aplicación Directa de la Directiva 2003/109 a los nacionales de terceros Estados que acrediten ser titulares del estatuto de los residentes de larga duración en otros Estados miembros de la UE", *Revista de Derecho Migratorio y Extranjería*, Vol. 19, pp. 81–98.

[60] Sentencia 117/07 del Juzgado Contencioso administrativo número 3 de Santander, 26 April 2007.

[61] A. Kocharov (2008), "What intra-Community Mobility for Third-Country Workers?", *European Law Review*, Vol. 33 (6), pp. 912–926, at 919.

[62] This Article has been renumbered as 20 by the TFEU.

the application of those limits was subject to judicial review and, therefore, individuals could rely directly on that Article.[63]

The precise meaning of Article 6(3) of Decision No 1/80

The Court continued its argumentation as follows:

> Article 6(3) of Decision No 1/80 merely clarifies the obligation incumbent on the Member States to take such administrative measures as may be necessary for the implementation of that provision, without empowering them to make conditional or restrict the application of the precise and unconditional right which the provision grants to Turkish workers.[64]

This could certainly be also applicable in the case of Directive 2003/109. In fact, I would argue that Guild's interpretation of the provision in Article 14(3) is the correct one. The CJEU would probably apply the effectiveness and proportionality test to this provision, as will be seen in the next Chapters,[65] as an exception to the rule has to be interpreted narrowly. It would also look at the scope and objectives of the Directive. Certainly, the fact that the subject matter of the Directive, as established in Article 1, is to determine the terms of residence for a status-holder to reside in another Member State, as well as the mention of the "effective attainment of an internal market as an area in which free movement of workers is ensured", seem to be in line with the interpretation given by Guild. Hence, if a long-term resident in one Member State has a job offer in another Member State and provided there is no EU citizen or third-country national in the second Member State who could perform the job, the second Member State may apply the same national procedures in order to grant that status-holder a job permit, as it would apply to a third-country national coming from outside the EU. However, the second Member State cannot apply any requirement which is not included in the Directive (e.g. sickness insurance) as that would render the Directive meaningless and deprive it of its effectiveness. Hence, Member States cannot deny granting the work permit to the status-holder on the basis of national requirements, but they are obliged to grant it if the conditions in the Directive are fulfilled. This conclusion is also reached by Guèvremont, with whom I agree, who looks at the intention of the legislator as reflected in the preambles. In fact, she argues,

---

[63] Case C-413/99, *Baumbast and R v Secretary of State for the Home Department* [2002] ECR I-07091, paragraph 86.

[64] Case C-237/91, *Kazim Kus v Landeshauptstadt Wiesbaden*, 16 December 1992, ECR [1992] I-06781, paragraph 31.

[65] See Chapter 9 below.

Recital 11[66] read together with Recital 17[67] provide, by *a contrario* reasoning, that long-term residence permits give a right of access to reside in a second Member State.[68] Moreover, she continues, Recital 18, mentioned above, in which reference is made to the attainment of an internal market means that the legislator not only opposes obstacles to the residence of status-holders in a second Member State, but goes further by linking the effectiveness of the Directive to the free movement of "all" persons: long-term residents or European citizens.[69] Finally, she points out Article 19(1),[70] under which the national authorities of the second Member State do not have any discretion in granting the status-holder the residence permit.[71] All this leads her to conclude that entry into the second Member State is not subject to the granting of any kind of residence permit and that a status-holder could in fact exercise any other activities on which he would like to base his stay in that second Member State (e.g. working or studying) even before obtaining a residence permit.[72] If this is the interpretation upheld, countries like Germany, analysed above, will breach the Directive if they do not grant a work and residence permit to a status-holder with a job offer.

The rationale that I have put forward seems to be in line with a purposive interpretation of the Directive and the Court could certainly defend this thesis

[66] Recital 11 reads as follows: "The acquisition of long-term resident status should be certified by residence permits enabling those concerned to prove their legal status easily and immediately. Such residence permits should also satisfy high-level technical standards, notably as regards protection against falsification and counterfeiting, in order to avoid abuses in the Member State in which the status is acquired and in Member States in which the right of residence is exercised."

[67] Recital 17 reads as follows: "Harmonisation of the terms for acquisition of long-term resident status promotes mutual confidence between Member States. Certain Member States issue permits with a permanent or unlimited validity on conditions that are more favourable than those provided for by this Directive. The possibility of applying more favourable national provisions is not excluded by the Treaty. However, for the purposes of this Directive, it should be provided that permits issued on more favourable terms do not confer the right to reside in other Member States."

[68] S. Guèvremont (2009), *Vers un Traitement Équitable des Étrangers Extracommunautaires en Séjour Régulier. Examen des Directives sur le Regroupement Familial et sur les Résidents de Longue Durée*, Wöhrmann Print Service : Zutphen, p. 433.

[69] *Ibid.*, p. 434.

[70] Article 19(1) reads as follows: "The competent national authorities shall process applications within four months from the date that these have been lodged."

[71] S. Guèvremont (2009), *Vers un Traitement Équitable des Étrangers Extracommunautaires en Séjour Régulier. Examen des Directives sur le Regroupement Familial et sur les Résidents de Longue Durée*, Wöhrmann Print Service : Zutphen, p. 434.

[72] *Ibid.*, p. 434–35.

as it seems reasonable that the mobility of long-term residents should be upheld, based on the objective of the Directive itself. With regard to the Commission, it could also propose amendments to the Directive in order to clarify this matter.

5.2. *Integration Measures*

The possibility to require integration measures in the second Member State needs further elaboration. The Directive itself makes a distinction between integration conditions (Article 5(2)) and integration measures (Article 15(3)). This means that the second Member State may require the long-term resident to attend an integration course, for example, a language course, if he did not comply with any integration conditions in order to acquire long-term residence status in the first Member State. However, the second Member State cannot ask the status-holder to successfully complete such a course as a condition for admission or residence.[73]

This is inferred not only from the different wording used in Articles 5(2) and 15(3) of the Directive, but also from an analysis of the Directive's negotiations. Carrera has shown how some Member States, notably Germany, Austria and the Netherlands, were willing to include the same integration conditions in Article 15 as in Article 5. Due to the opposition of other Member States, especially Belgium, France, Italy and Sweden, a compromise was reached to word the Directive in the way in which it was finally adopted.[74]

Finally, there is no reason to believe that the CJEU would interpret this provision in a different way from the one suggested here. So far, the Court, in its judgments on other measures adopted under Title IV, has repeatedly referred to the preambles, the purpose of the measure, the purpose of the area of freedom, security and justice and the *effet utile* of a provision.[75] A brief analysis of these elements confirms that the interpretation suggested by Groenendijk, among others, is the correct one. The preamble of the Directive refers to the aim of granting long-term resident third-country nationals "a set of uniform rights which are as near as possible to those enjoyed by citizens of the European Union". With regard to the purpose of the measure, it has already been revealed that one of the goals of the Directive is to determine "the terms of residence in

[73] K. Groenendijk (2004), "Legal Concepts of Integration in EU Migration Law", *European Journal of Migration and Law*, Vol. 6, pp. 111–126, at 124.

[74] S. Carrera (2009), *In Search of the Perfect Citizen? The Intersection between Integration, Immigration and Nationality in the EU*, Martinus Nijhoff: Leiden/Boston, at 175–183.

[75] K. Groenendijk (2006), "Family Reunification as a Right under Community Law", *European Journal of Migration and Law*, Vol. 8. (2), pp. 215–230, at 226.

Member States other than the one which conferred long-term status on them for third-country nationals enjoying that status". With reference to the area of freedom, security and justice, the Directive signals in its first Recital in the preamble that in order to progressively establish it, there is the need to adopt measures relating to immigration, "and safeguarding the rights of third-country nationals". Finally, with regard to the *effet utile* of the Directive, to add an extra condition not present in the Directive would take away its *effet utile*.[76] The CJEU has already expressed in other judgments the importance of not interpreting the provisions of a Directive restrictively in order to not deprive it of its effectiveness.[77]

Therefore, those countries requiring compliance with integration conditions for those long-term residents who have already fulfilled integration conditions in the first Member State and who move to reside in their territory, such as France, would not be in conformity with the Directive. The European Commission has the opportunity to point that out by using infringement proceedings.

6. *Conclusion*

Mobility rights for long-term residents in the EU are a crucial factor in the integration of third-country nationals. It must be first said that this Chapter of the Directive is an innovation, as free movement rights for third-country nationals for a period longer than three months did not previously exist. If this Chapter is seen from this perspective it is clearly a great advancement. Nonetheless, the way in which some Member States are making use of the optional limitations in the Directive makes it difficult for long-term residents to enjoy the possibility to go and work, study or reside for other purposes in another Member State. This might have important consequences for the identification of long-term residents with Europe, as they see how one of the most important rights for European citizens is limited. It also has negative outcomes for the attainment of an internal market and a Union's employment market. On the positive side, some Member States have not made use of the optional limitation clauses in the Directive. In that way they grant a proper right of

[76] For a discussion of the application of the *effet utile* in the area of free movement of persons see A. Woltjer (2005), "Free Movement of Persons in the European Union- the Evolutive Approach of the Court of Justice EC" in F. Stroink and E. van der Liden (eds.), *Judicial Lawmaking and Administrative Law*, Intersentia: Antwerpen/Oxford, pp. 81–96, at 84–90.

[77] Case C-127/08, *Blaise Baheten Metock and Others v Minister for Justice, Equality and Law Reform*, 25 July 2008, [2008] ECR I- 06241, Paragraph 93.

entry to long-term residents from other Member States in order to work, study or reside for other purposes. The doubts that some authors expressed with regard to the real usefulness of this Chapter of the Directive seem to be fair when scrutinising the implementation in some Member States, whereas in others a proper right of entry has been established.[78] This could fall short of one of the two objectives of the Directive, which is to give long-term residents the right to move around the Union for periods longer than three months.[79]

I have argued, however, that the CJEU has the opportunity to correctly interpret some of the most controversial elements, such as the precise meaning of Article 14(3) or the introduction of integration measures, in order not to render the Directive meaningless by depriving it of its effectiveness. The Commission also has the opportunity to look at the way some Member States have transposed these provisions, and to propose amendments to this Chapter. A big step forward would be to completely eliminate the possibility to require a work permit for a status-holder in order to move to reside in another Member State as well as the integration measures. As Groenendijk and Guild point out, "before we start recruiting new workers from outside the Union, we should first offer third-country nationals with long residence in the EU the opportunity to fulfil the vacancies".[80]

---

[78] This could change in the future as there no standstill clauses applying to this Chapter apart from the one provided in Article 14(4) on the possibility to impose a quota.

[79] S. Boelaert-Suominen (2005), "Non-EU Nationals and Council Directive 2003/109/EC on the Status of Third-Country Nationals who are Long-Term Residents: Five Paces Forward and Possibly Three Paces Back", *Common Market Law Review*, Vol. 42 (4), pp. 1011–1052, at 1030.

[80] K. Groenendijk and E. Guild (2001), "Converging Criteria: Creating an Area of Security of Residence for Europe's Third Country Nationals", *European Journal of Migration and Law*, Vol. 3, pp. 37–59, at 51–52.

Section IV

The Integration Conditions

Chapter 7

Origin and Development of the Integration Conditions

1. *Introduction*

This Section, which comprises Chapters 7, 8 and 9, deals with the integration conditions in Article 5. Chapter 8 summarises and categorises the political motivations for the introduction of these integration conditions, in order to acquire the long-term residence status, in different Member States, whereas Chapter 9 analyses their possible interpretation by the CJEU.

In this first Chapter I will look at the conditions that third-country nationals have to fulfil in order to acquire long-term residence status. My main interest here is to explore the possibility of requiring the third-country national to comply with some kind of integration before the permit is granted.

I will begin by briefly exploring their origin in the citizenship legislations of some Member States. Interestingly enough, in some countries, such as the Netherlands and the UK, the same test applies in order to become naturalised as to obtain permanent residence. This seems to be an unconscious recognition by Member States that long-term residence status is, in fact, equivalent to EU citizenship in all material respects.

I will then succinctly point out the way in which integration is also being used in another European instrument, notably the Family Reunification Directive, although that Directive allows for integration measures and not integration conditions, as will be seen below.

I will later explore the integration conditions by following the same structure as in the previous Chapters in Section III. Thus, I will first begin by explaining how a third-country national can obtain the long-term residence permit and what are the other conditions, apart from integration, that need to be fulfilled. I will then scrutinise the integration conditions required in order to obtain that permit, and I will see whether or not they were present in the Commission's proposal. I will briefly consider the situation of European citizens when they move to another country in order to see if they also have to accomplish any kind of integration. Also, under this second point, I will analyse the critiques by other academics of these integration conditions, after which I will examine how Member States are implementing the integration possibility. Due to the importance of this provision, I will give a general overview of what all Member States are doing, including those not bound by the Directive, paying special attention to the most problematic examples and to my four case studies. I will sum up with some final reflections on the issue.

Hence, the questions for this Chapter are the following:

1. What are the origins of the integration conditions in the legislations of Member States? Is there a similar trend of requiring a higher integration threshold in citizenship laws?
2. How has integration been interpreted in the other European Directive which refers to it, the Family Reunification Directive? How are Member States implementing that possibility?
3. What are the conditions, apart from integration, that a third-country national has to fulfil in order to be granted long-term residence status?
4. What is understood by the integration conditions? Was it present in the Commission's proposal? Is there any similar condition for European citizens when they move to reside in another Member State? What have been the main criticisms by other academics?
5. How are Member States implementing these integration conditions? Have their legislations changed with regard to the situation before the adoption of the Directive?

2. *The Origins of Integration Conditions: Citizenship Legislations*

The integration conditions in the Long-term Residence Directive have a precise antecedent in the citizenship legislations of some Member States, which require integration (usually in the form of language proficiency and knowledge of the country) in order to obtain citizenship.[1] After 2000, several Member States introduced language tests and examinations on the knowledge of different aspects of the receiving country (history, myths, traditions, etc.) as an unavoidable requirement for acquiring citizenship. This trend is not absolute, though, as there is at least one country moving in the opposite direction: Belgium.[2] In order to obtain a clearer picture it is

---

[1] See R. Bauböck, E. Ersbøll, K. Groenendijk and H. Waldrauch (2006), *Acquisition and Loss of Nationality/ Volumes 1 and 2 Policies and Trends in 15 European Countries*, Amsterdam University Press: Amsterdam.

[2] Belgium abolished language and integration requirements in its Belgian Act of 1st March 2000 amending its Nationality Code. See on this M.C. Foblets and Z. Yanasmayan (2010),

important to take a brief look at these new requirements in some of the Member States.[3]

Knowledge of different aspects of the country
This knowledge varies and can include history, culture, tradition, legal system, Constitution, geography, etc. In the years following the Tampere Conclusions, some countries introduced this prerequisite. This occurred, for example, in the United Kingdom in 2002,[4] Denmark in 2002,[5] France in 2003,[6] the Netherlands in 2003,[7] Austria in 2005[8] and Luxembourg in 2008.[9]

Proficiency in the country's official language
Here, the same situation arose with some Member States implementing this prerequisite. This happened, for instance, in Austria and Germany, which introduced it only after 1999. Moreover, since 2002, at least five Member States,

---

"Language and Integration Requirements in Belgium: Discordances Between the Flemish Policy of 'Inburgering' and the Federal Legislators' View(s) on the Integration of Newcomers and Migrants", in R. van Oers, E. Ersbøll and D. Kostakopoulou (eds.), *A Re-definition of Belonging? Language and Integration Tests in Europe*, Martinus Nijhoff: Leiden, pp. 271–306, at 277–78.

3 Here, I intend to offer some examples and not an exhaustive account of each Member State which has introduced language or civic knowledge requirements in order to acquire citizenship. To obtain a complete picture see R. Bauböck, E. Ersbøll, K. Groenendijk and H. Waldrauch (2006), *Acquisition and Loss of Nationality. Volumes 1 and 2 Policies and Trends in 15 European Countries*, Amsterdam University Press: Amsterdam; R. Bauböck, B. Perchinig and W. Sievers (eds.) (2009), *Citizenship Policies in the New Europe*, Amsterdam University Press: Amsterdam.

4 D. Kiwan (2008), "A Journey to Citizenship in the United Kingdom", *International Journal on Multicultural Societies*, Vol. 10, pp. 60–75.

5 S. Adamo (2008), "Northern Exposure: The New Danish Model of Citizenship Test", *International Journal on Multicultural Societies (IJMS)*, Vol. 10, pp. 10–28; A. Wiesbrock (2009), "Discrimination Instead of Integration? Integration Requirements for Immigrants in Denmark and Germany", in E. Guild, K. Groenendijk and S. Carrera (eds.), *Illiberal Liberal States. Immigration, Citizenship and Integration in the EU*, pp. 299–314.

6 A. Fornerod (2008), "La Langue Française en Droit de la Nationalité et en Droit des Étrangers", *R.F.D.A.*, November-December, p. 1097–1109.

7 R. Van Oers, (2008), "From Liberal to Restrictive Citizenship Policies: the Case of the Netherlands", *International Journal on Multicultural Societies (IJMS)*, Vol. 10, pp. 40–59.

8 C. Hofhansel (2008), "Citizenship in Austria, Germany and Switzerland: Courts, Legislatures and Administrators", *International Migration Review*, Vol. 42, pp. 163–192.

9 See Loi du 23 octobre 2008 sur la nationalité luxembourgeoise (publiée au Mémorial A - N° 158 du 27 octobre 2008) which entered into force 1 January 2009, Article 7.

including Austria, have increased the requirements: Denmark, Luxembourg, the Netherlands, the United Kingdom[10] and Austria.[11]

This brief account shows how many Member States have recently introduced integration conditions in their citizenship legislations. These conditions have consequently been implemented in their national legislations regarding the acquisition of long-term residence permits. Sometimes, the conditions required in order to acquire a long-term residence permit are the same as those needed to acquire citizenship. Such is the case, for example, in the Netherlands and the United Kingdom. Sometimes, the integration conditions required in order to acquire permanent residence are more lenient.[12] In any case, the intention in highlighting these developments is to illustrate that there has been a transition by which integration conditions to obtain citizenship have gradually also been adopted for the acquisition of permanent residence. This transition has also affected family reunification, as will be seen in the next point.

3. *Integration in Other European Instruments: the Family Reunification Directive*

The Family Reunification Directive was mentioned in Chapter 2 as one of the most important European instruments in the area of immigration. It is important to briefly analyse Directive 2003/86, as it also includes an integration provision that Member States have implemented in different ways. Furthermore, the political rationale for the introduction of integration conditions, in order to acquire long-term residence, is in many cases interlinked with

10 A language requirement in order to acquire citizenship had existed in the UK since 1914. However, this language ability was simply assumed unless there was any reason to doubt it. See B. Ryan (2009), "The Integration Agenda in British Migration Law", in E. Guild, K. Groenendijk, and S. Carrera (eds.) *Illiberal Liberal States. Immigration, Citizenship and Integration in the EU*, Ashgate: Surrey, pp. 277–298, at 278–80.

11 H. Waldrauch (2006) "Acquisition of Nationality" in R. Bauböck *et al. Acquisition and Loss of Nationality. Policies and Trends in 15 European Countries*, Amsterdam University Press: Amsterdam, extensive online version of Chapter 3, *at* http://www.imiscoe.org/natac/.

12 According to my research there would not be a Member State in which the integration conditions in order to acquire citizenship are easier than those required in order to be granted a long-term residence permit. In the UK though, there was a proposal in 2008 by which citizenship would be obtained sooner than permanent residence. See on this, B. Ryan (2009), "The Integration Agenda in British Migration Law", in E. Guild, K. Groenendijk, and S. Carrera (eds.) *Illiberal Liberal States. Immigration, Citizenship and Integration in the EU*, Ashgate: Surrey, pp. 277–298, p. 289.

the integration required from family members in order to be reunited with the sponsor.

The purpose of the Directive "is to determine the conditions for the exercise of the right to family reunification by third country nationals residing lawfully in the territory of the Member States" (Article 1). Indeed, family reunification, reads Recital 4 of the Directive, enhances integration:

> Family reunification is a necessary way of making family life possible. It helps to create sociocultural stability facilitating the integration of third country nationals in the Member State, which also serves to promote economic and social cohesion, a fundamental Community objective stated in the Treaty.

The mention of economic and social cohesion is remarkable.[13] According to the Recital, this cohesion comes from making family reunification possible. As the Recital points out, this is a fundamental Community objective stated in the Treaty, notably in Article 174 TFEU. It will be seen in the next Chapter, though, that the discourse on social cohesion is usually employed by Member States in the opposite direction. In other words, it is used to further restrict immigration legislations.

The Directive applies "where the sponsor is holding a residence permit issued by the Member State for a period of validity of one year or more who has reasonable prospects of obtaining the right of permanent residence" (Article 3). Article 4 specifies which family members can enter the Member State and divides them into the nuclear family (spouse and minor children) and other family members (first-degree relatives in the direct ascending line, adult unmarried children etc...). Chapter V establishes the process of family reunification of refugees with better guarantees. Chapter VI describes the rights that family members obtain once their application has been accepted. Finally, the Directive sets up the possibilities for Member States to reject or withdraw a family member's residence permit, as well as the obligation to ensure that the sponsor or the members of his/her family have the right to mount a legal challenge in such cases (Article 16–18).[14]

---

[13] Recital 4 of the Long-term Residence Directive also makes reference to social cohesion.

[14] For a concise analysis of the Directive see: H. Oosterom-Staples (2007), "The Family Reunification Directive: A Tool Preserving Member State Interest or Conducive to Family Unity?" in A. Baldaccini, E. Guild and H. Toner (eds.), *Whose Freedom, Security and Justice?*, Hart Publishing: Oxford/Portand, pp. 451–488; S. Peers (2004), "Family Reunion and Community Law", in N. Walker (ed.) *Europe's Area of Freedom, Security and Justice*, Oxford University Press: Oxford, pp. 143–197; For an analysis of the implementation see K. Groenendijk, R. Fernhout, D. van Dam, R. van Oers and T. Strik (2007), *The Family Reunification Directive in EU Member States. The First Year of Implementation*, Nijmegen Wolf Legal Publishers: Nijmegen; For a comparative analysis with European citizens see D. Acosta

Chapter IV of the Directive deals with the requirements for the exercise of the right to family reunification which are the following: proper accommodation, sickness insurance, stable and regular resources and integration measures.

I will only deal here with the integration measures. Article 7(2) of Directive 2003/86 reads as follows: "Member states may require third-country nationals to comply with integration measures, in accordance with national law". As will be analysed in Chapter 9,[15] the CJEU pronounced on this in *Parliament v. Council.*[16]

Three of the Member States bound by the Directive[17] apply integration conditions before entry for family members of third-country nationals. The legality of this is unclear. According to Groenendijk, under the terms of the Directive, Member States can offer language courses where available, although they cannot oblige a third-country national to pass an examination in order to be admitted.[18] This seems to be also the position of the Commission as stated in its report on the implementation of the Directive.[19] Nonetheless, some Member States are not satisfied with this interpretation, notably those that are already using this provision to require integration for family members before joining the sponsor.

The Netherlands was the first one to implement this measure. The Integration Abroad Act came into force on 15 March 2006.[20] The Act concerns any family member, aged between 16 and 65, who wishes to live in the Netherlands on a long-term basis, except for citizens of the USA, Canada, Australia, New Zealand, Japan, South Korea, Switzerland, the Vatican and Monaco. According to the Act, such persons must learn about the Netherlands and speak some Dutch. In order to evaluate these requirements, the Civic Integration Examination Abroad must be taken in the country of residence before arrival in the Netherlands. The examination is oral and tests basic knowledge of the Dutch language and of Dutch society. It takes place at a Dutch Embassy or Consulate General and costs 350 euros. In case of failure, it can be re-taken,

(2009), "Immigration in the European Union: Family Reunification after the Metock Case", *UCD Law Review*, Vol. 9, pp. 64–88.

15 See below Chapter 9.

16 Case C-540/03 *European Parliament v Council of the European Union* [2006] ECR I-5769.

17 These are the Netherlands, France and Germany.

18 K. Groenendijk (2007), "Integration Tests Abroad as a Condition for Family Reunification in the EU?" Immigration Law Practitioner's Association (ILPA), European Update June 2007.

19 Commission Report, On the Application of Directive 2003/86/EC on the Right to Family Reunification, COM (2008) 610 final, 8.10.2008.

20 Wet inburgering in het buitenland, Wib (Civic Integration Abroad Act).

but the fee must be paid again.[21] A visa will not be granted until the examination is successfully undertaken. The test became more difficult to pass as of 15 March 2008. This Dutch policy has been strongly criticised by academics as well as by non-governmental organisations.[22] The Dutch example is currently being followed, in a less restrictive manner, by France and Germany.[23]

France requires, first of all, that the sponsor be integrated.[24] Second, according to a 2007 modification of the immigration law,[25] family members are required to follow a sort of preparation in the country of origin.[26] The modified law requires that the family member who is being sponsored have his/her knowledge of French and the values of the Republic evaluated. If the candidate fails the examination, the administrative authorities provide a course for a maximum of two months, after which the third-country national is evaluated once again. In order to obtain a visa, the third-country national is obliged to take the course.[27] This legislative provision was implemented by a decree adopted in October 2008[28] and a by-law of December 2008.[29]

---

[21] See on the issue of fees for Turkish workers Case C-92/07, *European Commission v Kingdom of the Netherlands*, 29 April 2010, [2010]; Case C-242/06, *Minister voor Vreemdelingenzaken en Integratie v T. Sahin*, 17 September 2009, [2009] ECR I-08465.

[22] Human Rights Watch (2008), "The Netherlands: Discrimination in the Name of Integration. Migrants' Rights under the Integration Abroad Act", Briefing Paper Number 1 May 2008.

[23] Austria has also debated the possibility to introduce a pre-entry requirement for spouses. See R. van Oers, E. Ersbøll and D. Kostakopoulou (2010), "Mapping the Redefinition of Belonging in Europe" in R. van Oers, E. Ersbøll and D. Kostakopoulou (eds.), *A Re-definition of Belonging? Language and Integration Tests in Europe*, Martinus Nijhoff: Leiden, pp. 307–332, at 307; B. Perchinig (2010), "Country Report Austria", INTEC Project, Centre for Migration Law, Radboud University Nijmegen, p. 16.

[24] According to Article L 411-5 of the CESEDA, family reunification can be refused if the sponsor "ne se conforme pas aux principes essentiels qui, conformément aux lois de la République, régissent la vie familiale en France, pays d'accueil."

[25] It was modified by the Loi no 2007-1631 du 20 novembre 2007 relative à la maîtrise de l'immigration, à l'intégration et à l'asile, JORF n°270 du 21 novembre 2007.

[26] Article L 411-8 of the CESEDA.

[27] See on this Y. Pascouau (2010), "Integration Measures in France: An Evolving Process between Integration and Migration Issues", in R. van Oers, E. Ersbøll and D. Kostakopoulou (eds.), *A Re-definition of Belonging? Language and Integration Tests in Europe*, Martinus Nijhoff: Leiden, pp. 153–184, especially at 161–63 and 171–182.

[28] Décret no 2008-1115 du 30 octobre 2008 relatif à la préparation de l'intégration en France des étrangers souhaitant s'y installer durablement, JORF 1 novembre 2008.

[29] Arrêté du 1 décembre 2008 relatif à l'évaluation dans leur pays de résidence du niveau de connaissance, par les étrangers, de la langue française et des valeurs de la République et aux formations prescrites dans ces domaines conformément aux articles R.311-30-1 à R.311-30-11 du code de l'entrée et du séjour des étrangers et du droit d'asile, JORF 5 décembre 2008.

In Germany, legislation provides that a third-country national's spouse must be able to communicate in basic German to be granted a residence permit. Nationals of Australia, Canada, Israel, Japan, the Republic of Korea, New Zealand and the USA are exempted from this requirement. Exceptions apply if the marriage existed when the third-country national established his/her residency in Germany, the spouse's need for integration is minimal or the spouse is unable to provide evidence of a basic knowledge of German on account of a physical or mental illness.[30] Knowledge of German is shown by submitting an A1 German language proficiency certificate, which must be paid for by the migrant him or herself.[31] In addition, there is also an integration condition for children aged between 16 and 18 years. They may only be granted a residence permit if they speak German or if they show that they will integrate into German society on the basis of their education and way of life to date.[32]

In Denmark, which is not bound by Directive 2003/86, a test in the Danish language and society has also been adopted. The Aliens Act, which was amended by, inter alia, Act No 379 of 25 April 2007, introduced the possibility of a test based on proficiency in the Danish language and knowledge of Danish society as a condition for issuing a residence permit in most cases of family reunification. The test had not yet entered into force as of 1 December 2010 due to some technical difficulties. The test is oral and consists of a Danish language and a societal knowledge one. An important difference with the previous examples is that the test takes place in Denmark. Basically, those applicants subjected to a visa requirement will receive a 3 month visa and have to take the test during the first two months and a half after the arrival in Denmark. If the test is not successfully passed during those first 3 months family reunification will be refused and a date of departure will be established.[33]

In the UK, which is also not bound by the Directive, a debate was sparked by a consultation paper launched in December 2007. The Paper considered whether it was necessary to introduce a pre-entry English requirement for spouses. This, according to the Government, was in order to assist the spouse's integration into British society at an early stage.[34] In July 2009, the Government produced a consultation paper in which it announced its intention to introduce

[30] German 2004 Residence Act Article 30.

[31] Human Rights Watch (2008), "The Netherlands: Discrimination in the Name of Integration. Migrants' Rights under the Integration Abroad Act", Briefing Paper Number 1 May 2008, at footnote 27.

[32] German 2004 Residence Act Article 32(2).

[33] E. Ersbøll and L.K.Gravesen (2010), "Country Report Denmark", INTEC Project, Centre for Migration Law, Radboud University Nijmegen, pp. 19–20.

[34] Home Office (Border and Immigration Agency) (2007), "Marriage Visas: Pre-entry English Requirements for Spouses", Consultation Paper, December 2007.

this requirement in the summer of 2011.[35] The new Government elected in May 2010 announced its intention to introduce this requirement in autumn 2010.[36] Finally the test was introduced from 29 November 2010. The level required is A1 in spoken English.[37]

The validity of these requirements under Directive 2003/86 is doubtful. In 2008, the Commission expressed reservations in its report on the implementation of the Directive:

> Their admissibility under the Directive depends on whether they serve this purpose and whether they respect the principle of proportionality. Their admissibility can be questioned on the basis of the accessibility of such courses or tests, how they are designed and/or organised (test materials, fees, venue, etc.), whether such measures or their impact serve purposes other than integration (e.g. high fees excluding low-income families).[38]

These reservations have been further reinforced by the CJEU in *Chakroun*, which will be analysed in Chapter 9. Moreover, in the case of family reunification, the fact that the Directive refers to *integration measures* and not to *integration conditions* seems to presuppose that Member States may require a lower level of engagement for family members. According to Groenendijk, integration conditions may include passing tests, whereas integration measures only allow a requirement that family members make a certain effort.[39]

As will be revealed in the next Chapter, the motivations for the introduction of integration for family members sometimes overlap with the rationale underlying the same conditions for obtaining long-term residence. The next part of this Chapter analyses the conditions to be fulfilled in order to acquire long-term residence.

4. *Conditions for Acquiring Long-Term Residence Status*

In this part of the Chapter, I will look at the conditions to be fulfilled in order to acquire long-term residence. Here, I will analyse how the integration conditions present in Article 5 of Directive 2003/109 constitutes its most

---

35 See Home Office UK Border Agency (2009), "Earning the Right to Stay. A New Points Test for Citizenship", Consultation Paper, July 2009, at 23.

36 M. Gower (2010), "Immigration: spouses, civil partners and fiancé(e)s", House of Commons Library, Home Affairs Section, Standard Note: SN/HA/862, at 8.

37 See on this B. Ryan (2010), "Country Report United Kingdom", INTEC Project, Centre for Migration Law, Radboud University Nijmegen, p. 10.

38 Commission Report, On the Application of Directive 2003/86/EC on the Right to Family Reunification, COM (2008) 610 final, 8.10.2008, pp. 7–8.

39 K. Groenendijk (2006), "Family Reunification as a Right under Community Law", *European Journal of Migration and Law*, Vol. 8 (2), pp. 215–230, at. 224.

critical aspect. Chapter 9 will then look at how the CJEU could interpret them in light of its previous case law.

A third-country national who would like to acquire long-term residence status has to fulfil certain conditions. The first one, a period of five years' legal residence, has already been analysed in Chapter 4.[40] According to Article 4(3), the third-country national may be absent from the territory for a maximum period of six consecutive months or ten months in total during those five years, although Member States may accept a longer period of absence.[41] This is slightly different for EU Blue Card Holders (highly skilled workers).[42] Once the long-term residence status has been acquired, it will be withdrawn "in the event of absence from the territory of the Community for a period of 12 consecutive months".[43] Article 6 lays down that Member States may refuse to grant a long-term residence permit on grounds of public policy or public security. Finally, Article 5 of the Directive introduces three additional conditions. I will look at the first two:

Stable and regular resources

Third-country nationals have to fulfil this condition to maintain themselves and their dependent family members, without recourse to the social assistance system of the Member State concerned.[44] In turn, European citizens need to

---

[40] See Chapter 4 above.

[41] This is desirable in light of the current debates about circular migration and its benefits. See for instance, A. Portes (2006), "Migration and Development: A conceptual review of the Evidence", The Centre for Migration and Development, Princeton University, CMD Working Paper # 06–07; F. Docquier (2006), "Brain Drain and Inequality Across Nations", FNRS, IRES, Université Catholique de Louvain and IZA Bonn, Discussion Paper No. 2440; L.T. Katseli, R.E.B. Lucas and T. Xenogiani (2006), "Effects of Migration on Sending Countries: What do We Know?" OECD Development Centre, Working Paper No. 250.

[42] According to Article 16 of Council Directive 2009/50 on Highly Qualified Workers, an EU Blue Card Holder is allowed to accumulate periods of residence in different Member States, in order to fulfil the requirement of the duration of residence, if he has lived the last two years in the Member State in which he is submitting his application. Moreover, EU Blue Card Holders have the possibility to abandon the territory of the EU for 12 consecutive months or a maximum period of 18 months. Member States may require that this absence is due to the exercise of an economic activity, the performing of a voluntary service or pursuing studies in the country of origin.

[43] Article 9 (c) Directive 2003/109. It is probable that the Commission will propose an extension of this period to two or three years. See Commission Communication on Circular Migration and Mobility Partnerships between the European Union and Third Countries, COM (2007) 248 final, 16.5.2007. In fact, EU Blue Card holders may extend their period of absence to 24 months, according to Article 16(4) of Directive 2009/50.

[44] See on this M. Bell (2007), "Civic Citizenship and Migrant Integration", *European Public Law*, Vol. 13(2), pp. 311–333, at 328.

show sufficient resources for themselves and their family members not to become a burden on the social assistance system of the host Member State during their period of residence, if they are not workers or self-employed persons.[45] However, the test for EU citizens is completely different and much lower since, according to Article 8(4) of Directive 2004/38, the amount that they have to show "shall not be higher than the threshold below which nationals of the host Member State become eligible for social assistance, or (...) higher than the minimum social security pension paid by the host Member State." This same level was in fact proposed by the Commission for third-country nationals but it was rejected in the final version of the Directive adopted by the Council. However, the CJEU considered in Chakroun that a third-country national who was on unemployment benefits which supplemented his resources fulfilled the requirement in Directive 2003/86 on the right to family reunification of having "stable and regular resources which are sufficient to maintain himself/herself... without recourse to the social assistance of the Member State concerned".[46] The CJEU understood that:

> The concept of 'social assistance'...must be interpreted as referring to assistance which compensates for a lack of stable, regular and sufficient resources, and not as referring to assistance which enables exceptional or unforeseen needs to be addressed.[47]

There is no doubt that the CJEU will use the same interpretation for the same terms in Directive 2003/109.

It is also important to note that a European citizen who works or who is a job-seeker does not have to demonstrate that he/she has sufficient resources, whereas a third-country national in the same situation does.

Sickness insurance

Third-country nationals need to have sickness insurance in respect of all the risks normally covered for the citizens of the Member State concerned. This condition was also present in the Commission's proposal. With regard to European citizens, those who are not workers or self-employed persons also need to have comprehensive sickness insurance cover in the host Member State.[48]

These two conditions seem to be quite objective and do not offer Member States wide room for interpretation. They seem in that sense reasonable as a

---

45 Article 7(1) of Directive 2004/38.

46 Case C-578/08, Rhimou Chakroun v Minister van Buitenlandse Zaken, [2010], paragraph 52.

47 *Ibid.*, paragraph 49.

48 Article 7(1) Directive 2004/38.

third-country national who has already regularly resided for a period of five years in a Member State, and who has stable and regular resources and sickness insurance seems to be an ideal candidate for obtaining a more secure status. However, the Council introduced a further condition which was not present in the Commission's proposal: integration.

5. *The Integration Conditions*

As was mentioned in Chapter 3, during the negotiations on the Long-term Residence Directive, the Council added a very relevant provision in Article 5(2):

> Member States may require third-country nationals to comply with integration conditions, in accordance with national law.

This was introduced mainly on the initiative of Austria, Germany and the Netherlands[49] and is considered by many commentators to be the "real Achilles heel of the Directive." This is because there are no stated limits on the significance of the integration conditions and there is no standstill provision.[50]

This condition did not appear in the Commission's proposal. Moreover, there is obviously nothing similar for European citizens when they move to reside in another Member State. The only limitation that might be imposed on European citizens concerns language requirements when the post to be filled requires specific language knowledge.[51] In addition to that, the situation with Turkish workers is not so clear after the case *Commission v the Netherlands*.[52] This case established that a system for the issue of residence permits for Turkish nationals providing for charges, which are disproportionate in relation to those imposed on nationals of Member States for the issue of similar documents, was contrary to Article 9 of the Association Agreement, Article 41 of the Additional Protocol and Articles 10(1) and 13 of Decision No 1/80. This prompts Carrera and Wiesbrock to argue that this prohibition also comprises

---

[49] See Chapter 3 above.

[50] S. Boelaert-Suominen (2005), "Non-EU Nationals and Council Directive 2003/109/EC on the Status of Third-country Nationals who are Long-term Residents: Five Paces Forward and possibly Three Paces Back", *Common Market Law Review*, Vol. 42 (4), pp.1011–1052, at 1023.

[51] Article 3(1) of Regulation (EEC) No. 1612/68 of the Council of 15 October 1968 on freedom of movement for workers within the Community OJ 1968 L 257/2. See on this Case 379/87 *Groener v Minister for Education* [1989] ECR 03967.

[52] Case C-92/07, *European Commission v Kingdom of the Netherlands*, 29 April 2010, [2010].

any other additional requirement such as integration and language requirements.[53] In fact, based on that precedent, a Dutch Court has established that requiring Turkish nationals to comply with integration conditions is contrary to Article 9 of the Association Agreement and to Articles 10(1) and 13 of Decision No. 1/80.[54] This decision has been appealed and the final result will be extremely important to see whether these tests can be imposed on Turkish workers or not.

The result has been that the most vehement critiques by academics have been addressed to integration conditions under Article 5(2) of the Directive. For example, Guild describes it as follows:

> The Directive on the status of third country nationals who are long-residents reveals another aspect of the nightmare of Otherness. The Member States are permitted to apply an integration obligation to be tested at the national level to a third country national before acknowledging his or her status as an EU long-term resident...what it means is that before the third country national can enjoy security of residence from EU law...he or she must prove to the Member State that he or she is no longer the dangerous Other.[55]

In turn, Groenendijk points out that,

> if Member States refrain from introducing the possible integration condition or from using it as an instrument for blocking access to that status, almost half of all third-country nationals lawfully living in the Union could qualify for this new status.[56]

Hence, the main question is to assess in what way Member States are implementing the integration conditions. The importance of this matter means that my analysis here will be more general and will cover to a certain extent every single Member State, paying more in-depth attention to the most relevant cases. This is so, as the integration conditions could close the door to accessing long-term residence status to many third-country nationals and, therefore, it is the most relevant provision in the Directive.

---

[53] S. Carrera and A. Wiesbrock (2010), "Whose European Citizenship in the Stockholm Programme? The Enactment of Citizenship by Third Country Nationals in the EU", *European Journal of Migration and Law*, Vol. 12(3), pp. 337–359, at 350.

[54] LJN: BN3934, Rechtbank Rotterdam, 08/4934.

[55] E. Guild (2004), *The Legal elements of European Identity: EU citizenship and Migration Law*, Kluwer Law Internacional, European Law Library: The Hague, pp. 216–17.

[56] K. Groenendijk, (2006) "Citizens and Third-Country Nationals: Differential Treatment or Discrimination?" in J.Y. Carlier, E. Guild & B. Coulie (eds.), *The Future of Free Movement of Persons in the EU* Brussel: Bruylant, pp. 79–101, at 98.

6. *Implementation*

A number of Member States have implemented the integration conditions into their national legislations. In 1999, only Germany and Hungary required sufficient knowledge of the language to obtain a permanent residence permit.[57] That has changed with the transposition of the Directive. These integration conditions vary from country to country and can be divided between language requirements and civic knowledge requirements.[58] Depending on the existence of conditions and on when these conditions were imposed, Member States may be divided into three categories.

6.1. *Integration before Acquiring Long-Term Residence*

A first group of Member States includes those which require integration before the third-country national is eligible to acquire the long-term residence permit, usually by signing an integration agreement. Here France, Germany, Italy, Luxembourg, the Netherlands and Denmark (which is not bound by the Directive) can be mentioned. Austria would be an intermediate case between this first group and the second one as will be seen below.

France is pertinent to highlight the pattern of tightening requirements over a period of time. A permanent residence status had been in place since the immigration law of 1984. This law was quite liberal and provided many possibilities for third-country nationals to acquire this status. There were no integration conditions.[59] However, the requirements for acquiring this status changed in November 2003 when the Loi Sarkozy[60] entered into force.[61] In fact, this law introduced integration conditions in order to acquire a residence card which could be requested after five years of residence. Later,

---

[57] K Groenendijk, E. Guild and H. Dogan (1998), *Security of Residence of Long-term Migrants. A Comparative Study of Law and Practice in European Countries*, Council of Europe, Strasbourg, at 99.

[58] C. Adam and A. Devillard (2008), *Comparative Study of the Laws in the 27 EU Member States for Legal Migration*, European Parliament Study, Policy Department C: Citizens' Rights and Constitutional Affairs: Brussels, at 52–53.

[59] D. Lochak (2005), "L'Intégration Alibi de la Précarisation", *Plein Droit* 59–60, pp. 3–6.

[60] Law no. 2003–1119, Article 8 (Loi n. 2003–119 du 26 novembre 2003 relative à la maîtrise de l'immigration, au séjour des étrangers en France et à la nationalité), NOR: INTX 0300040L, Journal Officiel de la République française, 27 novembre 2003.

[61] For an in-depth analysis of the French legislative modifications see Y. Pascouau (2010), "Integration Measures in France: An Evolving Process between Integration and Migration Issues", in R. van Oers, E. Ersbøll and D. Kostakopoulou (eds.), *A Re-definition of Belonging? Language and Integration Tests in Europe*, Martinus Nijhoff: Leiden, pp. 153–183.

the 2006 legislation made the integration contract compulsory, requiring the third-country national to attend a civic formation course, and a linguistic one if needed.[62] The signing of this contract has been compulsory since 1 January 2007. Although it is true that the courses are free of charge, and that there are some exceptions to the obligation to sign the contract (for example, when the foreigner has attended a French school for three years), it should be noted that on the first renewal of the residence permit the administrative authorities will take into consideration the non-respect of the integration contract.[63]

In ***Germany*** an integration course has to be successfully completed to show adequate knowledge of the German language and basic knowledge of the legal and social system and the way of life. This course is compulsory for some third-country nationals (notably those who do not speak German, receive benefits or have special integration needs).[64] The number of hours that have to be followed increased in 2008 from 600 to 900 hours of language courses and from 30 to 45 hours of civic education. Also, the final language examination became compulsory.[65] Although sanctions are not always applied, they include the non-extension of a temporary residence permit or the non-granting of a permanent residence one.[66] There are certain exceptions to the obligation to participate in these courses.[67]

Italy introduced integration conditions in order to obtain a long-term residence permit in 2009. According to the 2009 Security Law,[68] which modified the 1998 Immigration Act,[69] a third-country national entering Italy for the

[62] Law 2006-911 (Loi n. 2006-911 du 24 juillet 2006 relative à l'immigration et l'intégration), NOR : INTX 0600037L, Journal Officiel de la République française, 25 juillet 2006.

[63] Article L311-9 Aliens Code as modified by Law 2006-911, Ordonnance n°2004-1248 du 24 novembre 2004 relative à la partie législative du Code de l'entrée et du séjour des étrangers et du droit d'asile (CESEDA). NOR: INTX0400217R, Journal Officiel de la République française, 25 novembre 2004, entered into force 1 March 2005.

[64] See Section 9 and 43-45 of the AufenthG (Residence Act).

[65] I. Michalowski (2010), "Integration Tests in Germany. A communitarian Approach?" in R. van Oers, E. Ersbøll and D. Kostakopoulou (eds.), *A Re-definition of Belonging? Language and Integration Tests in Europe*, Martinus Nijhoff: Leiden, pp. 185-210, at 194.

[66] A. Wiesbrock (2009), "Discrimination Instead of Integration? Integration Requirements for Immigrants in Denmark and Germany", in E. Guild, K. Groenendijk and S. Carrera (eds.), *Illiberal Liberal States. Immigration, Citizenship and Integration in the EU*, Ashgate: Surrey, pp. 299-314, at 306.

[67] See Verordnung über die Durchführung von Integrationskursen für Ausländer und Spätaussiedler (Integrationskursverordnung-IntV), 13.12.2004, Section 4(2).

[68] Legge 15 luglio 2009, n. 94, Disposizioni in materia di sicurezza pubblica. (09G0096), Gazzetta Ufficiale n. 170 del 24-7-2009.

[69] Decreto Legilslativo 25 luglio 1998, n. 286, Testo unico delle disposizioni concernenti la disciplina dell'immigrazione e norme sulla condizione dello straniero (Supplemento ordinario n.139 alla Gazzetta Ufficiale n.191 del 18.08.1998).

first time would have to sign an integration contract. That integration contract establishes a number of credits to be given to the third-country national, as well as the integration objectives for a certain period. If the person concerned does not fulfil the integration conditions he will begin to lose credits. If he loses all his credits, he will be expelled from Italy. The precise details of this integration contract had not been adopted as of 1 December 2010 and the Government will have to pass secondary legislation to regulate it. Moreover, the 2009 modification to the Immigration Act also introduced the need to pass a language test in order to obtain the long-term residence permit. This language test has been regulated by a 2010 Decree.[70] The third-country national has to attain a level of knowledge of Italian equivalent to an A2.[71] This can be proved by passing an examination or by showing a certificate from certain institutions specified in the Decree.[72] There are also some exceptions for third-country nationals who do not have to pass the test, e.g. those who are under 14 years old and those who suffer from limitations to learning a language due to their age or physical condition.[73] A Ministerial Order adopted in November 2010 provided that the test will be applicable from 9 December 2010.[74]

In ***Luxembourg***, the 2008 law on immigration,[75] which derogates from the 1972 legislation, includes a voluntary integration contract in order to obtain the long-term residence permit.[76] The integration contract had not been introduced as of 1 December 2010. Nevertheless, it includes a linguistic and civic formation course and lasts for a maximum period of two years. The language courses will be available in Luxemburgish, German and French. The price of the course will be symbolic (5 Euros). It is important to note that this is a voluntary course and it is not clear what the consequences of not attending it will be.

The case of *the* ***Netherlands*** is very relevant. In 1998, a first law was passed entitled "Act on the Integration of New Immigrants".[77] The Act provided for an

[70] Decreto 4 giugno 2010 Modalita di svolgimento del test di conoscenza della lingua italiana, previsto dall'articolo 9 del decreto legislativo 25 luglio 1998, n. 286, introdotto dall'articolo 1, comma 22, lettera i) della legge n. 94/2009. (10A07303) (GU n. 134 del 11-6-2010).

[71] *Ibid.*, Article 2(1).

[72] *Ibid.*, Articles 3 and 4.

[73] *Ibid.*, Article 1(3).

[74] Circolare n. 7589 del 16 novembre 2010 Ministero dell'Interno.

[75] Loi du 29 août 2008 portant sur la libre circulation des personnes et l'immigration.

[76] Article 81 of the Law. See also Art 11 of the Règlement grand-ducal du 5 septembre 2008 portant exécution de certaines dispositions relatives aux formalités administratives prévues par la loi du 29 août 2008 sur la libre circulation des personnes et l'immigration.

[77] Wet inburgering nieuwkomers (Act on the Integration of New Immigrants). It entered into force on 30 September 1998 but was later repealed by the new Civic Integration Act.

integration programme of 600 hours comprising language courses and courses on Dutch society. There was an administrative fine for those who did not participate in the programme.[78] However, on 1 January 2007, the "Civic Integration Act"[79] replaced the 1998 Act.[80] The 2007 Act has the same objective of providing courses on Dutch language and society to the newcomers. Nonetheless, it has three important differences. First, the Act also applies to some old-comers.[81] Second, the person involved has to pass an examination and not merely follow a course. The penalty for not passing the examination adds, to the administrative pecuniary sanction, a more severe one, such as the impossibility of acquiring long-term residence status. Third-country nationals may continue to reside on a temporary permit but their residence status remains more insecure. Third, it is the third-country national who has to pay for the examination and the course and not the government, as was previously the case.[82] Those who think that they possess enough knowledge of Dutch and the Netherlands can take a test without attending the course. The period within which the candidates have to pass the examination varies from three and half years, if the candidate has already passed a basic examination abroad, to five years in other cases. Interestingly enough, as of 15 March 2008 it became more difficult to pass the spoken Dutch test, as candidates were required to answer more questions correctly in order to pass.[83] There are certain exceptions for some third-country nationals who do not have to pass the test,

---

[78] L. Besselink (2006), "Unequal Citizenship: Integration Measures and Equality", in S Carrera (ed.), *The Nexus between Immigration, Integration and Citizenship in the EU*, CHALLENGE Collective Conference Volume, Centre for European Policy Studies, CEPS: Brussels, pp. 14–19, at 15.

[79] We inburgering, Wi (Civic Integration Act).

[80] See on this L. Besselink (2009) "Integration and Immigration – The Vicissitudes of Dutch 'Inburgering" in K. Groenendijk, S. Carrera and E. Guild (eds.), *Illiberal Liberal States: Immigration, Citizenship and Integration in the EU*, Ashgate: Surrey, pp. 241–258.

[81] In effect, the Act provides that the old-comers who do not have a Dutch passport, are between 16 and 65 years old, have lived in the Netherlands before 1 January 2007, have lived in the Netherlands for fewer than eight years when they were of school age and have no diplomas to prove that they have an appropriate knowledge of Dutch and the Netherlands, must also undergo integration.

[82] The Act provides that some municipalities will issue a so-called "integration grant" paying for the preparation course for those without enough resources. Basically, the Act defines them as those on social benefits, those who have no income or those who have a religious function.

[83] This integration has been applicable in the Netherlands since 1 January 2010. See Royal Decree of 29 December 2008, Staatsblad 605 (see Article I under R of that Decree) in Article 9.2(2) and (3) of Besluit Inburgering (Royal Decree on Integration). The date of entry of the obligation under Article 21(1)(k) Aliens Act was changed from 21 September 2009 to 1 January 2010.

including those younger than 16 or older than 65, those who have stayed for at least eight years in the country during the age of compulsory education and those who have a physical or mental disability.[84]

In ***Denmark,*** which is not governed by the Directive, a third-country national has to sign an integration contract when he is granted a residence permit.[85] In that contract, signed with the local council, it is decided the degree and content of the programme. In order to obtain a permanent residence permit,[86] a third-country national must have completed this introduction programme and passed a test in the Danish language.[87] The permanent residence rules were newly modified in 2010 with the aim of making it possible for "well-integrated immigrants" to obtain permanent residence after 4 years (instead of 7) while introducing new requirements making it harder for "poorly integrated migrants".[88]

Finally, Austria is an interesting example which is half way between this first group of countries and the next one. In ***Austria*** third-country nationals who have an initial settlement permit or who apply for an additional settlement permit have to comply with the integration agreement,[89] although some exemptions may apply to some of them.[90] The integration agreement consists of two modules: one is a 75 hours course on the acquisition of the ability to read and write for those who need it and another one of 300 hours on knowledge of German and acquisition of the capacity to participate in the social economic and cultural life in Austria.[91] The interesting thing about Austria is that there are many categories of third-country nationals who are considered to have fulfilled the integration agreement per se without having to follow the

---

[84] See Article 5 of the We inburgering, Wi (Civic Integration Act).

[85] See for a more in depth analysis on Denmark: E. Ersbøll (2010), "On Trial in Denmark", in R. van Oers, E. Ersbøll and D. Kostakopoulou (eds.), *A Re-definition of Belonging? Language and Integration Tests in Europe*, Martinus Nijhoff: Leiden, pp. 107–152.

[86] This is usually granted only after seven years, although there are some exceptions. See Art 11 (3) AA of Aliens Act No. 243 of 27 March 2006, as amended by Act no. 379 of 25 April 2007.

[87] C. Adam and A. Devillard (2008), *Comparative Study of the Laws in the 27 EU Member States for Legal Migration*, European Parliament Study, Policy Department C: Citizens' Rights and Constitutional Affairs: Brussels, at 197–98.

[88] See on this E. Ersbøll and L.K.Gravesen (2010), "Country Report Denmark", INTEC Project, Centre for Migration Law, Radboud University Nijmegen, pp. 26–30. See Act no. 572 of 31 May 2010.

[89] 2006 Austrian Settlement and Residence Act, Art 14 (3).

[90] *Ibid.*, Art 14 (4) refers to minors and those who cannot fulfil the obligation because of health reasons.

[91] *Ibid.*, Art 14 (2).

course.[92] This includes, among others, those considered as "key workers",[93] those who have pursued certain studies in Austria or those who can provide sufficient knowledge of German language.[94] The course costs between 1500 and 2500 Euros, although some discounts apply if the examination is taken within the first 24 months after immigration.[95] It is interesting to mention that the language requirements have increased in difficulty.[96] In order to obtain a long-term residence permit the third-country national has to have complied with the integration agreement.[97] The agreement needs to be fulfilled within the first five years of residence. This would prompt me to include Austria in the following groups of countries. However, the Austrian government has announced its intention to reduce that period to two years.[98] In cases of non-compliance with the integration requirement, expulsion is contemplated in the law as a last resort.[99] There were three deportation orders issued in Austria in 2009. All three were appealed and are pending a final decision.[100]

6.2. *Integration at the Moment of Acquiring Long-Term Residence*

A second group of Member States includes those which only impose integration conditions when the third-country national is seeking to apply for a long-term residence permit. Here nine Member States can be mentioned: Estonia,

92 B. Perchinig (2010), "Country Report Austria", INTEC Project, Centre for Migration Law, Radboud University Nijmegen, p. 14.

93 Key workers are those who hold key managerial or technical functions and earn more than 2,466 EUR fourteen times a year. *Ibid.*, p. 14.

94 2006 Austrian Settlement and Residence Act, Article 14(5).

95 R. Van Oers, E. Ersbøll and D. Kostakopoulou (2010), "Mapping the Redefinition of Belonging in Europe" in R. van Oers, E. Ersbøll and D. Kostakopoulou (eds.), *A Re-definition of Belonging? Language and Integration Tests in Europe*, Martinus Nijhoff: Leiden, pp. 307–332, at 313.

96 An A2 level of German knowledge instead of the previous A1 is required to be allowed to stay in the country. K. König and B. Perchinig (2005), "Austria", in J. Niessen, Y. Schibel and C. Thompson (eds.), *Current Immigration Debates in Europe,* Migration Policy Group: Brussels, *at* http://www.migpolgroup.com/public/docs/141.EMD_Austria_2005.pdf (accessed 1 December 2010), at 11.

97 2006 Austrian Settlement and Residence Act, Art 45.

98 B. Perchinig (2010), "Country Report Austria", INTEC Project, Centre for Migration Law, Radboud University Nijmegen, p. 16.

99 Austrian Alien Police Act, Art 54(4).

100 B. Perchinig (2010), "Country Report Austria", INTEC Project, Centre for Migration Law, Radboud University Nijmegen, p. 23.

Czech Republic, Portugal, Latvia, Romania, Greece, Lithuania, Slovakia and the UK (which is not bound by the Directive).

In ***Estonia*** there is a language test to prove that the third-country national can speak Estonian at least at a B1 level.[101] Pursuant to Act No. 326/1999 Coll., on the Residence of Foreigners in the ***Czech Republic***, a foreigner is – from 1 January 2009 – required to submit a permanent residence application accompanied by a certificate proving that he/she has successfully passed a Czech language test at an A1 level.[102] ***Portugal*** requires basic knowledge as well.[103] The same occurs in ***Latvia,*** which requires sufficient basic knowledge of the Latvian language (equivalent to level A2) in order to grant long-term residence status.[104] The fees to be paid for the examination are around 14 Euros.[105] There are some exemptions to these requirements for people who have studied in Latvia or who have a health impediment.[106] Similar to this is the case in ***Romania*** with a satisfactory level required.[107] In ***Greece***, before applying, third-country nationals must pass a Greek test. Third-country nationals who have completed secondary school or its equivalent in Greece are exempt from this requirement.[108] In ***Lithuania*** civic knowledge is required in addition to language.[109] In ***Slovakia***, the level of the third-country nationals' integration

---

[101] This situation follows on from the 2006 amendment to the Aliens Act. The language requirement has been in place since 1 June 2007. Aliens Act (Välismaalaste seadus) (1993), RTI, no 44, Article 14[5]

[102] Act No. 326/1999 Coll., Foreigner's Residence Act.

[103] Portuguese Immigration Law, Art 126(1)(e), Lei n.o 23/2007 de 4 de Julho, Aprova o regime jurídico de entrada, permanência, saída e afastamento de estrangeiros do território nacional, Diário da República, 1.a série—N.o 127—4 de Julho de 2007

[104] Art 3(1)(2) of the Law "Long-term resident status of the European Community in Latvia". See also Cabinet Regulations 733 July 2009, Section 10.

[105] For more information on the Latvian case see: K. Kruma, (2010), "Latvian Integration Policy: Lost in Translation", in R. van Oers, E. Ersbøll and D. Kostakopoulou (eds.), *A Re-definition of Belonging? Language and Integration Tests in Europe*, Martinus Nijhoff: Leiden, pp. 241–270, at 262–264. Cabinet Regulations 733 July 2009, Section 63.

[106] Cabinet Regulations 733 July 2009, Section 12.

[107] Romanian Immigration Act Art 70(e), Law amending the Government Emergency Ordinance No. 194/2002 regarding the Legal Status of Aliens in Romania, Official Gazette of Romania, Section I, No. 1116/November 27, 2004, entered into force 1 January 2007.

[108] See Art 26 paragraph 7 Law 3879/2010 modifying Law 3386/2005 entitled "Entry, residence and social inclusion of third country nationals in Greek territory", Articles 67–69, Official Journal 212/A 23.8.2005 and Presidential Decree 150/2006, Official Journal 160/A 31.7.2006.

[109] Article 53(6) of the Law on the Legal Status of Aliens of 29 April 2004 No. IX-2206 as last amended by 22 July 2009 – No XI-392, provides that in order to acquire the long-term residence status, a third-country national "has passed the examination in state language and in the fundamentals of the Constitution of the Republic of Lithuania".

into Slovak society is considered when granting this permit. This notion of integration is vague as the law does not detail it.[110] In the ***UK***, which is not bound by the Directive, in order to obtain a settlement permit (long-term residence) the third-country national has to pass a language and knowledge of life in the UK test. This requirement has been in place since 2 April 2007.[111]

6.3. *No Integration Conditions in order to Acquire Long-Term Residence*

A last group of Member States will include those which do not use an exclusionary mechanism - they might offer language courses or other integration courses (mostly free) or might do nothing. Here 11 Member States which do not require the passing of an examination to obtain a long-term residence permit can be mentioned: ***Belgium***, ***Bulgaria***,[112] ***Cyprus***,[113] ***Finland***,[114] ***Hungary***,[115] ***Malta***,[116] ***Poland***, ***Slovenia***, ***Spain***, ***Sweden*** and ***Ireland***[117] (which is not bound

110 C. Adam and A. Devillard (2008), *Comparative Study of the Laws in the 27 EU Member States for Legal Migration*, European Parliament Study, Policy Department C: Citizens' Rights and Constitutional Affairs: Brussels, at 410. See Act on Residence of Foreigners 48/2002, official journal 23/2002, p. 518 as amended by Act 8 November 2005, official journal 558/2005.

111 See on this B. Ryan (2009), "The Integration Agenda in British Migration Law", in E. Guild, K. Groenendijk, and S. Carrera (eds.) *Illiberal Liberal States. Immigration, Citizenship and Integration in the EU*, Ashgate: Surrey, pp. 277–298, especially at 285–287. The test might become more difficult to pass according to a consultation document by the British Government in 2009: Home Office. UK Border Agency. July 2009. *Earning the Right to Stay. A New Points Test for Citizenship.*

112 See Law on the Foreigners in the Republic of Bulgaria, Prom. SG. 153/23 December1998, last amendments dated SG 103/29 December 2009.

113 N. Trimikliniotis (2010), "Country Report: Cyprus", EUDO Citizenship Observatory, January 2010, revised April 2010, p. 18.

114 Finnish Aliens Act 301/2004 (Ulkomaalaislaki) as amended by the Act 358/2007.

115 See on Hungary: J. Toth (2010), "Ethnic Citizenship- Can it be Obtained and Tested?" in R. van Oers, E. Ersbøll and D. Kostakopoulou (eds.), *A Re-definition of Belonging? Language and Integration Tests in Europe*, Martinus Nijhoff: Leiden, pp. 211–240, at 229–231. See Act II of 2007 on entry and residence of third country nationals and Government Decree No. 114 of 2007, 24 May on implementation rules to the Act II of 2007.

116 It is interesting to note that Malta does not impose any integration conditions in order to acquire the long-term residence permit. Nevertheless, it may require long-term residents from other EU Member States coming to Malta to attend and successfully complete a Maltese language course. L.N. 278 of 2006, Immigration Act (CAP. 217) Status of Long-term Residents (Third Country Nationals) Regulations, 2006, Article 14(3).

117 In Ireland, which is not governed by this Directive, a third-country national has to demonstrate a reasonable competence to communicate in English or Irish and has to show that he has made reasonable efforts to integrate into Irish society according to a bill which had not

by the Directive). In ***Spain***, the 2009 modification to the Immigration Law does not provide for any kind of examination before acquiring long-term residence. Article 32 of the Immigration Law only refers to the period of five years' residence in the Spanish territory. In **Sweden**, the Immigration law does not provide for integration conditions in order to acquire long-term residence status. According to Section 1 of Chapter 5a, the person has to have spent five years in Sweden. Moreover, stays outside Sweden for a period shorter than six consecutive months and not adding up to more than ten months are not considered to interrupt the stay within Sweden. Section 2 provides that the applicant has to be fully able to support himself or herself and his or her family members. Finally section 3 establishes that those applicants who are a threat to public order or security may not be granted this status.

Finally, with reference to ***Belgium***, it is important to note that it is included in this group as there is no integration requirement in order to acquire the long-term residence permit. However, since 2003, the Flemish Community has imposed a policy called "civic integration". By virtue of this, the third-country national who registers for the first time in the Commune has to sign a contract of civic integration and follow a course on the duties and values of Flemish society, a 20-hour vocational guidance course and a Dutch language course of between 120 and 240 hours. In case of non-compliance with this requirement, an administrative fine can be imposed, which ranges from 50 to 5,000 Euros.[118] Some third-country nationals are exempted from this obligation including those who have a serious illness or a mental or physical disability, those over the age of 65 and those who can prove that they are already integrated by producing certain certificates or diplomas.[119]

7. *Conclusion*

In this Chapter I have evaluated Article 5(2) of the Directive on the possibility of introducing integration conditions in order to acquire long-term residence status. I have begun by looking at the origin of these integration conditions in

been adopted by 1 December 2010. See Immigration, Residence and Protection Bill 2010, S 46 (4) (d) (ii) and (iii).

118 There are also some other third-country nationals who might have to follow these courses. See on this: M.C. Foblets and Z. Yanasmayan (2010), "Language and Integration Requirements in Belgium: Discordances Between the Flemish Policy of 'Inburgering' and the Federal Legislators' View(s) on the Integration of Newcomers and Migrants", in R. van Oers, E. Ersbøll and D. Kostakopoulou (eds.), *A Re-definition of Belonging? Language and Integration Tests in Europe*, Martinus Nijhoff: Leiden, pp. 271–306, at 285–290.

119 *Ibid.*, at 288.

the citizenship legislations of some Member States. I have continued by assessing how some Member States are implementing integration measures under the Family Reunification Directive. I have then seen how these kinds of conditions have been included in one way or another in 14 of the 24 Member States implementing Directive 2003/109, as well as in two of the other three Member States which are not bound by it. Academics have regretted this and expressed their concerns. Besselink, for example, argues that these developments show that the "discourse about integration has become discourse about admission and residence, and is now even extended to be a discourse about expulsion."[120] In that sense, some Member States try to use integration to avoid giving a more secure status to citizens who have been established for a long time in their territories. There are various reasons for this trend but it seems that there is a certain concern about cultural attributes.

> Concern for the cultural, linguistic and ethnic integration of aliens may send a signal which accentuates both the otherness of the alien and an intolerance of the dominant culture towards such otherness.[121]

Hence, before the immigrant is allowed entrance into a more secure status "he or she must abandon attributes of being a third country national."[122]

However, the validity of these integration requirements seems doubtful if they do not respect certain general principles of Union law that the CJEU has always taken into consideration when interpreting a Directive, as will be seen below in Chapter 9.

---

120 L. Besselink (2006), "Expulsion and Integration: Erecting Internal Borders within the Kingdom of the Netherlands", Challenge Liberty and Security, September 2006, *at* http://www.libertysecurity.org/article1096.html (accessed 01 December 2010), at 5.

121 J.H.H. Weiler (1992), "Thou Shalt not Oppress the Stranger: On the Judicial Protection of the Human Rights of Non-EC Nationals" *European Journal of International Law*, Vol. 3, 67.

122 E. Guild (2004), *The Legal elements of European Identity: EU citizenship and Migration Law*, Kluwer Law International, European Law Library: The Hague, at 234.

Chapter 8

Political Motivations for the Introduction of Integration Requirements

1. *Introduction*

In this Chapter, I will analyse the political motivations that have made it possible to introduce integration conditions in various Member States.

In the previous pages, I assessed different elements of the implementation of Directive 2003/109. It was established that there were mainly four controversial Articles which had been widely criticised by scholars. However, it was also mentioned that the most critical provision in the Directive comes in Article 5 with the possibility to introduce integration conditions in accordance with national law before obtaining a long-term residence permit.

As was mentioned previously, 14 Member States (plus two other Member States not bound by the Directive)[1] require third-country nationals to show some level of integration before being granted a long-term residence permit. These integration conditions vary considerably from country to country but share the characteristic that they have been mainly introduced within a seven-year period (from 2003 to 2009). Evidently, integration is part of a larger political discourse which goes far beyond the implementation of this particular Directive and which intertwines with other debates, such as those around identity or nationalism. One question is, thus, pertinent: What is the political rationale behind such a widespread practice? I will explain here how I intend to answer this question and why I consider it to be extremely relevant from a legal point of view.

In looking at the political motivations behind the introduction of these integration conditions, I will mostly rely on the work done by other academics. In this Chapter though, I will not constrain myself to the analysis of my four case studies but I will, on the contrary, look at those practices which exemplify better the trends that I would like to highlight.

---

[1] These are Austria, Czech Republic, Estonia, France, Germany, Italy, Latvia, Lithuania, Luxembourg, the Netherlands, Portugal, Romania, Slovakia and Slovenia, as well as Denmark and the United Kingdom (which are not bound by the Directive). See Chapter 7 above.

The importance of this analysis lies in the fact that Member States have to pursue a legitimate objective when requiring integration conditions from third-country nationals. This has been made clear by the CJEU in its 2010 ruling in *Chakroun* in which the Court interpreted certain conditions in order to exercise the right to family reunification under Directive 2003/86. In fact, as will be seen in the next Chapter, since granting a long-term residence permit after five years of regular residence is the general rule, any condition has to be interpreted strictly. The margin of manoeuvre which Member States have in implementing the Directive cannot be used in a manner which could undermine the objective of the Directive or its effectiveness. Consequently, what happens when the integration conditions have the result of excluding certain third-country nationals as some authors argue? This raises several questions regarding not only the principles of effectiveness, proportionality and respect for fundamental rights, but also regarding the principle of non-discrimination. I will pose several of these questions in the next Chapter below as it is very probable that the CJEU and the Commission will take them into consideration when looking at the individual integration conditions in those Member States which impose them.

However, in this Chapter, I intend to answer the following two questions: What are the different political motivations behind the introduction of integration conditions in order to acquire the long-term residence permit? Is it possible to identify common trends?

2. *A Categorisation of the Political Motivations for the Introduction of Integration Conditions in order to Acquire Long-Term Residence Status*

As I have mentioned, I will provide an analysis of different political motivations that could explain the introduction of integration conditions in various Member States in recent years. In order to do that, I will mostly rely on the work done by other academics who have already scrutinised this phenomenon.[2]

The main motivation for the presence of integration conditions in the Directive was the insistence by Germany, the Netherlands and Austria to

[2] Orgad, for example, has posed the question: what is the goal of these policies? According to his analysis, there are six possible goals: national security, restricting migration, protecting the welfare state system, promotion of social cohesion, encourage democratic participation and, lastly, to help migrants prepare for their new life by enriching their civic experience. L. Orgad (2010), "Illiberal Liberalism Cultural Restrictions on Migration and Access to Citizenship in Europe", *the American Journal of Comparative Law*, Vol. 58, pp. 53–106, at 74–79.

introduce them.[3] This was important for these three Member States as it was compatible with their national legal orders where integration conditions were already present.[4] This explains why the integration conditions were included in the final Directive adopted but it does not give an account of why so many different Member States have introduced them in their national legislation.[5] Despite the fact that it might be difficult to identify a grand narrative which explains the reproduction of integration conditions, I suggest that some factors have played an important role, at least in some countries.

In the following pages I will argue that the rise of far right parties in some Member States has been essential in centring the debate on immigration around a supposed lack of integration by third-country nationals. This has gone hand in hand with renewed calls for the preservation of allegedly essential national identities. The response by more mainstream parties to these ideas has been central in seeing the kind of immigration and integration legislation that has been adopted. Moreover, many Governments have also referred to the discussion on integration by pointing to the importance of social cohesion, as well as to the need for having more selective immigration, notably of highly skilled workers. Finally, these ideas have been spread around Europe via networks of government officials.

2.1. *The Discourse of Far Right Populist Parties*

The influence of far right political parties is a recurrent explanation for the introduction of integration conditions.[6] Sometimes these parties are part of a Government coalition. On many other occasions they are not but they, nonetheless, play a role in drawing the contours of the political agenda on immigration, as will be seen below. In any case, some academics point out that the turn to civic integration "has certainly been aggravated by the rise of right-wing populism across Europe".[7] While it is true that far right-wing parties existed in the 1970s and 1980s, it was particularly in the early 1990s that immigration emerged as an issue "dominating the extreme right propaganda".[8]

[3] See above Chapter 3.

[4] S. Carrera (2009), *In Search of the Perfect Citizen? The Intersection between Integration, Immigration and Nationality in the EU*, Martinus Nijhoff: Leiden/Boston, p. 178 and p. 181.

[5] See above Chapter 7.

[6] See on this D. Acosta (2010), "A Belief in the Purity of the Nation: The Possible Dangers of its Influence on Migration Legislation in Europe", *Studies in Ethnicity and Nationalism*, Vol. 10(2), pp. 234–254.

[7] C. Joppke (2004), "The Retreat of Multiculturalism in the Liberal State: Theory and Policy", *the British Journal of Sociology*, Vol. 55 (2), pp. 237–257, at 249.

[8] C. Mudde (1999), "The Single-Issue Party Thesis: Extreme Right Parties and the Immigration Issue", *West European Politics*, Vol. 22(3), pp. 182–197, at 190.

In fact, there are authors who have argued that immigration is the sole political issue that unites all populist right-wing parties which have been successful in recent years.[9]

Howard has convincingly shown that there is a bigger risk of having a restrictive immigration policy in countries with a powerful far right-wing party.[10] Denmark, where the Danish Peoples' Party influenced the Government in 2005 on the adoption of new restrictive guidelines on immigration, constitutes a relevant example of this. Those measures "stress the adherence to Danish cultural values as a precondition for a permanent residence in the country".[11] This was also the case in Austria where the Freedom Party (FPÖ, *Freiheitliche Partei Österreichs*) played a leading role in the introduction of integration requirements[12] and the Netherlands,[13] where, after the appearance of the Fortuyn party, most political parties were compelled to adapt their discourse on immigration.[14] It is also true that, by contrast, Germany introduced more stringent integration requirements without the presence of right-wing populist parties.[15]

A similar argument is also put forward by Joppke, who argues that left-wing parties are in favour of a policy of increasing rights for migrants (what he labels as "de-ethnicization"), whereas right-wing parties are in favour of giving

9 E. Ivarsflaten (2008), "What Unites Right-Wing Populists in Western Europe? Re-Examining Grievance Mobilization Models in Seven Successful Cases", *Comparative Political Studies*, Vol. 41 (1), pp. 3–23.

10 M. Howard (2006) "Comparative Citizenship: An Agenda for Cross-National Research"', *Perspectives on Politics*, Vol. 4, pp. 443–455.

11 S. Adamo (2008), "Northern Exposure: The New Danish Model of Citizenship Test", *International Journal on Multicultural Societies (IJMS)*, Vol. 10, pp. 10–28, at 11; See also: E. Ersbøll (2010), "On Trial in Denmark", in R. van Oers, E. Ersbøll and D. Kostakopoulou (eds.), *A Re-definition of Belonging? Language and Integration Tests in Europe*, Martinus Nijhoff Publishers: Leiden, pp. 107–152.

12 B. Perchinig (2010), "All You Need to Know to Become an Austrian: Naturalisation Policy and Citizenship Testing in Austria" in R. van Oers, E. Ersbøll and D. Kostakopoulou (eds.), *A Re-definition of Belonging? Language and Integration Tests in Europe*, Martinus Nijhoff: Leiden, pp. 25–50; B. Perchinig (2010), "Country Report Austria", INTEC Project, Centre for Migration Law, Radboud University Nijmegen, p. 11–16.

13 C. Joppke (2007), "Beyond National Models: Civic Integration Policies for Immigrants in Western Europe", *West European Politics*, Vol. 30, pp. 1–22, at 18.

14 M. Bruquetas-Callejo, B. Garcés-Mascareñas, R. Penninx and P. Scholten (2007), "Policy-making related to Immigration and Integration. The Dutch Case", *IMISCOE Working Paper 15: Country Report*.

15 I. Michalowski (2010), "Integration Tests in Germany. A communitarian Approach?" in R. van Oers, E. Ersbøll and D. Kostakopoulou (eds.), *A Re-definition of Belonging? Language and Integration Tests in Europe*, Martinus Nijhoff: Leiden, pp. 185–210.

more rights to emigrants abroad (what he calls "re-ethnicization").[16] The picture is probably more complex. As Howard mentions, there are two important factors. The first is "not simply whether a right-of-centre government is in power, but whether it is mobilized on the issue of immigration and citizenship reform".[17] Italy is an example of a country where the Government is clearly mobilised in that direction. In fact, the introduction in 2009 of an integration contract, as well as the requirement to pass an Italian language examination before acquiring long-term residence status, were proposed by the Lega Nord, which is part of the Italian Government coalition, and whose restrictive opinions on immigration and on migrants' rights are well known.[18] The Lega Nord has indeed always positioned itself in an ethno-nationalist attitude by which it essentialised cultural differences to turn them into "quasi-genetic characteristics".[19]

The second factor is "the reaction of more mainstream conservative parties to the challenge of the far right's message".[20] This is probably the case in France where, according to Carrera, Nicolas Sarkozy usurped many of the ideas of the Front National. In fact, the Front National managed to centre the immigration debate on the integration of third-country nationals and to reactivate the discourse on French national identity.[21] Also in Belgium, the Vlaams Belang has played a significant role in framing the debate on immigration.[22] It is important though to look not only at the reaction of other conservative parties but also of other centre-left ones.[23]

---

16 C. Joppke (2003), "Citizenship between de- and re-ethnicization", *European Journal of Sociology*, Vol. 44, pp. 429–58.

17 M. Howard (2006) "Comparative Citizenship: An Agenda for Cross-National Research", *Perspectives on Politics*, at 450.

18 Il Corriere della Sera, *L'Idea della Lega Nord: "Permesso di Soggiorno a Punti. Via chi Sbaglia"*, 7 October 2008.

19 D. Albertazzi and D. McDonell (2005) "The Lega Nord in the Second Berlusconi Government: In a League of its Own", *West European Politics*, Vol. 28 (5), pp. 952–972, at 964.

20 M. Howard (2006) "Comparative Citizenship: An Agenda for Cross-National Research", *Perspectives on Politics*, Vol. 4, pp. 443–455, at. 451.

21 S. Carrera (2009), *In Search of a Perfect Citizen? The Intersection between Integration, Immigration and Nationality in the EU*, Martinus Nijhoff: Leiden/Boston, pp. 315–320.

22 P. Loobuyck and D. Jacobs (2006), "The Flemish Immigration Society: Political Challenges on Different Levels", in L. d'Haenens, M. Hooghe, D. Vanheule, H. Gezduci (eds.), *New Citizens, New Policies? Developments in Diversity Policy in Canada and Flanders*, Academia Press: Gent, pp. 105–118, at 106.

23 Saskia Bonjour has showed how in the Dutch case all political parties (including the left wing opposition except for the Greens) accepted the introduction of integration requirements. See S. Bonjour (2010), "Between Integration Provision and Selection Mechanism. Party Politics, Judicial Constraints, and the Making of French and Dutch Policies of Civic Integration Abroad", *European Journal of Migration and Law*, Vol. 12(3), pp. 299–318, at 308–312.

2.2. *Identity Issues*

I have mentioned above how a far right party, the Front National, managed to centre the debate on immigration around the issues of integration and identity. In fact, in 2009, the French Government began the process of searching for the values of the Republic[24] and even expanded the debate into a more controversial area of searching for what it means to be French. Indeed, it seems that since the mid-1990s there has been an official promotion of national identity and alleged national values in various Member States.[25] Indeed, identity issues also seem to play an important role in the introduction of integration requirements. There are some authors, though, who do not agree with this rationale. Joppke, for instance, suggests that even if "the turn to civic integration is indeed driven by the attempt to commit and bind newcomers to the particular society that is receiving them" the values that are embedded in that integration stands for "the universal creed of liberty and equality", at least in the case of the Netherlands and the UK.[26]

I argue, however, that a certain understanding of national identity and the nation also plays a role in the introduction of integration conditions. As Kostakopoulou mentions:

> In the eyes of governmental elites, social cohesion, national unity and belonging can be bolstered by requiring migrants to learn to speak the language of the host state and by re-educating them so that they can embrace a country's history and institutions, its values and the national way of life.[27]

In fact, these tests send a clear message that Member States will only accept those new citizens or long-term residents who are not only harmless and financially independent but who have also gone through an apprenticeship on the values of the nation. It is remarkable, though, how the official discourse

---

[24] See Haut Conseil à l'intégration (2009), *Faire Connaitre les Valeurs de la République*, April 2009.

[25] D. Kostakopoulou (2010), "Matters of Control: Integration Tests, Naturalisation Reform and Probationary Citizenship in the United Kingdom", *Journal of Ethnic and Migration Studies*, Vol. 36 (5), pp. 829–846, at 830. See also on this D. Schnaper (1991), *La France de l'Intégration. Sociologie de la Nation en 1990*. Gallimard: Paris; D. Schnaper (1994), *Community of Citizens. On the Modern Idea of Nationality*. Transaction Publishers: New Brunswick and London.

[26] C. Joppke (2004), "The Retreat of Multiculturalism in the Liberal State: Theory and Policy", *The British Journal of Sociology*, Vol. 55 (2), pp 237–257, at 253.

[27] D. Kostakopoulou (2010), "Introduction" in R. van Oers, E. Ersbøll and D. Kostakopoulou (eds.), *A Re-definition of Belonging? Language and Integration Tests in Europe*, Martinus Nijhoff: Leiden, pp. 1–24, at 1.

always denies that these tests are about assimilation[28] and tries, instead, to depict them as necessary in the name of national or community cohesion.[29] Indeed, there is an anxiety about social cohesion which is highlighted by the rush to integrate new arrivals and future citizens through language and civic knowledge courses which are, especially the language ones, easy to sell to the electorate.[30] I mention citizenship here because, although I am dealing with long-term residence, the tendency in some Member States, such as the Netherlands and the United Kingdom, is to require the same conditions for those third-country nationals who would like to become naturalised as for those who would like to obtain long-term residence status.[31] Consequently, it seems that the motivations for the introduction of the integration conditions both in citizenship tests and for long-term residence have a similar rationale. It is undeniable, in any case, that the debate surrounding citizenship "negatively influenced the 'immigration debate', and led to more language and political-cultural assimilation preconditions for entry and residence".[32]

Despite the fact that there is an extended assumption among academics to consider nations as modern constructs which only arose in the last two

---

[28] D. Jacobs, and A. Rea (2007), "The End of National Models? Integration Courses and Citizenship Trajectories in Europe", *Paper Prepared for the EUSA-Conference, Montreal, 17–19 May 2007*, at 9.

[29] There are several references to social cohesion in the preparatory documents to immigration reforms. See for example in France : *Présentation du projet de loi relatif à l'immigration, à l'intégration et à la nationalité*, Ministère de l'immigration, de l'intégration, de l'identité nationale e du développent solidaire, Paris, 1 April, 2010. See on the UK: Home Office. UK Border Agency. July 2009. *Earning the Right to Stay. A New Points Test for Citizenship*. See for an academic debate on this: R. Van Oers (2010), "Citizenship Tests in the Netherlands, Germany and the UK", in R. van Oers, E. Ersbøll and D. Kostakopoulou (eds.), *A Re-definition of Belonging? Language and Integration Tests in Europe*, Martinus Nijhoff: Leiden, pp. 51–106; B. Ryan (2009), "The Integration Agenda in British Migration Law", in E. Guild, K. Groenendijk, and S. Carrera (eds.) *Illiberal Liberal States. Immigration, Citizenship and Integration in the EU*. Ashgate: Surrey, pp. 277–298.

[30] A. Blackledge and S. Wright (2010), "Testing for Citizenship: Why tests and why now?" *Communicating European Citizenship, 22 March 2010*, Lancaster House, London, p. 13.

[31] For the UK case see R. Van Oers (2010), "Citizenship Tests in the Netherlands, Germany and the UK", in R. van Oers, E. Ersbøll and D. Kostakopoulou (eds.), *A Re-definition of Belonging? Language and Integration Tests in Europe*, Martinus Nijhoff: Leiden, pp. 51–106, at 68. For the Dutch case see, S. Carrera and A. Wiesbrock (2009), "Civic Integration of Third-Country Nationals. Nationalism versus Europeanisation in the Common EU Immigration Policy", Centre for European Policy Studies, CEPS: Brussels, at 29.

[32] K. McGauran (2007), "Germany's Immigration Amendment Act of 2007: Achieving Integration of Foreigners?" *Journal of Immigration Asylum and Nationality Law*, Vol. 21 (4), pp. 295–310, at 296.

centuries,[33] it is also probably true, as Kostakopoulou mentions, that "the idea that ethno-history determines the quality, scope and intensity of national identity still exerts considerable influence..."[34] This rationale portrays the nation as a "unitary, seamless transhistorical cultural community which is imbued with timeless qualities."[35] This line of thinking has two fundamental flaws: First, it disregards the cultural interaction that has been the norm in the construction of every country in Europe. Second, it creates a worrying problem for the future as national identities are seen as immutable, thus complicating the integration of the new Europeans with an immigrant background. As Guild explains:

> The moment this idea of national culture becomes dominant...the separation of those who do not share the elements of the 'newly' national culture from those who do takes the form of dividing those who belong and the minorities and immigrants who are different.[36]

This can be seen in the way the tests are presented, as aspirant citizens (as well as long-term residents) "are often required to display their understanding of the 'imagined community' of the nation".[37] In addition to showing an understanding of an idea of the nation, they also have to increasingly show knowledge of the language.

Guibernau links these debates, with the previous discussion on the centrality of populist parties, by pointing out that "renewed calls for preserving the 'purity' of national identities are on the rise"[38] and some political parties are portraying foreigners as a "potential threat to the stability, order, prosperity and/or well being of the nation state".[39] At the same time, Guibernau goes on, these parties are "promoting an organic conception of the nation which regards 'foreign bodies' as a threat to its life and health".[40] Again, Guild warns

---

[33] See among others E. Hobsbawm (1990), *Nations and Nationalism since 1780,* Cambridge University Press: Cambridge; B. Anderson (1991), *Imagined Communities. Reflections on the Origin and Spread of Nationalism,* Verso: London, New York; E. Gellner (1983), *Nations and Nationalism,* Basil Blackwell: Oxford; U. Özkirimli (2005), *Contemporary Debates on Nationalism. A Critical Engagement,* Palgrave Mcmillan: New York.

[34] D. Kostakopoulou (2001), *Citizenship, Identity and Immigration in the European Union. Between Past and Future,* Manchester University Press: Manchester, at 6.

[35] *Ibid.,* at 23.

[36] E. Guild, (2005), "Cultural and Identity Security. Immigrants and the Legal Expression of National Identity" in E. Guild and J. Van Selm (eds.) *International Migration and Security. Opportunities and Challenges,* Routledge: Oxon, pp. 101–112, at 103.

[37] S. Wright (2008) "Citizenship Tests in Europe- Editorial Introduction", *International Journal on Multicultural Societies (IJMS),* Vol. 10, pp. 1–9, at 3.

[38] M. Guibernau (2007), *The Identity of Nations,* Polity Press: Cambridge, at 6.

[39] *Ibid.,* at 30.

[40] *Ibid.,* at 151.

against the results of the nationalist theory. This theory would produce, according to her view, a "need to protect the national culture by endowing it with its own state-protector; the need to unmask, neutralise and drive out the foreigners, who wish to destroy and debase that culture".[41] Integration, in that sense, "becomes another tool for the state to manage the nation and to determine who belongs to its imagined community."[42] Or as Carrera and Wiesbrock point out, integration is not seen,

> as a process of social inclusion and equalisation of rights and freedoms, but rather as a state requirement for the TCN to disappear into the homogeneous national wholeness and another way for the state to promote national identity and nationalism within and beyond its territorial borders.[43]

As other authors mention, these "ideological narratives about the alleged destiny of the nation" as well as "discourses about the need to maintain the 'social cohesion'...preclude credible policy options".[44] In fact, they seem to have contributed to a more restrictive immigration policy, at least in the area of integration. This is extremely relevant as the implementation of a harsher immigration policy would not be a legitimate objective under the Directive. Thus, this is the next point that must be analysed.

2.3. *Restrictive Immigration Policy*

There seem to be two contradictory tendencies in some Member States since the entry into force of the Treaty of Amsterdam. On the one hand, there appears to be an emphasis on recruiting new migrants in certain sectors with shortages, with a clear preference for highly skilled ones.[45] On the other hand,

---

41 E. Guild (2005), "Cultural and Identity Security. Immigrants and the Legal Expression of National Identity", in E. Guild and J. Van Selm (eds.) *International Migration and Security. Opportunities and Challenges*, Routledge: Oxon, pp 101–112, at 102.

42 E. Guild, K. Groenendijk and S. Carrera (2009), "Understanding the Contest of Community: Illiberal Practices in the EU?" in E. Guild, K. Groenendijk and S. Carrera (eds.) *Illiberal Liberal States. Immigration, Citizenship and Integration in the EU*, Ashgate: Surrey, pp. 1–25, at 16.

43 S. Carrera and A. Wiesbrock (2009), "Civic Integration of Third-Country Nationals. Nationalism versus Europeanisation in the Common EU Immigration Policy", Centre for European Policy Studies, CEPS: Brussels, at 4.

44 R. van Oers, E. Ersbøll and D. Kostakopoulou (2010), "Mapping the Redefinition of Belonging in Europe", in R. van Oers, E. Ersbøll and D. Kostakopoulou (eds.), *A Re-definition of Belonging? Language and Integration Tests in Europe*, Martinus Nijhoff: Leiden, pp. 307–332, at 329–30.

45 J. Apap (2002), "Shaping Europe's Migration Policy. New Regimes for the Employment of Third Country Nationals: A Comparison of Strategies in Germany, Sweden, the Netherlands and the UK", *European Journal of Migration and Law*, Vol. 4, pp. 309–328.

Governments have been quite keen to assert full control over the entitlement of who lives in their territory[46] in order to manage what Joppke labels as a challenge to their sovereignty.[47] Thus, requiring new citizens (or long-term residents) "to be coached as if they were joining the homogeneous monolithic nation state system of the past" could be explained as "an exercise of nation state power simply because naturalisation is an area where the nation does still have sovereign power".[48] That is, however, not the case with regard to permanent residence where the discretionary power to grant it has been limited through the adoption of the Long-term Residence Directive.

This contradiction between liberal and restrictive policies has been well explained by Castles:

> The strength of nationalism and racism in immigration countries has made it easier to mobilize public opinion against immigration than for it. This can mean that politicians are content to provide anti-immigration rhetoric while actually pursuing policies that lead to more immigration, because this meets important economic or labour market objectives. This explains the hidden agendas in many migration policies- that is, policies which purport to follow certain objectives, while actually doing the opposite.[49]

Integration conditions are a case in point when discussing hidden agendas. Despite the fact that some Member States explicitly mentioned migration control as one of the motivations for their introduction,[50] there has been official rhetoric referring to promoting integration and making third-country

46 A. Favell and R. Hansen (2002), "Markets against Politics: Migration, EU Enlargement and the idea of Europe", *Journal of Ethnic and Migration Studies*, Vol. 28(4), pp. 581–601, at 582. See also this ambivalent position in the case of Latvia: K. Kruma (2010), "Latvian Integration Policy: Lost in Translation", in R. van Oers, E. Ersbøll and D. Kostakopoulou (eds.), *A Re-definition of Belonging? Language and Integration Tests in Europe*, Martinus Nijhoff: Leiden, pp. 241–270, at 261.

47 C. Joppke (1998), "Immigration Challenges the Nation-State", in C. Joppke (ed.), *Immigration in Western Europe and the United States*, Oxford University Press: Oxford, pp. 5–48, at 10. See also on this: W. A. Cornelius, P.L. Martin and J.F. Hollifield (eds.) (1994), *Controlling Immigration. A Global Perspective*, Stanford University Press: Stanford. See for a review of these debates: L. Schuster and J. Solomos (2002), "Rights and Wrongs across European Borders: Migrants, Minorities and Citizenship", *Citizenship Studies*, Vol. 6(1), pp. 37–54.

48 A. Blackledge and S. Wright (2010), "Testing for Citizenship: Why tests and why now?", *Communicating European Citizenship, 22 March 2010, Lancaster House, London*, p. 10.

49 S. Castles (2004), "Why Migration Policies Fail", *Ethnic and Racial Studies*, Vol. 27(2), pp. 205–227, at 214.

50 R. van Oers, E. Ersbøll and D. Kostakopoulou (2010), "Mapping the Redefinition of Belonging in Europe" in R. van Oers, E. Ersbøll and D. Kostakopoulou (eds.), *A Re-definition of Belonging? Language and Integration Tests in Europe*, Martinus Nijhoff: Leiden, pp. 307–332, at 312.

nationals self-sufficient.[51] It is difficult to agree with this, however, if one considers that "the failure to comply with the integration obligations results in the refusal of a (permanent) residence permit…or in the imposition of financial sanctions".[52] This is also the case when the level that has to be attained is increased once "too many applicants" pass the test, as in the case of the Netherlands' examination abroad for family members.[53] In fact, some authors argue that the Dutch government "has taken the view that a restrictive immigration policy is a necessary condition for a successful integration process".[54]

Thus, a restrictive immigration policy to reduce the number of family migrants and to restrict access to security of residence (or nationality) seems to be the most important motivation behind their introduction in several European cases.[55]

It is important to differentiate at the outset between the implementation of a restrictive immigration policy in the country of origin and its implementation in the Member State itself.

With regard to the first one, as has been seen, three Member States have introduced integration conditions for family members, which seem to have as

[51] This argument has been put forward for example in the UK, Netherlands and Germany. See B. Ryan (2009), "The Integration Agenda in British Migration Law", in E. Guild, K. Groenendijk, and S. Carrera (eds.) *Illiberal Liberal States. Immigration, Citizenship and Integration in the EU*, Ashgate: Surrey, pp. 277–298, at 277; S. Carrera and A. Wiesbrock (2009), "Civic Integration of Third-Country Nationals. Nationalism versus Europeanisation in the Common EU Immigration Policy", Centre for European Policy Studies, CEPS: Brussels, at 12; A. Wiesbrock (2009), "Discrimination Instead of Integration? Integration Requirements for Immigrants in Denmark and Germany", in E. Guild, K. Groenendijk and S. Carrera (eds.), *Illiberal Liberal States. Immigration, Citizenship and Integration in the EU*, pp. 299–314, at 309.

[52] R. van Oers, E. Ersbøll and D. Kostakopoulou (2010), "Mapping the Redefinition of Belonging in Europe" in R. van Oers, E. Ersbøll and D. Kostakopoulou (eds.), *A Re-definition of Belonging? Language and Integration Tests in Europe*, Martinus Nijhoff: Leiden, pp. 307–332, at 318. See also: L.F.M. Besselink (2009), "Integration and Immigration: The Vicissitudes of Dutch 'Inburgering'", in E. Guild, K. Groenendijk and S. Carrera (eds.), *Illiberal Liberal States. Immigration, Citizenship and Integration in the EU*, Ashgate: Surrey, pp. 241–257, at 248.

[53] S. Carrera and A. Wiesbrock (2009), "Civic Integration of Third-Country Nationals. Nationalism versus Europeanisation in the Common EU Immigration Policy", Centre for European Policy Studies, CEPS: Brussels, at 13.

[54] B.P. Vermeulen and K.M. de Vries (2008), "Citizenship in the Netherlands: Changing Policies and Concepts", *Canadian Diversity/Diversité Canadienne*, Vol. 6(4), pp. 86–90, at 88.

[55] See on the Dutch case: *Ibid.*, at 241; E. Guild, K. Groenendijk and S. Carrera (2009), "Understanding the Contest of Community: Illiberal Practices in the EU?", in E. Guild, K. Groenendijk and S. Carrera (eds.) *Illiberal Liberal States. Immigration, Citizenship and Integration in the EU*, Ashgate: Surrey, pp. 1–25, at 8.

their goal a reduction in the number of migrants.[56] Carrera and Wiesbrock mention the case of the Netherlands. They point out that the high fee (350 Euros) that a migrant has to pay acts as a deterrent. Moreover, they argue that the Netherlands increased the level of language proficiency that candidates had to achieve in 2008, after the Government realised that too many were being successful. Carrera and Wiesbrock conclude that this is a clear element in proving that behind the integration tests there is an objective to reduce the number of family migrants.[57] In fact, between 2004 and 2007 the number of persons requesting visas dropped from 29.000 to 12.000.[58] In France, the reduction in the number of applications for family reunification was also one of the goals that the Government pursued with the introduction of integration measures abroad.[59] A similar situation may be mentioned in the case of Denmark, where their introduction seems to be motivated by the same rationale. Nevertheless, the minister for integration argued that a reduction in the number of family members was not behind their future applicability.[60] A closely related argument has been put forward by Michalowski, who argues that tests for family members in Germany and the Netherlands are a tool for the selection of more skilled migrants rather than for integration.[61]

In fact, most Member States show a clear preference for highly skilled workers[62] in line with what the French President labelled as "une immigration

[56] I. Michalowski and A. Walter (2008), "Family Reunification between EC Law and National Integration Policy", in: Anita Böcker et al. (ed.), *Migration Law and Sociology of Law, collected essays in honour of Kees Groenendijk*, Wolf Legal Publishers: Nijmegen, pp 103–120, at 111; S. Carrera (2009), "Nationality, Immigration and 'the Republican Integration' in France", in K. Groenendijk, S. Carrera and E. Guild (eds.), *Illiberal Liberal States: Immigration, Citizenship and Integration in the EU*, Ashgate: Surrey, pp. 315–335, at 331.

[57] S. Carrera and A. Wiesbrock (2009), "Civic Integration of Third-Country Nationals. Nationalism versus Europeanisation in the Common EU Immigration Policy", Centre for European Policy Studies, CEPS: Brussels, p. 13.

[58] B.P. Vermeulen and K.M. de Vries (2008), "Citizenship in the Netherlands: Changing Policies and Concepts", *Canadian Diversity/Diversité Canadienne*, Vol. 6(4), pp. 86–90, at 89.

[59] *Ibid.*, p. 15.

[60] E. Ersbøll (2010), "On Trial in Denmark", in R. van Oers, E. Ersbøll and D. Kostakopoulou (eds.), *A Re-definition of Belonging? Language and Integration Tests in Europe*, Martinus Nijhoff: Leiden, p. 107–152, at 129.

[61] I. Michalowski (2010), "Integration Tests in Germany. A communitarian Approach?" in R. van Oers, E. Ersbøll and D. Kostakopoulou (eds.), *A Re-definition of Belonging? Language and Integration Tests in Europe*, Martinus Nijhoff: Leiden, pp. 185–210, at 192.

[62] I. Michalowski (2007), "Modelos de acogida en Alemania, Francia y los Países Bajos: diseño y efectividad de los programas de acogida e integración", in: Fundació CIDOB (ed.), *Políticas y modelos de acogida. Una mirada transatlántica: Canadá, Alemania, Francia y los Países Bajos*, Documentos CIDOB Migraciones 12 June 2007, pp. 67–92, at 88.

choisie" in order to have "une integration réussie".[63] Although the Long-term Residence Directive does not provide for any independent right of entry,[64] some scholars argue that the implicit objective of the civic and language integration criteria is to reduce the number of migrants, as there would be fewer who would be able to achieve the level required.[65] Those who do not achieve that level will have to leave the country or remain with a temporary residence permit, and it might be expected that better educated and highly skilled workers obtain higher passing rates.[66]

It has been proven in any case that the introduction of integration conditions for family reunification and citizenship have resulted in a reduction in the number of applications.[67] The effect might be similar in the case of long-term residence applications. This will certainly run contrary to the final objective of the Directive and raises a number of questions regarding the principles of effectiveness, proportionality and respect for fundamental rights, as will be addressed below. Moreover, if the empirical results show that migrants of certain nationalities or from certain socio-economic backgrounds have more difficulties in passing the tests, this might also raise the issue of indirect discrimination.[68] If, as Ryan argues, "the focus of integration policy is no longer on the equalisation of opportunity, but rather on the discouragement and

---

63 I. Michalowski (2009), "Liberal states – privatised integration policies?" in E. Guild, K. Groenendijk and S. Carrera (eds.), *Illiberal Liberal States. Immigration, Citizenship and Integration in the EU*, Surrey: Ashgate, pp. 259–276, at 271.

64 See Chapter 4 above.

65 S. Carrera and A. Wiesbrock (2009), "Civic Integration of Third-Country Nationals. Nationalism versus Europeanisation in the Common EU Immigration Policy", Centre for European Policy Studies, CEPS: Brussels, p. 22.

66 An opposite argument could be that highly skilled workers under the 2009 Directive enjoy a number of derogations from the Long-term Residence Directive which makes it easier for them to obtain this status. However, there is no derogation from the integration requirement which is also applicable to them. Interestingly, family members of highly skilled workers may only be subject to integration measures once they are reunited in the host Member State. See Article 15(3) of Directive 2009/50/EC of 25 May 2009 of the Council on the Conditions of Entry and Residence of Third-country Nationals for the Purposes of Highly Qualified Employment, OJ 2009 L 155/17, 18.6.2009.

67 See on this R. van Oers, E. Ersbøll and D. Kostakopoulou (2010), "Mapping the Redefinition of Belonging in Europe" in R. van Oers, E. Ersbøll and D. Kostakopoulou (eds.), *A Re-definition of Belonging? Language and Integration Tests in Europe*, Martinus Nijhoff: Leiden, pp. 307–332, at 322–24.

68 For example, in the UK, certain nationalities such as Afghanis, Bangladeshis, Iraqis or Turkish, have a considerably lower level of success in passing the life in the UK test leading to citizenship or permanent residence. See B. Ryan (2009), "The Integration Agenda in British Migration Law", in E. Guild, K. Groenendijk, and S. Carrera (eds.) *Illiberal Liberal States. Immigration, Citizenship and Integration in the EU*, Ashgate: Surrey, pp. 277–298, at 297.

penalisation of migrants who do not posses certain attributes",[69] one may wonder about the legitimacy of such tests in light of the Directive.

2.4. *Spread of the Tests*

The fourth step in explaining how integration conditions have been adopted by such a variety of Member States has to do with the way in which the tests have spread. Some authors have highlighted the key role played by the National Contact Points on Integration, which is a network of experts from the national administrations.[70] This network has facilitated the exchange of information and produced a "paradigm shift" by which Member States have mimicked each other's practices.[71] This has also happened with the introduction of citizenship tests in some countries, where it was argued that it was just a common trend already established in other countries.[72] This was also the case in Germany,[73] France,[74] Denmark[75] and the UK[76] where the Dutch model was used by these Member States to propose the introduction of integration requirements for family members. With regard to long-term residence integration conditions, the experience of other Member States was mentioned in Latvia[77] and

---

69 B. Ryan (2008), "Integration Requirements: A New Model in Migration Law", *Journal of Immigration, Asylum and Nationality Law*, Vol. 22(4), pp. 303–316, at 312.

70 S. Carrera (2009), In Search of a Perfect Citizen? The Intersection between Integration, Immigration and Nationality in the EU, Martinus Nijhoff: Leiden/Boston, p. 63.

71 E. Guild, K. Groenendijk and S. Carrera (2009), "Understanding the Contest of Community: Illiberal Practices in the EU?" in E. Guild, K. Groenendijk and S. Carrera (eds.) *Illiberal Liberal States. Immigration, Citizenship and Integration in the EU*, Ashgate: Surrey, pp. 1–25, at 7.

72 For example in Denmark, see S. Adamo (2008), "Northern Exposure: The New Danish Model of Citizenship Test", *International Journal on Multicultural Societies (IJMS)*, Vol. 10, pp. 10–28, at 22.

73 I. Michalowski (2009), "Liberal states – privatised integration policies?", in E. Guild, K. Groenendijk and S. Carrera (eds.), *Illiberal Liberal States. Immigration, Citizenship and Integration in the EU*, Ashgate: Surrey, pp. 259–276, at 270.

74 Y. Pascouau (2010), "Integration Measures in France: An Evolving Process between Integration and Migration Issues", in R. van Oers, E. Ersbøll and D. Kostakopoulou (eds.), *A Re-definition of Belonging? Language and Integration Tests in Europe*, Martinus Nijhoff Publishers: Leiden, pp. 153–183, at 173.

75 S. Carrera and A. Wiesbrock (2009), "Civic Integration of Third-Country Nationals. Nationalism versus Europeanisation in the Common EU Immigration Policy", Centre for European Policy Studies, CEPS: Brussels, at 13.

76 Home Office. UK Border Agency. July 2009. *Earning the Right to Stay. A New Points Test for Citizenship*, at 23.

77 K. Kruma (2010), "Latvian Integration Policy: Lost in Translation", in R. van Oers, E. Ersbøll and D. Kostakopoulou (eds.), *A Re-definition of Belonging? Language and Integration Tests in Europe*, Martinus Nijhoff: Leiden, pp. 241–270, at 262–63.

Austria.[78] Some other Member States, such as France, have also advanced the implementation of EU migration law as a reason.[79] In this way, the EU has been "instrumentalised for backing up the development of innovative national political priorities of restrictive nature".[80] Nonetheless, it is precisely because integration conditions are enshrined in a European Directive that certain principles have to be respected in their implementation. Those limits have been stressed by the CJEU in its ruling in *Chakroun*.

3. *Conclusion*

In this Chapter, I have looked at the political debates surrounding the introduction of integration conditions in order to acquire a long-term residence permit in several Member States. I have chosen to look at these particular debates as it has been revealed that integration is the main obstacle for third-country nationals to enjoyment of the rights provided in the Directive. It is in that sense the most important and controversial issue around Directive 2003/109.

I have mostly argued that the rise of far right parties in some Member States has been essential in centring the debate on immigration around a supposed lack of integration by third-country nationals. This has gone hand in hand with renewed calls for the preservation of allegedly essential national identities. The response by more mainstream parties to these ideas has been key in seeing the kind of immigration and integration legislation that has been adopted. Moreover, many Governments have also referred to the discussion on integration by pointing to the importance of social cohesion, as well as to the need for having more selective immigration, notably of highly skilled workers. Finally, these ideas have been spread around Europe via networks of government officials.

The next Chapter will look at the legitimacy of the integration conditions under the Directive, taking into account the debates for their introduction that have been presented in this Chapter.

---

78 B. Perchinig (2010), "All You Need to Know to Become an Austrian: Naturalisation Policy and Citizenship Testing in Austria" in R. van Oers, E. Ersbøll and D. Kostakopoulou (eds.), *A Re-definition of Belonging? Language and Integration Tests in Europe*, Martinus Nijhoff: Leiden, pp. 25–50, at 31.

79 S. Carrera (2009), "Nationality, Immigration and 'the Republican Integration' in France", in K. Groenendijk, S. Carrera and E. Guild (eds.), *Illiberal Liberal States: Immigration, Citizenship and Integration in the EU*, Ashgate: Surrey, pp. 315–335, at 330.

80 *Ibid.*, at 334.

Chapter 9

Possible Interpretation of the Integration Conditions by the CJEU

1. *Introduction*

After having analysed the implementation of the integration conditions in the different Member States in Chapter 7, as well as the political motivations for their introduction in Chapter 8, I can now consider how the CJEU could interpret the integration conditions. The Court could follow a number of steps in order to acknowledge whether or not the integration conditions applied by some Member States are in line with the Directive. In the following pages, I will attempt to enumerate those steps in order to make sense of this complex issue of interpretation and see the way in which the validity of those integration conditions could be challenged before national courts and the possible response that the CJEU could give if required to decide on a preliminary ruling.

Thus the questions for this Chapter are:

1. How could the CJEU interpret the integration conditions?
2. What are the possible legal questions raised by the political motivations mentioned in the previous Chapter with regard to the principles of effectiveness, proportionality, respect for fundamental rights or non-discrimination? How has the Court interpreted other conditions in the Family Reunification Directive? What lessons can be learned from the ruling in *Chakroun*?

2. *Possible Steps in the Interpretation of the Integration Conditions*

Here I will look at the possible steps that the CJEU could take in order to interpret the integration conditions.[1]

---

[1] See for a very brief analysis of these issues D. Acosta (2011), "Directive 2003/109 on Long-term Residence for Third-Country Nationals: Possible Future Interpretation by the European Court of Justice" in C. Murphy and P. Green (eds.), *Law and Outsiders: Norms, Processes and Othering in the 21st Century*, Hart: Oxford, pp. 143–165.

2.1. *Integration is not a Blank Cheque*

The CJEU decided in *Parliament v Council* that Member States could not use integration as a blank cheque. It stated that:

> The fact that the concept of integration is not defined cannot be interpreted as authorising the Member States to employ that concept in a manner contrary to general principles of Community law, in particular to fundamental rights.[2]

The Court is saying two important things here. The first is that it does not matter whether or not integration is defined in the Directive. The second thing it mentions is that the fact that the concept of integration is not defined does not exonerate its application from one important limit: the general principles of Union law and, specially, fundamental rights. The Court, when mentioning fundamental rights, is certainly refereeing to the right to family life, as this case was about Directive 2003/86 on the right to family reunification. However, the right to private life is also important. There are nonetheless three other important principles: the principle of effectiveness, the principle of proportionality and the principle of non-discrimination.

2.2. *The Context and Objectives of Directive 2003/109*

Once the CJEU establishes that integration is not a blank cheque, it could certainly follow by looking at the context and objective of the Directive. In order to see the context and objectives of a Directive the Court looks at the operative part as well as the preamble. This has been made clear in previous cases such as *Metock*[3] where the Court took preambles very seriously while interpreting the meaning of a Directive. The context comes within the framework of the Tampere Conclusions, as Recital 2 refers to them. Therefore, third-country nationals have to be treated as far as possible as European citizens. What is the objective of the Directive? Article 1 establishes that the Directive determines "the terms for conferring and withdrawing long-term resident status granted by a Member State in relation to third-country nationals legally residing in its territory, and the rights pertaining thereto". Therefore, the objective is to grant third-country nationals who fulfil a number of conditions a long-term residence status. The main criterion for granting this long-term residence status, reads Recital 6 of the preamble, is the duration of residence in the territory of a Member State. Consecutively, Recital 7 mentions that third-country nationals

---

[2] Case C-540/03, *European Parliament v. Council*, 27 June 2006, [2006] ECR I-5769, paragraph 70.

[3] Case C-127/08 *Metock* [2008] ECR I-06241, paragraphs 4,59 and 82.

also have to prove that they have adequate resources and sickness insurance, while Recital 8 establishes that these third-country nationals should not constitute a threat to public policy or public security. The integration conditions are not mentioned in the preamble.

Accordingly, it is clear that the objective of the Directive is to grant those third-country nationals who have regularly resided for five years in the territory of a Member State, who are not a threat and who have regular and stable resources as well as sickness insurance, a long-term residence permit. The CJEU would have to take into account the context and objectives of this Directive in order not to interpret it restrictively so that the Directive is not deprived of its effectiveness. As will be seen below, the Court decided in *Chakroun* that any condition applying to the general rule has to be interpreted strictly. Nonetheless, a question arises: How could the CJEU interpret the integration conditions themselves?

2.3. *The Integration Conditions in Article 5(2)*

Article 5(2) of the Directive provides that "Member States may require third-country nationals to comply with integration conditions, in accordance with national law". As has already been revealed, there is no definition on the meaning of integration provided in the Directive. In addition to that, the integration conditions may be applied in accordance with national law. There are thus two interpretation difficulties: what is the definition of integration? And how should the words "in accordance with national law" be interpreted?

The Definition of Integration

The CJEU has already faced situations in the past where a concept was not defined. This happened, for instance, with the concept of worker in *Levin*.[4]

Mrs Levin was a British national who applied for a permit to reside in the Netherlands. The Dutch authorities refused to grant the permit arguing that Mrs Levin was not engaged in a gainful occupation in the Netherlands. The Court, thus, had to interpret the provision in Article 48 (now Article 45 TFEU) on free movement of workers, which had been implemented inter alia by Regulation 1612/68[5] and Council Directive 68/360.[6] The concept of worker was however not defined anywhere. Hence, the Court took a number of steps to determine its meaning. I will see whether those steps could be applicable to

[4] Case 53/81, *D.M. Levin v Staatssecretaris van Justitie*, 23 March 1982, [1982] ECR 01035.

[5] This Regulation has been partly repealed by Directive 2004/38.

[6] It has been repealed by Directive 2004/38.

a possible interpretation of the integration conditions under Directive 2003/109:

Generally recognised principles of interpretation
The Court begins by acknowledging that in order to determine the meaning of worker, the generally recognised principles of interpretation should be used "beginning with the ordinary meaning to be attributed to those terms in their context and in the light of the objectives of the Treaty".[7] Here the Court reiterates its well-established teleological interpretation tool by looking at the context and objectives of the Treaty. This understanding is also pertinent when assessing Directive 2003/109.

EU law meaning
In Levin, several Member States argued that national criteria should be applied in order to ascertain concepts such as minimum wage, in order to see if a person was a worker or not. The Court turned down this argument and established that the concept of worker had an EU law meaning. Otherwise, the Court continued,

> the meaning of those terms could be fixed and modified unilaterally, without any control by the Community institutions, by national laws which would thus be able to exclude at will certain categories of persons from the benefit of the Treaty.[8]

Do integration conditions have an EU law meaning? As has been seen, Article 5(2) refers to national law. According to Peers, whenever the Directive does not refer to national law, the provision would have an EU law meaning.[9] Hence, he seems to argue that integration conditions would not have an EU law meaning since they refer to national law. Accordingly, could Member States introduce any integration requirement in accordance with their own national laws? The answer to this question must be in the negative. The Court has, in fact, already encountered situations where it had to interpret what a provision referring to national legislation meant. In the case just mentioned above, *Parliament v. Council*, the CJEU stated that integration is not a blank cheque. The Court was interpreting how integration could be framed in Directive 2003/86, more specifically in Article 4(1), which is worded as follows:

---

[7] Case 53/81, *D.M. Levin v Staatssecretaris van Justitie*, 23 March 1982, [1982] ECR 01035, paragraph 9.

[8] *Ibid.*, paragraph 11.

[9] S. Peers, (2004), "Implementing Equality? The Directive on Long-term Resident Third Country Nationals", *European Law Review*, Vol. 29(4), p. 437–460, at 444.

> By way of derogation, where a child is aged over 12 years and arrives independently from the rest of his/her family, the Member State may, before authorising entry and residence under this Directive, verify whether he or she meets a condition for integration provided for by its existing legislation on the date of implementation of this Directive.

Thus, Article 4(1) is making a reference to national legislations. Similarly, Article 7(2) of Directive 2003/86 also makes a reference to the national legal orders when it provides that:

> Member States may require third country nationals to comply with integration measures, in accordance with national law.

As mentioned earlier, the Court declared that this concept had to be applied in line with general principles of Union law. This is irrespective of the fact that these integration measures may be implemented in accordance with national law. Thus, even if the Court would consider that integration conditions do not have an EU law meaning, Member States would not be able to legislate contrary to the general principles of Union law, such as effectiveness, proportionality, fundamental rights or non-discrimination.

The importance of the EU law meaning
The Court explained in Levin the importance of giving an EU law meaning to the term worker. It clarified that:

> If that were not the case, the Community rules on freedom of movement for workers would be frustrated, as the meaning of those terms could be fixed and modified unilaterally, without any control by the Community institutions, by national laws which would thus be able to exclude at will certain categories of persons from the benefit of the Treaty.[10]

The Court continued its argumentation by adding that if that were the case:

> [T]he field of application rationae personae of the Community rules on this subject might vary from one Member State to another. (Consequently) The meaning and the scope of the terms "worker"....should thus be clarified in the light of the principles of the legal order of the Community.[11]

The Court here is just reinforcing the importance of giving an EU law meaning to the term worker. If integration conditions could not be considered to have an EU law meaning, that would not give Member States a free hand to impose those integration conditions in any way they wished, but they would

[10] Case 53/81, *D.M. Levin v Staatssecretaris van Justitie*, 23 March 1982, [1982] ECR 01035, paragraph 11.
[11] *Ibid.*, paragraph 12.

have to respect the general principles of Union law such as fundamental rights, and they would be clarified in light of those principles.

2.4. *What is the Meaning of Integration according to the CJEU's Case Law on Turkish Workers?*

The next logical step is to see the way in which the CJEU has interpreted the concept of integration itself in the past. I have made clear up to here that the aim and broad logic of the Directive is the integration of third-country nationals who are long-term residents (Recital 4) by granting them a genuine instrument of integration after the acquisition of a permit by which they get to enjoy equality of treatment in many areas (Recital 12). It is now time to examine what integration itself means. The Court has on a number of occasions touched upon this concept when interpreting Decision No 1/80 for Turkish workers. It is important to consider some of these cases to acknowledge the parallelisms that could be drawn. I will refer to two cases. The first, *Wählergruppe Gemeinsam,*[12] concerned Article 10(1) of Decision No 1/80 regarding the principle of non-discrimination.[13] In brief, Austria required Austrian nationality in order to be eligible to stand for election to the general assembly of chambers of workers. Thus, the main issue was to see whether this was compatible with Article 10 mentioned above. The Court first established that this Article had direct effect.[14] It then considered that "national legislation which makes eligibility for election to a body representing and defending the interests of workers…subject to the possession of the nationality of the host Member State must be considered to be incompatible with Article 10(1)…"[15] It is very interesting for our purposes what the Court declared immediately afterwards:

> Moreover, as the Commission rightly pointed out, the above interpretation is the only one consistent with the aim and broad logic of Decision No 1/80, which is intended to secure progressively freedom of movement for workers and to promote the integration in the host Member State of Turkish workers who satisfy the conditions laid down in that decision and thus enjoy the rights conferred on them by it (see *Kurz*, paragraphs 40 and 45). *Granting Turkish workers legally employed in the territory of a Member State entitlement to the same conditions of*

[12] Case C-171/01, *Wählergruppe "Gemeinsam Zajedno/Birlikte Alternative und Grüne GewerkschafterInnen/UG" and Bundesminister für Wirtschaft und Arbeit and Others*, of 8 May 2003, ECR [2003] I-04301.

[13] Article 10(1) reads as follows: "The Member States of the Community shall as regards remuneration and other conditions of work grant Turkish workers duly registered as belonging to their labour forces treatment involving no discrimination on the basis of nationality between them and Community workers".

[14] Case C-171/01, *Wählergruppe*, paragraph 58.

[15] *Ibid.*, paragraph 78.

> *work as those enjoyed by workers who are nationals of the Member States is an important step towards creating an appropriate framework for the gradual integration of migrant Turkish workers* (emphasis added).

Hence, the Court declares that integration comes by giving Turkish workers rights, and not by denying them those same rights. A similar situation arose in *Commission v Austria.*[16] Once again, only Austrian nationals were permitted to stand for election to workers' chambers. The Court, in line with its previous judgment, ruled that this was contrary to the principle of non-discrimination present in Article 10 of Decision No 1/80.[17] It stated:

> Moreover, the above interpretation is the only one consistent with aim and broad logic of the agreements concerned, since granting workers who are nationals of the non-member States party to such agreements and who are legally employed in the territory of a Member State entitlement to the same conditions of work as those enjoyed by workers who are nationals of the Member States is an important step towards creating an appropriate framework for the gradual integration of those migrant workers in the host Member State...[18]

Consequently the same idea is made explicit here: integration arises from the granting of rights. Interestingly enough, as Guild points out when referring to the ruling by the Court in *Nazli,*[19] "the Court focuses exclusively on the economic integration into the labour force. Neither here nor elsewhere in the judgment does it assess any other type of integration, for instance social or cultural integration".[20] This is important as certain Member States are using integration in order to measure cultural integration, for example. The Directive, however, expresses this same rationale of integration deriving from rights in Recital 12 of the preamble, which, it is worth reminding, reads as follows:

> In order to constitute a genuine instrument for the integration of long-term residents into society in which they live, long-term residents should enjoy equality of treatment with citizens of the Member State in a wide range of economic and social matters, under the relevant conditions defined by this Directive.

Thus, the Directive itself is portraying the rationale that the Court has defended for the integration of Turkish workers under Decision No 1/80. Hence, it is

---

16 Case C-465/01, *Commission of the European Communities v Republic of Austria*, 16 September 2004, ECR [2004] I-08291.

17 *Ibid.*, paragraph 49.

18 *Ibid.*, paragraph 53.

19 Case C-340/97 *Nazli v Stadt Nürnberg*, ECR [2000] I-00957. See on this case Chapter 5 above.

20 E. Guild (2001), "Security of Residence and Expulsion of Foreigners: European Community Law" in E. Guild and P. Minderhoud, *Security of Residence and Expulsion: Protection of Aliens in Europe*, Kluwer Law International: The Hague/London/Boston, pp. 59–80, at 77.

certainly arguable that while interpreting the Directive the Court would follow the same line of reasoning.

2.5. *General Principles of Union Law*

The general principles of Union law are "unwritten principles of law which underlie the Community law edifice."[21] According to Steiner and Woods, general principles of law are used in different ways. First, EU law cannot be interpreted in a way which may conflict with these principles. Second, they may be invoked by individuals to challenge Community action. Third, and most importantly for our purposes, "general principles may also be invoked as a means of challenging action by a Member State...where the action is performed in the context of a right or obligation arising from Community law".[22] As Carrera rightly points out, general principles of EU law apply when Member States are implementing a Directive in their national legal orders.[23] This is further emphasised by the fact that the Union and the Member States have to pursue the principle of sincere cooperation when carrying out tasks which flow from the Treaties.[24] The CJEU has already pronounced on this on a number of occasions and I will come back to this issue below.[25]

There is a large amount of literature on this area.[26] Consequently, I will limit myself to seeing the ways in which the principles of effectiveness and proportionality may affect the implementation by Member States of the integration possibility.

---

[21] T. Tridimas (2006), *The General Principles of EC Law*, Oxford University Press: Oxford, 2nd edition, p. 3.

[22] J. Steiner and L. Woods (2009), *EU Law*, Oxford University Press: Oxford (10th edition), p. 133.

[23] S. Carrera (2009), In Search of a Perfect Citizen? The Intersection between Integration, Immigration and Nationality in the EU, Martinus Nijhoff: Leiden/Boston, p. 361.

[24] Article 4(3) TEU reads as follows: "The Member States shall take any appropriate measure, general or particular, to ensure fulfilment of the obligations arising out of the Treaties or resulting from the acts of the institutions of the Union. The Member States shall facilitate the achievement of the Union's tasks and refrain from any measure which could jeopardise the attainment of the Union's objectives".

[25] Case C-212/04, *Konstantinos Adeneler and Others v Ellinikos Organismos Galaktos (ELOG)*, [2006] ECR I-06057; Case C-422/05, *Commission of the European Communities v Kingdom of Belgium*, [2007] ECR I-04749.

[26] U. Bernitz and J. Nergelius (2000), *General Principles of European Community Law*, Kluwer Law International: the Hague; A. Arnull (1990), *The General Principles of EEC Law and the Individual*, Leicester University Press: Leicester.

The Principle of Effectiveness

Effectiveness is a general principle of Union law.[27] "It requires the effective protection of Community rights and, more generally, the effective enforcement of Union law in national courts".[28] Effectiveness "derives from the distinct characteristics of Community law, primacy and direct effect".[29] The Court has already referred to it in a number of cases dealing with the free movement provisions for European citizens. The Court, for instance, established in *Metock* that:

> Having regard to the context and objectives of Directive 2004/38, the provisions of that directive cannot be interpreted restrictively, and must not in any event be deprived of their effectiveness.[30]

The Court of Justice mentions two things here. First, it explains how in order to understand the meaning of a Directive one has to look at its objectives and context. It has already been seen above what the context and objective of Directive 2003/109 are. Second, it establishes the important standard that Directives cannot be deprived of their effectiveness. Before that, it mentions that Directive 2004/38 cannot be interpreted restrictively. With regard to the impossibility of interpreting this Directive restrictively, the Court makes reference to a previous ruling in *Eind,* which reads as follows:

> First of all, the basis for requiring such a right is not laid down, expressly or by implication, in any provision of Community law relating to the right of residence in the Community of third-country nationals who are members of the families of Community workers. According to settled case-law of the Court of Justice, secondary Community legislation on movement and residence cannot be interpreted restrictively (see, inter alia, in respect of Regulation No 1612/68, Case 267/83 *Diatta* [1985] ECR 567, paragraphs 16 and 17, and Case C-413/99 *Baumbast and R* [2002] ECR I-7091, paragraph 74).[31]

The fact that secondary Community legislation on movement and residence cannot be interpreted restrictively, as the Court says, is important for our purposes because Recital 2 of the preamble to Directive 2003/109 makes reference to the Tampere Conclusions where it states, as has been mentioned, that

---

[27] See on the principle of effectiveness: M. Ross (2006), "Effectiveness in the European Legal Order(s): Beyond Supremacy to Constitutional Proportionality?, *European Law Review*, Vol. 31(4), pp. 476–498.

[28] T. Tridimas (2006), *The General Principles of EC Law*, Oxford University Press: Oxford, 2nd edition, p. 276.

[29] *Ibid.*, p. 276.

[30] Case C-127/08, *Metock* [2008] ECR I-06241, paragraph 84.

[31] Case C-291/05, Minister voor Vreemdelingenzaken en Integratie v R.N.G. Eind, [2007] ECR I-10719, paragraph 43.

"the legal status of third-country nationals should be approximated to that of Member States' nationals".[32] This is remarkable, as the provisions in the Directive "will have to be interpreted by the national courts and the Court of Justice, in light of the aims and the instructions of the Tampere Council".[33] Therefore, "to give a different meaning to similar provisions in two Directives has to be justified. It cannot be taken for granted".[34] Moreover, as will be seen below in *Chakroun*, the CJEU has also referred to the principle of effectiveness when interpreting Directives for third-country nationals.

Proportionality

The second important principle to be mentioned here is proportionality. The principle of proportionality has been understood as one of the general principles of EU law. It has been established by the jurisprudence of the CJEU.[35] The principle has been discussed at length in the literature[36] and "requires that the means used to achieve a given end must be no more than that which is appropriate and necessary to achieve that end".[37] It has been applied by the CJEU to measures adopted by Member States when implementing EU law. In fact, it has even been argued that the level of scrutiny by the Court in these cases is more intense than when reviewing Community measures. Jacobs has justified this by pointing out that "the scrutiny of national measures may need to be more demanding where they are likely to impair the effectiveness of Community measures".[38] Hence, proportionality is intrinsically linked to the principle of effectiveness just explained. The principle is composed of three different elements or tests: suitability, necessity and proportionality *stricto sensu*. These principles may be described as follows:

---

[32] See Chapter 2 above.

[33] K. Groenendijk (2007), "The Long-Term Residents Directive, Denizenship and Integration", in A. Baldaccini, E. Guild and H. Toner (eds.), *Whose Freedom, Security and Justice? EU Immigration and Asylum Law and Policy*, Hart Publishing: Oxford, pp. 429–450, at 440–41.

[34] *Ibid.*, at 441.

[35] See Case 11/70, *Internationale Handelsgesellschaft mbH v Einfuhr- und Vorratsstelle für Getreide und Futtermittel*, [1970] ECR 1125.

[36] N. Emiliou (1996), *The Principle of Proportionality in European Law. A Comparative Study*, Kluwer Law International: The Hague; E. Ellis (1999) (ed.), *The Principle of Proportionality in the Laws of Europe*, Hart Publishing: Oxford; G. de Burca (1993), "The Principle of Proportionality and its Application in EC Law", *Yearbook of European Law*, Vol. 13, pp. 105–150.

[37] J. Steiner and L. Woods (2009), *EU Law*, Oxford University Press: Oxford (10th edition), p. 147.

[38] F. G. Jacobs (1999), "Recent Developments in the Principle of Proportionality in European Community Law", in E. Ellis (ed.), *The Principle of Proportionality in the Laws of Europe*, Hart Publishing: Oxford, pp. 1–21, at 21.

a. Suitability: Here, "the means employed by the measure must be suitable, namely reasonably likely, to achieve its objectives".[39]
b. Necessity: Here, "the adverse consequences that the measure has on an interest worthy of legal protection" are assessed so the Court can determine "whether those consequences are justified in view of the importance of the objective pursued".[40] Moreover, "the more severely a measure affects private interests, the more difficult it is to establish its necessity".[41]
c. Proportionality *stricto sensu*: The third test would establish whether "the measure does not have an excessive effect on the applicant's interests" even if there are no less restrictive means.[42]

Carrera has applied the analysis of the principle of proportionality to the French case and to its integration contract, explained above, to obtain the long-term residence permit. Carrera arrived at the conclusion that the binding nature of the contract and the set of sanctions attached to it in case of non-compliance made it possible to argue that "the French implementing laws appear to be very far from those guiding Council Directive 2003/109, and therefore cannot be considered as increasing the protection of the rights envisaged by it".[43] The principle of proportionality will have to be confronted on a case by case basis with each of the measures applying integration conditions in the different Member States. Moreover, as Groenendijk rightly explains, the meaning of concepts such as integration "will undoubtedly be influenced by the meaning of those or similar concepts in other Directives in the migration field or in other fields of Community law".[44]

I will return to the analysis of certain practices in some Member States below, once I have explained the ruling in *Chakroun*.

Fundamental Rights

The question of fundamental rights regarding long-term residents is a very relevant one[45] and arose in the case of the ECtHR *Sisojeva and Others*

39 T. Tridimas (1999), "Proportionality in Community Law: Searching for the Appropriate Standard of Scrutiny", in in E. Ellis (ed.), *The Principle of Proportionality in the Laws of Europe*, Hart Publishing: Oxford, pp. 65–84, at 68.

40 *Ibid.*, at 68.

41 *Ibid.*, at 76.

42 *Ibid.*, at 68.

43 S. Carrera (2009), In Search of a Perfect Citizen? The Intersection between Integration, Immigration and Nationality in the EU, Martinus Nijhoff: Leiden/Boston, p 404.

44 K. Groenendijk (2006), "Family Reunification as a Right under Community Law", *European Journal of Migration and Law*, Vol. 8, pp. 215–230, at 221.

45 See on this D. Thym (2008), "Respect for Private and Family Life under Article 8 ECHR in Immigration Cases: a Human Right to Regularize Illegal Stay?", *International and Comparative Law Quarterly*, Vol. 57(1), pp. 87–112.

v Latvia.[46] It has to be recalled at the outset that Recital 3 of the preamble to Directive 2003/109 reads as follows:

> This Directive respects the fundamental rights and observes the principles recognised in particular by the European Convention for the Protection of Human Rights and Fundamental Freedoms and by the Charter of Fundamental Rights of the European Union.

The case in *Sisojeva* is hence important. The applicants alleged that the refusal of the Latvian authorities to grant them a residence permit despite the long period of time that they had lived there amounted to a violation of their right to private life under Article 8 of the ECHR. The Court agreed.

The facts are the following. The applicants, Svetlana Sisojeva and Arkady Sisojev, were a married couple. The third applicant, Aksana Sisojeva, was their daughter. The first two applicants arrived in Latvia in 1969 and 1968 respectively. Their daughter was born in Latvia. In 1993, the first two applicants requested permanent residence permits but they were only granted temporary ones. After going through different judicial instances, they were required to leave Latvia in 2000. Later, in 2003, the Interior Ministry's Nationality and Migration Directorate sent a letter to the applicants with a procedure that they could use in order to regularise their situation. Nevertheless, none of the applicants complied with that procedure.

The Court found that Latvian authorities, contrary to their claims, had not afforded redress for the damage caused to the applicants.[47] In fact, the applicants claimed that they had been victims of a violation of Article 8 ECHR. The Court rejected their first claim, based on the right to family life, under that Article. Since the third applicant, their daughter, was already an adult, the first two applicants could not claim the existence of family life.[48] Therefore, the Court turned to the analysis of the second argument under Article 8 ECHR: the right to private life.

Regarding the right to private life, the Court started by acknowledging that the main objective of Article 8 was the protection of the individual against arbitrary interference by the public authorities. However, this negative obligation also had another side of the coin, which under certain circumstances, might be a positive obligation. Or as the Court mentioned:

> In other words, it is not enough for the host State to refrain from deporting the person concerned; it must also, by means of positive measures if necessary,

[46] Case of *Sisojeva and others v. Latvia*, Application no. 60654/00, 16 June 2005.

[47] *Ibid.*, paragraph 54.

[48] *Ibid.*, paragraph 103.

> afford him or her the opportunity to exercise the rights in question without interference.[49]

And then the Court pointed out that:

> [T]he prolonged refusal of the Latvian authorities to grant the applicants the right to reside in Latvia on a permanent basis constitutes an interference with the exercise of their right to respect for their private life.[50]

The Court finally concluded that none of the possible legitimate aims of the second paragraph of Article 8 had been pursued. In fact the Court argued that:

> While it recognises the right of each State to take effective steps to ensure compliance with immigration laws, it considers that a measure of the kind imposed on the applicants could be considered to be proportionate only if the applicants had acted in a particularly dangerous manner.[51]

Consequently, the Court found that Latvia had violated Article 8 of the Convention.

The ruling opens an interesting path for those third-country nationals who, having resided for a long period of time in the EU, and not being a threat to public policy or public security, are denied the long-term residence permit. The ECtHR has however made it clear in *Mendizabal* that Article 8 does not grant the right to a particular residence permit (permanent, temporary or other).[52] Nevertheless, the right to be granted a long-term residence permit would come from Directive 2003/109 itself. Moreover, the ECtHR also recognized in the same case that not being granted a secure residence permit had several material and moral consequences such as the impossibility to obtain a permanent job or the risk of facing social and financial difficulties.[53] This is certainly the case when a third-country national does not obtain a long-term residence permit since the situation with a temporary permit is much more precarious with regards to, for example, access to employment or access to services such as procedures for obtaining housing.[54]

This is thus extremely relevant jurisprudence on the right to private life that the CJEU has to bear in mind when interpreting the integration conditions.

---

49 *Ibid.*, paragraph 104.

50 *Ibid.*, paragraph 105.

51 *Ibid.*, paragraph 108.

52 Affaire *Aristimuño Mendizabal c. France*, Requête no. 51431/99, 17 janvier 2006, paragraph 66.

53 *Ibid.*, paragraph 71.

54 See Article 11 Directive 2003/109.

3. *The CJEU's Ruling in* Chakroun

The 2010 CJEU's *Chakroun* judgment on Directive 2003/86 on the right to family reunification offers an excellent opportunity to recapitulate the grounds on which certain integration conditions imposed by some Member States may be in breach of the Directive. I will first explain the facts in *Chakroun* to, subsequently, look at four possible ways to challenge integration conditions: effectiveness, respect for fundamental rights, proportionality and non-discrimination.

Mr Chakroun was a Moroccan national who had resided in the Netherlands since 21 December 1970 and held an indefinite period residence permit. At the time of the ruling, he had been receiving unemployment benefits since 12 July 2005. Mrs Chakroun, also a Moroccan national, married Mr Chakroun in 1972. In 2006, she applied for a provisional residence permit to live with her husband. However, that permit was refused on the ground that her husband was not in receipt of sufficient income according to Dutch legislation, notably the 2000 Decree on Aliens law. Directive 2003/86 on the right to family reunification provides in Article 7(1)(c), as one of the conditions to be fulfilled, that the sponsor needs to have "stable and regular resources which are sufficient to maintain himself/herself and the members of his/her family, without recourse to the social assistance system of the Member State concerned". That clause was implemented in the Dutch legal order by Article 3.74 of the 2000 Decree on Aliens,[55] which basically provides that "the means of support…are sufficient if the net income is equal to…120% of the minimum wage" in the case of family formation.[56]

After a series of objections and appeals the matter arrived before the Raad van State, which referred two questions to the CJEU. It is important to look here at the first of those questions:

> Should the phrase "recourse to the social assistance system" in Article 7(1)(c) of the Directive be interpreted as permitting a Member State to make an arrangement in respect of family reunification which results in family reunification not being granted to a sponsor who has provided evidence of having stable and regular resources to meet general subsistence costs, but who, given the level of such resources, will nevertheless be entitled to claim special assistance to meet

[55] Decree on Aliens of 2000 (Vreemdelingenbesluit 2000; "the Vb 2000") as amended by Royal Decree of 29 September 2004 (Staatsblad 2004, p. 496).

[56] 120% of the minimum wage amounts to 1,441.44 euros per month, including holiday allowance, whereas Mr Chakroun's unemployment benefit was only 1,322.73 euros net per month, inclusive of holiday allowance.

> exceptional, individually determined, essential living costs, income-related remission of charges by municipal authorities, or income-support measures in the context of municipal income policies ["minimabeleid"]?[57]

The CJEU answered in the negative to this question. However, I am mostly interested in the argumentation put forward in order to arrive at that conclusion. Those arguments, as will be seen, sustain many of the findings present in this book with regard to how the CJEU might interpret the provisions of the Long-term Residence Directive, including the integration conditions. I will explain the Court's line of reasoning on this matter of family reunification and I will apply it by analogy to long-term residence. Underlying this is the key question which has already been posed by Pascouau: "Are integration measures geared towards an integration purpose or do they serve as a tool for the management of migration flows?"[58]

3.1. *Effectiveness*

The CJEU re-stated its commitment to enforce respect for the general principles of Union law. In the observations submitted by the parties, both Mrs Chakroun and the European Commission argued "that the discretion left to the Member States in implementing the Directive must not adversely affect its objectives or effectiveness".[59] The CJEU agreed by following a three-step argumentation, which could certainly be applicable in the case of the Long-term Residence Directive with regard to, for example, integration conditions. The first two steps refer to the principle of effectiveness:

What is the objective of the Directive?

The Court began by establishing the objective of the Directive, which is, according to Article 4(1), "to authorise family reunification of certain members of the sponsor's family, without being left a margin of appreciation". Similarly, the objective of the 2003/109 Directive is, according to Article 4, to grant a long-term residence permit to those third-country nationals who "have resided legally and continuously within its territory for five years immediately prior to the submission of the relevant application".

---

[57] Case C-578/08, *Rhimou Chakroun v Minister van Buitenlandse Zaken*, [2010], paragraph 31.

[58] Y. Pascouau (2010), "Integration Measures in France: An Evolving Process between Integration and Migration Issues", in R. van Oers, E. Ersbøll and D. Kostakopoulou (eds.), *A Re-definition of Belonging? Language and Integration Tests in Europe*, Martinus Nijhoff Publishers: Leiden, pp. 153–183, at 156.

[59] Case C-578/08, *Rhimou Chakroun v Minister van Buitenlandse Zaken*, [2010], paragraph 8.

What are the conditions?

The CJEU acknowledged that the objective of the Directive (to grant family reunification) was subject to compliance with certain conditions which are enumerated in Article 7. Likewise, granting a long-term residence permit is subject to compliance with certain conditions present in Article 5 of Directive 2003/109. Most importantly, the Court referred to these conditions in the following way:

> Since authorisation of family reunification is the general rule, the faculty provided for in Article 7(1)(c) of the Directive must be interpreted strictly. Furthermore, the margin for manoeuvre which the Member States are recognised as having must not be used by them in a manner which would undermine the objective of the Directive, which is to promote family reunification, and the effectiveness thereof.[60]

This line of reasoning is also certainly valid for Directive 2003/109. The general rule is granting a long-term residence permit to those third-country nationals who have regularly resided for a period of five years in a Member State. Hence, any condition has to be interpreted strictly in order not to run contrary to the objective of the Directive and its effectiveness. Any integration condition which might make it too cumbersome to obtain the long-term residence permit, undermining the objective of the Directive, might be challenged before a national court. Examples of this include various practices, such as the lack of availability of integration courses necessary to obtain long-term residence or excessive fees being charged in order to attend these courses as it is the case in Austria.[61] In fact, in 2009, the Commission sent a reasoned opinion to the Netherlands in which it stated that excessive fees levied in order to obtain a long-term residence permit ran contrary to the principle of effectiveness of the Directive. A Dutch Court ruled in the same direction after pointing out the Commission's reasoned opinion and the Commission finally brought the Netherlands before the Court of Justice on this issue.[62] This kind of practice might also raise proportionality issues.

3.2. *Respect for Fundamental Rights*

The Court continued its argumentation by referring to Recital 2 of the Preamble to the Directive on Family Reunification.[63] Recital 2 provides

---

60 *Ibid.*, paragraph 43.

61 See Chapter 7 above.

62 LJN: BJ3776, Rechtbank 's-Gravenhage, zittingsplaats Rotterdam, Awb 08/42722. See Action brought on 25 October 2010 - European Commission v Kingdom of the Netherlands (Case C-508/10).

63 The CJEU also mentions at a later point Recital 6 of the preamble, reinforcing once again the importance it gives them when interpreting a Directive.

that the Directive respects fundamental rights as enshrined particularly in Article 8 ECHR and in the Charter.[64] Therefore, the CJEU established that the provisions of the Directive, especially its conditions, must be interpreted in the light of fundamental rights.[65] In the same way, Recital 3 of Directive 2003/109 provides for the respect for fundamental rights and the principles recognised in the ECHR and in the Charter. Hence, there is no reason why the Court would not apply this same principle when interpreting the conditions in the Long-term Residence Directive. This is important, as has been previously analysed,[66] when looking at the right to private life enshrined in Article 8 ECHR. This could be certainly invoked in cases where a third-country national who has resided for a long period of time in a Member State (five years) is denied access to a long-term residence permit because of lack of compliance with integration conditions and threaten with expulsion as in the Austrian case.[67]

3.3. *Proportionality*

In *Chakroun,* the Court did not find it necessary to scrutinise whether the Dutch provisions were proportionate as it established that they ran contrary to the principle of effectiveness. As has been stressed, though, Member States have to pursue a legitimate objective. However, even when Member States pursue a genuine integration objective, which is non-discriminatory, they have to comply with the principle of proportionality. The devil is in the detail and among the practices which throw doubt on whether or not they respect the principle of proportionality, the following can be mentioned:

The level or difficulty of the content[68]
The test cannot be so difficult as to impede many third-country nationals from attaining the necessary level. Is the practice by some Member States, such as the Netherlands or Lithuania, of requiring the same test to become a citizen as to become a long-term resident proportionate?

---

64 Case C-578/08, *Rhimou Chakroun v Minister van Buitenlandse Zaken,* [2010], paragraph 44.
65 *Ibid.,* paragraph 44.
66 See above in this Chapter.
67 The Austrian Constitutional Court has already decided that after a period of residence of five years it would only allow deportation in exceptional cases due to Article 8 ECHR. See B. Perchinig (2010), "Country Report Austria", INTEC Project, Centre for Migration Law, Radboud University Nijmegen, p. 16.
68 S. Carrera and A. Wiesbrock (2009), "Civic Integration of Third-Country Nationals. Nationalism versus Europeanisation in the Common EU Immigration Policy", Centre for European Policy Studies, CEPS: Brussels, at 33.

The length of the preparation courses[69]
The courses should not be so lengthy as to impede the third-country national concerned from engaging in other activities such as working, looking after his/her family or others. Would the CJEU consider it to be proportionate to impose a condition by which a third-country national willing to obtain long-term residence has to undertake a 900- hour language course and a 45-hour civic education one, such as is the case in Germany?

The fees for the course
The courses or the final examination should not be so expensive as to impede some third-country nationals from attending or registering for them. Is asking between 1.500 and 2.500 Euros as in Austria, proportionate?

Fines
Fines for not attaining the level required in the contracts or for not passing the examinations do not seem to be in line with the integration rationale but denote a punitive perspective. Are fines proportionate?

Denial of the long-term residence permit[70]
As with fines, the denial of the residence permit shows the exclusionary perspective of some of these practices. Moreover, the possibility of expulsion, as in the Austrian case, is even clearer of a non-integrative perspective. Is the automatic denial of a long-term residence permit in case of non-fulfilment of the integration conditions, such as is the case in France, Germany and the Netherlands, or expulsion, such as in Austria, proportionate?

The mandatory nature of the tests[71]
Is it really suitable in order to facilitate the acquisition of the long-term residence permit by third-country nationals to impose mandatory tests? Would it not be more in line with the principle of proportionality that Member States could impose mandatory courses (with a reasonable price, length and content), which would be sufficient in order to be granted long-term residence?

The Court will certainly look individually at the practices in each of the Member States. The message is, however, clear: any single element which is

[69] *Ibid.*, p. 33.
[70] *Ibid.*, p. 33.
[71] *Ibid.*, p. 33.

not proportionate might be subject to review by the CJEU in order to confront it with the principle of proportionality.

3.4. *Non-discrimination*

In *Chakroun,* Advocate General Sharpston referred to the principle of non-discrimination.[72] She specifically referred to Recital 5 of the Directive, which is the same for Directive 2003/109, and reads as follows:

> Member States should give effect to the provisions of this Directive without discrimination on the basis of sex, race, colour, ethnic or social origin, genetic characteristics, language, religion or beliefs, political or other opinions, membership of a national minority, fortune, birth, disabilities, age or sexual orientation.

That allowed her to conclude that, in order to respect the principle of non-discrimination, legislation such as the one in the Netherlands should be precluded.[73]

This argument has already been raised by some authors with regard to the practice, mentioned above,[74] by which the Netherlands and Germany do not require family members of certain nationalities to comply with integration conditions. This would raise questions about their compatibility with Articles 14 ECHR and 18 TFEU.[75]

A similar reasoning is put forward by other authors regarding the French integration contract (which has to be fulfilled in order to obtain long-term residence) from which those third-country nationals whose residence permit mentions competences and skills are exempted.[76] Would such practices be in line with the principle of non-discrimination or would they be indirect discrimination on grounds of nationality or social origin? Could the integration and language tests be considered indirectly discriminatory as applicants from

---

[72] Opinion of Advocate General Sharpston delivered on 10 December 2009, paragraph 40.

[73] *Ibid.*, paragraph 43.

[74] See above Chapter 7.

[75] E. Guild, K. Groenendijk and S. Carrera (2009), "Understanding the Contest of Community: Illiberal Practices in the EU?", in E. Guild, K. Groenendijk and S. Carrera (eds.) *Illiberal Liberal States. Immigration, Citizenship and Integration in the EU,* Ashgate: Surrey, pp. 1–25, at 10; K. Groenendijk (2006), "Citizens and Third Country Nationals: Differential Treatment or Discrimination?", in J.Y. Carlier, E. Guild & B. Coulie (eds.), *The Future of Free Movement of Persons in the EU,* Collection du Centre des Droits de L'Homme de l'Université Catholique de Louvain, Bruylant, Brussels, pp 79–101, at 84–86.

[76] S. Carrera and A. Wiesbrock (2009), "Civic Integration of Third-Country Nationals. Nationalism versus Europeanisation in the Common EU Immigration Policy", Centre for European Policy Studies, CEPS: Brussels, at 35.

a certain social background have more difficulty passing them, especially considering the tendency of increasingly requiring a higher threshold in order to successfully take them?[77] Would it be possible to argue that the Austrian practice of considering integrated those third-country nationals who earn a particular amount of money per year, as well as their family members, constitute direct discrimination on grounds of social origin?[78]

4. *Conclusion*

In this Chapter, I have looked at the way in which the CJEU could interpret the integration conditions. I will briefly summarise what the possible lessons that can be obtained from my previous analysis are. First, it has been made clear that integration is an optional clause which does not give Member States a blank cheque. In fact, the objective of such measures has to be to facilitate the integration of third-country nationals and have to respect the principles of effectiveness and proportionality, as well as fundamental rights. Second, as the Commission rightly pointed out in its report on the implementation of Directive 2003/86 on the right to family reunification,[79] "their admissibility under the Directive depends on whether they serve this purpose and whether they respect the principle of proportionality". The Commission went on by stating that:

> Their admissibility can be questioned on the basis of the accessibility of such courses or tests, how they are designed and/or organised (test materials, fees, venue, etc.), whether such measures or their impact serve purposes other than integration (e.g. high fees excluding low-income families).

The Commission clearly limits here the discretion that Member States have to impose integration without any interference from the Community. In fact, as Guild, Groenendijk and Carrera argue:

> By expressly inserting integration inside their provisions, the Member States have seen their discretional powers diminished when determining the content and

[77] A. Wiesbrock (2009), "Discrimination Instead of Integration? Integration Requirements for Immigrants in Denmark and Germany", in E. Guild, K. Groenendijk and S. Carrera (eds.), *Illiberal Liberal States. Immigration, Citizenship and Integration in the EU*, Ashgate: Surrey, pp. 299–314, at 312.

[78] See on the Austrian case Chapter 7 above. Other questions might be relevant. For example: How will the CJEU interpret Article 21 of the Charter of Fundamental Rights considering that it became legally binding with the adoption of the Treaty of Lisbon?

[79] Commission Report, On the Application of Directive 2003/86/EC on the Right to Family Reunification, COM (2008) 610 final, 8.10.2008, pp. 7–8.

> reach of integration as an exceptional condition for having access to European rights and guarantees applicable to certain groups of TCNs. The inclusion of the category of integration inside the main body of the EU Directives creates a fundamental Community interest when assessing and monitoring the member states' application…in their respective domestic legal systems. It is also here where the force played by the general principles of EC law restricting Member States' discretion at times of national implementation comes sharply into focus once taken seriously by national lawyers and judges.[80]

Hence the Court has to assess on a case by case basis whether Member States are respecting the principles of proportionality and effectiveness in their transposition of the Directive. The European Commission also has the possibility to shed some light on the matter by pointing out what practices may not be in line with the Directive.

Member States have to pursue a legitimate objective when establishing integration conditions in order to acquire long-term residence in their national legislations. This has been made clear by the ruling in *Chakroun*. This judgment is extremely valuable as it confirms the positions defended in the previous Chapters with regard to how the Court will interpret Directive 2003/109. The central point is to see that the general rule is to grant a long-term residence permit to those third-country nationals who have regularly resided for a period of five years in a Member State. Any conditions to that general rule have to be interpreted strictly. Member States cannot impose any condition in a way which could hamper the final objective of the Directive and deprive it of its effectiveness. Any State practice has to comply not only with the principle of effectiveness, but also with the principles of respect for fundamental rights, proportionality and non-discrimination. Therefore, there appears to be several State practices which are not in line with these principles and which could be challenged before the national courts of Member States, which would probably have to refer a question to the CJEU. This is a useful perspective for lawyers and migrant organisations working in the national arena in those countries which impose integration conditions.

---

[80] E. Guild, K. Groenendkijk and S. Carrera (2009), "Understanding the Contest of Community: Illiberal Practices in the EU?" in E. Guild, K. Groenendijk and S. Carrera (eds.), *Illiberal Liberal States. Immigration, Citizenship and Integration in the EU*, Ashgate, pp. 1–25, at 5.

Section V

Conclusion

Chapter 10

Conclusion

1. *Is the European Union Constructing a "Legal Other"?*

This work has scrutinised to what extent the EU is constructing a "Legal Other" through its immigration law. It has assessed the implementation and possible interpretation by the CJEU of the Long-term Residence Directive in order to conclude that long-term residence status has the potential to become a subsidiary form of EU citizenship which escapes direct control by Member States. Hence, this Directive brings the prospect of transforming Member States' control over the relationship between territory and population.

While some Member States seem to be willing to reduce as much as possible the number of third-country nationals obtaining long-term residence, as well as the rights which are associated with that status, I have defended that a purposive interpretation by the CJEU will mean that long-term residents will obtain similar treatment to European citizens in a number of areas in line with the Tampere objective, re-affirmed in the Stockholm programme, of equal treatment.

Immigration is at the centre of the political debates of most EU Member States. With 20 million third-country nationals, out of a population of 500 million, it is crucial to see the way in which the EU deals with the legal status of these "new Europeans". In fact, as the European Commission has repeatedly mentioned, immigration, far from stopping, will continue to grow in future decades due to Europe's own needs. Thus, the purpose of this study has been to see how the EU treats those third-country nationals who have regularly resided for a period of, at least, five years within its territory. In other words, it has looked at the understanding by the EU of the legal integration of third-country nationals. The EU, it is worth highlighting once again, has been understood as an amalgam of actors (Commission, Parliament, Council, CJEU and European Council) with different interests and visions.

This book has examined certain aspects of the most important piece of legislation in the area of immigration that the EU has adopted since it obtained a clear-cut competence to regulate these matters with the Amsterdam Treaty in 1999. The Long-term Residence Directive grants third-country nationals equal rights in a number of areas, secure residence status as well as the possibility to move into, and reside in, another Member State. The analysis of the Directive has served to determine whether the EU is constructing a new "Legal Other" through its implementation and interpretation, or whether, on the contrary, this instrument is bridging the gap between the rights of European citizens and those of third-country nationals. By "Legal Other", I have meant those third-country nationals who do not have an independent right of entry to work in the EU.

I have arrived at the conclusion that the Long-term Residence Directive has the potential to become a subsidiary form of EU citizenship which escapes direct control by Member States. The fulfilment of that potentiality depends, however, on the way in which Member States have implemented the Directive with its numerous optional clauses and, ultimately, on how the CJEU will interpret the most controversial provisions in that implementation.

In order to assess this issue, I have used a comparative research method to investigate the content of the Directive and the way in which Member States have implemented four key provisions. These four central Articles establish who can acquire long-term residence status (Article 3), what the security of residence is once the status is granted (Article 12), what the possibilities to move into, and reside in, a second Member State in order to perform an economic activity are (Article 14) and, most importantly, what are the conditions that have to be fulfilled before obtaining a long-term residence permit (Article 5). I have then also used a comparative method to explore how the CJEU could interpret the Directive, taking into account similarities that could be drawn from its previous jurisprudence on Turkish workers, European citizens and on other immigration Directives.

In Chapter 4, Article 3, which defines the scope of the Directive, was examined. I gave special attention to the clause by which long-term residence may not be granted to those third-country nationals whose "residence permit has been formally limited". This clause, which was not present in the Commission's proposal and which is not applicable to European citizens, was criticised by various scholars. While looking at the implementation of the clause, two main problems arose: The first one was the practice by some Member States, e.g. Austria, of excluding at the outset whole categories of third-country nationals from qualifying to apply for the long-term residence permit. The second one concerned the position in some Member States, e.g. Cyprus, of those third-country nationals with consecutive limited and non-renewable permits who, nonetheless, fulfilled the requirement of five years' residence. A thorough review of the CJEU's case law on Turkish workers revealed how the Court would probably interpret that any third-country national who had regularly resided in a Member State for five years would be within the scope of the Directive and, therefore, entitled to apply for a long-term residence permit.

This was regardless of whether the third-country national was working in temporary employment, or whether the residence permit was for a limited period and non-renewable. Most Member States seemed to correctly interpret this provision in their national legal orders. The Commission has certainly, nonetheless, the possibility to point out problems in the transposition by bringing enforcement procedures against any Member State, such as Austria or Cyprus, which it considers to be in breach of its obligations under the Directive.

In Chapter 5, Article 12, which establishes the security of residence that long-term residents enjoy, was analysed. I paid particular attention to the scrutiny of the differences in the wording of Directive 2003/109 and Directive 2004/38 on European citizens. I showed how the wording of the provision establishing security of residence for long-term residents and the analogous one for European citizens was almost identical. I mentioned, however, the key divergences in both tests. The fundamental question was to see how the CJEU could interpret these slightly different provisions. It was defended that the Court would probably interpret that long-term residents enjoyed the same level of protection against expulsion as European citizens. This conclusion was achieved after thoroughly analysing the CJEU's case law on Turkish workers since its key case of *Nazli*.

The reading of the remaining two Articles proved more complicated. With regard to Article 14, I scrutinised in Chapter 6 the difficulty in assessing to what extent status-holders are able to move to reside and work in another Member State. I considered the possible meaning and extent of what was understood by the application of national procedures by Member States. I concluded that the CJEU would most likely apply the effectiveness and proportionality tests to this provision, which as an exception to the rule, had to be interpreted narrowly. It would also look at the scope and objectives of the Directive and to the fact that the preamble referred to the Union's employment market. Hence, if a long-term resident in one Member State received a job offer in another Member State, and provided that there was no EU citizen or third-country national in the second Member State who could perform the job, the second Member State would not be able to apply any requirement which had not been included in the Directive (e.g. sickness insurance) as that would render the Directive meaningless and deprive it of all its effectiveness. Linked to the uncertainty of what was meant by national procedures, was the fact that the second Member State might ask the status-holder to comply with integration measures. In fact, it was acknowledged that the main "Achilles' heel" of the Directive was the possibility to subject third-country nationals to integration conditions before granting the long-term residence permit.

Integration conditions were examined in Section IV. In Chapter 7, I looked at their origins in citizenship legislation as well as the development of integration measures in the family reunification Directive. Later, it was assessed how several Member States had made use of the possibility to impose integration conditions before obtaining a long-term residence permit. Those Member States that employed that prerogative had done it with different levels of intensity. The analysis of the political motivations and debates that preceded the introduction of integration conditions was the subject of Chapter 8. Those debates allowed me to anticipate whether the objective of the integration conditions was legitimate or whether, on the contrary, its implementation would run contrary to general principles of Union law such as proportionality, effectiveness, respect for fundamental rights or non-discrimination. The conclusion was that the CJEU might mitigate the meaning of this unclear provision in its future interpretation of the Directive. This conclusion was clearly reinforced by the 2010 ruling in *Chakroun*, where the CJEU, while interpreting the Family Reunification Directive, clearly stated that any restriction to the general rule (family reunification) had to be interpreted strictly in order not to deprive the Directive of its effectiveness. That rationale is certainly applicable to the interpretation of long-term residence, as I made clear in Chapter 9.

2. *Policy Recommendations*

I propose a number of recommendations, substantiated in the conclusions provided in the different Chapters in Sections III and IV. These recommendations are mainly addressed to national courts and the CJEU, as well as to national practitioners who may have an opportunity to challenge some of the contentious national practices before the national Courts. They are also of interest for the European Commission which may bring infringement proceedings against Member States. Finally, they are also important for the European Parliament as it has co-decision with the Council in the area.

2.1. *Eligibility*

It is submitted that:

- Member States should eliminate from their implementing legislations any exclusion of whole categories of third-country nationals at the outset from the scope of the Directive. Any third-country national who has regularly resided in a Member State for a period of five years and who has fulfilled the conditions in the Directive should be granted a long-term residence permit. The European Commission has to be attentive to the unilateral exclusion at the outset by some Member States of certain categories of third-country nationals who perform a particular profession from the scope of the Directive. In turn, the CJEU should interpret this in line with its previous jurisprudence on Turkish workers in cases such as *Ertanir*.

- Likewise, Member States should not exclude from the scope of the Directive third-country nationals who entered a Member State with non-renewable permits which were subsequently renewed to total a residence period of five years. It does not matter in that sense that the third-country national entered the Member State in order to work for a specific employer on a temporary basis. The fact that the third-country national was aware that his residence permit was non-renewable does not exclude the application of the Directive. Any third-country national who has regularly resided in a Member State for a period of five years, even if it was with consecutive non-renewable residence permits, should be included within the scope of the Directive. The CJEU should interpret this in line with its previous jurisprudence on Turkish workers in cases such as *Günaydin* or *Birden*. The European Commission could launch infringement proceedings against those Member States, such as Cyprus, which are in breach of the Directive.

2.2. *Security of Residence*

- The CJEU should interpret the provisions in Article 12 of the Directive regarding security of residence for long-term residents as it has previously done for European citizens and Turkish workers. The Court's previous case law with regard to Turkish workers since its decision in *Nazli* goes clearly in the direction of contributing to the coherence of Union law. Moreover, the Court has already taken the same position when interpreting the concept of public policy for Tunisian workers under the Euro-Mediterranean agreement in line with its previous case law on European citizens and Turkish workers. There is no doubt that the same interpretation could be applicable for Directive 2003/109.

2.3. *Possibility to Reside in a Second Member State*

- Member States should not impede the movement of long-term residents in the EU by imposing cumbersome procedures which go against the purpose of the Directive of contributing to the attainment of an internal market in which free movement of persons is ensured, as established in Recital 18.
- Those Member States which ask for a work permit even after the status-holder has worked in that second Member State for one year are in breach of the Directive. The European Commission could launch infringement proceedings in this respect.

- Member States should not impose integration conditions for status-holders who complied with those requirements when they obtained the long-term residence permit in the first Member State. These practices are in breach of the Directive and the European Commission could act accordingly.
- The CJEU should interpret Article 14 of the Directive as allowing Member States to apply their existing procedures regarding access to the labour market but not their requirements. The only requirements that can be imposed are those coming under the Directive itself. This will be in line with the previous jurisprudence of the Court on Turkish workers in cases such as *Kus*. Any other interpretation would render the Directive meaningless by depriving status-holders of the possibility to move to another Member State in order to exercise a paid activity. Hence, if a long-term resident in one Member State has a job offer in another Member State and, provided there is no EU citizen or third-country national in the second Member State who could perform the job, the second Member State may apply the same national procedures in order to grant that status-holder a job permit, as it would apply to a third-country national coming from outside the EU. However, the second Member State cannot apply any requirement which is not included in the Directive (e.g. sickness insurance) as that would render the Directive meaningless and deprive it of its effectiveness. Hence, Member States cannot deny granting the work permit to the status-holder on the basis of national requirements, but they are obliged to grant it if the conditions in the Directive are fulfilled.

2.4. *Integration Conditions*

- Those Member States who have used the possibility to impose integration conditions should not do it as a way to further restrict their immigration policy. A restrictive immigration policy is not a legitimate objective under the Directive and should not be used to limit migrants' rights under EU law. Moreover, Member States have to respect the general principles of Union law in their implementation of the integration conditions, especially effectiveness, proportionality, respect for fundamental rights and non-discrimination.
- The CJEU should follow its ruling in *Chakroun* in order to interpret the integration conditions in the Long-term Residence Directive. Since granting a long-term residence permit is the general rule, any condition has to be interpreted strictly in order not to deprive the Directive of its effectiveness. That effectiveness might be affected by some of the Member States'

practices, such as not providing enough courses to prepare or charging excessive fees.

- The CJEU will also have to be attentive so that Member States' practices do not conflict with the respect for fundamental rights, notably with the right to family and private life enshrined in Article 8 ECHR.
- The CJEU and the national courts will also have to analyse if required the proportionality of some of the measures imposed in Member States. There are various practices, such as expulsion if an integration contract is not fulfilled, the mandatory nature of the tests or the length of the courses which could be challenged by national practitioners on the basis of proportionality.
- Finally, some of the Member States' practices might raise issues of non-discrimination. This seems possible, for example, in the cases of Germany or the Netherlands where family members of third-country nationals from certain nationalities are not required to pass an integration test abroad.
- The European Commission has the opportunity to analyse these controversial practices and launch infringement proceedings if necessary. National NGOs could help in the process of providing information for the Commission on these integration conditions.
- National practitioners should make use of the possibility opened by the Treaty of Lisbon by which all national courts may refer a question to the CJEU. These give them opportunities to challenge these practices at the national level and ask the Court to refer a question to the CJEU if there are interpretation issues.

2.5. *Implementation*

- Member States should not escape their obligations under the Directive by incorrectly implementing its provisions. Creating a more inclusive society by granting long-term residence to third-country nationals who have resided for a number of years in a Member State will be beneficial for the migrants themselves as well as for the host society.

References

Books and Articles

Acosta, D. (2011), "Directive 2003/109 on Long-term Residence for Third-Country Nationals: Possible Future Interpretation by the European Court of Justice" in C. Murphy and P. Green (eds.), *Law and Outsiders: Norms, Processes and Othering in the 21st Century*, Hart: Oxford, pp. 143–165.

Acosta, D. (2010), "Migration and Borders in the European Union: The Implementation of the Returns Directive on Irregular Migrants in Spain and Italy", in E. Zapata (ed.), *Shaping the Normative Contours of the European Union: a Migration-Border Framework*, CIDOB Foundation: Barcelona, pp. 81–95.

Acosta Arcarazo, D. (2010), "La Nueva Ley de Inmigración en España. Un Primer Análisis de sus Aspectos Liberales y Restrictivos" in J. Roy and R. Domínguez (eds.), *España, la Unión Europea y la Integración Latinoamericana*, Florida European Union Centre/Jean Monnet Chair: Miami, pp. 51–61.

Acosta, D. (2010), "A Belief in the Purity of the Nation: The Possible Dangers of its Influence on Migration Legislation in Europe", *Studies in Ethnicity and Nationalism*, Vol. 10(2), pp. 234–254.

Acosta, D. (2009), "Immigration in the European Union: Family Reunification after the Metock Case", *UCD Law Review*, Vol. 9, pp. 64–88.

Acosta Arcarazo, D. (2009), "Latin American Reactions to the Adoption of the Returns Directive", Centre for European Policy Studies, CEPS: Brussels, 13 November 2009.

Acosta, D. (2009), "The Good, the Bad and the Ugly in EU Migration Law: Is the European Parliament Becoming Bad and Ugly (The Adoption of Directive 2008/115: The Returns Directive)", *European Journal of Migration and Law*, Vol. 11(1), pp. 19–39.

Adam, C. and A. Devillard (2008), *Comparative Study of the Laws in the 27 EU Member States for Legal Immigration*, IOM: Brussels.

Adamo, S. (2008), "Northern Exposure: The New Danish Model of Citizenship Test", *International Journal on Multicultural Societies (IJMS)*, Vol. 10, pp. 10–28.

Albertazzi, D. and D. McDonell (2005), "The Lega Nord in the Second Berlusconi Government: In a League of its Own", *West European Politics*, Vol. 28 (5), pp. 952–972.

Alexander, W. (1992), "Free Movement of Non-EC Nationals. A Review of the Case-Law of the Court of Justice", *European Journal of International Law*, Vol. 3(1), pp 53–64.

Alter, K.J. (1998), "Who are the 'Masters of the Treaty'? European Governments and the European Court of Justice", *International Organization*, Vol. 52, pp. 121–147.

Anderson, B. (1991), *Imagined Communities. Reflections on the Origin and Spread of Nationalism*, Verso: London, New York.

Apap, J. (2002), *The Rights of Immigrant Workers in the European Union*, Kluwer Law International: The Hague.

Apap, J. (2002), "Shaping Europe's Migration Policy. New Regimes for the Employment of Third Country Nationals: A Comparison of Strategies in Germany, Sweden, the Netherlands and the UK", *European Journal of Migration and Law*, Vol. 4 (3), pp. 309–328.

Arnull, A. (1990), *The General Principles of EEC Law and the Individual*, Leicester University Press: Leicester.

Avci, G. (1999), "Immigrant Categories: The Many Sides of the Coin?", *European Journal of Migration and Law*, Vol. 1 (2), pp. 199–213.

Baldaccini, A. (2009), "The Return and Removal of Irregular Migrants under EU Law: An Analysis of the Returns Directive", *European Journal of Migration and Law*, Vol. 11(1), pp 1–17.

Baldwin-Edwards, M. and A. Kraler (eds.) (2009), *REGINE. Regularisations in Europe*, Pallas Publications: Amsterdam.

Balzacq, T. and S. Carrera (eds.) (2006), *Security versus Freedom: A Challenge for Europe's Future?*, Ashgate Publishing: Hampshire.

Balzacq, T. and S. Carrera (2005), *Migration, Borders and Asylum. Trends and Vulnerabilities in EU Policy*, CEPS: Brussels.

Bauböck, R, B. Perchinig and W. Sievers (eds.) (2009), *Citizenship Policies in the New Europe*, Amsterdam University Press: Amsterdam.

Bauböck, R, E. Ersbøll, K. Groenendijk and H. Waldrauch (2006), *Acquisition and Loss of Nationality/ Volumes 1 and 2 Policies and Trends in 15 European Countries*, Amsterdam University Press: Amsterdam.

Bell, M. (2007), "Civic Citizenship and Migrant Integration", *European Public Law*, Vol. 13(2), pp. 311–333.

Bernitz, U. and J. Nergelius (2000), *General Principles of European Community Law*, Kluwer Law International: The Hague.

Besselink, L. (2009) "Integration and Immigration – The Vicissitudes of Dutch 'Inburgering" in K. Groenendijk, S. Carrera and E. Guild (eds.), *Illiberal Liberal States: Immigration, Citizenship and Integration in the EU*, Ashgate: Surrey, pp. 241–258.

Besselink, L. (2006), "Unequal Citizenship: Integration Measures and Equality", in S. Carrera (ed.), *The Nexus between Immigration, Integration and Citizenship in the EU*, CHALLENGE Collective Conference Volume, Centre for European Policy Studies, CEPS: Brussels, pp. 14–19.

Besselink, L. (2006), "Expulsion and Integration: Erecting Internal Borders within the Kingdom of the Netherlands", Challenge Liberty and Security, September 2006, *at* http://www.libertysecurity.org/article1096.html (accessed 01 December 2010).

Bicocchi, L. and M. Le Voy (2007), *Undocumented Migrants Have Rights! An Overview of the International Human Rights Framework*, PICUM: Brussels.

Blackledge, A. and S. Wright (2010), "Testing for Citizenship: Why tests and why now?", *Communicating European Citizenship*, 22 March 2010, Lancaster House, London.

Blake, N. QC and R. Husain (2003), *Immigration, Asylum and Human Rights*, Oxford University Press: Oxford.

Boelaert-Suominen, S. (2005), "Non-EU Nationals and Council Directive 2003/109/EC on the Status of Third-country Nationals who are Long-term Residents: Five Paces Forward and Possibly Three Paces Back", *Common Market Law Review*, Vol. 42(4), pp. 1011–1052.

Boeles, P. (2001), "Introduction: Freedom, Security and Justice for All" in E. Guild and C. Harlow (eds.), *Implementing Amsterdam. Immigration and Asylum Rights in EC Law*, Hart Publishing: Oxford, pp. 1–12.

Bonjour, S. (2010), "Between Integration Provision and Selection Mechanism. Party Politics, Judicial Constraints, and the Making of French and Dutch Policies of Civic Integration Abroad", *European Journal of Migration and Law*, Vol. 12(3), pp. 299–318.

Bruquetas-Callejo, M, B. Garcés-Mascareñas, R. Penninx and P. Scholten (2007), "Policymaking related to Immigration and Integration. The Dutch Case", *IMISCOE Working Paper 15: Country Report*.

Bulterman, M. (2008), *Common Market Law Review*, Vol. 45, pp. 245–259.

Cardwell, P. J. (2009), *EU External Relations and Systems of Governance. The CFSP, Euro-Mediterranean Partnership and Migration*, Routledge: Oxon.

Carrera, S. (2009), "Nationality, Immigration and 'the Republican Integration' in France", in K. Groenendijk, S. Carrera and E. Guild (eds.), *Illiberal Liberal States: Immigration, Citizenship and Integration in the EU*, Ashgate: Surrey, pp. 315–335.

Carrera, S. (2009), *In Search of the Perfect Citizen? The Intersection between Integration, Immigration and Nationality in the EU*, Martinus Nijhoff: Leiden/Boston.

Carrera, S. (2005), "What Does Free Movement Mean in Theory and Practice in an Enlarged EU?", *European Law Journal*, Vol. 11(6), pp. 699–721.

Carrera, S. (2005), "Integration as a Process of Inclusion for Migrants? The case of Long-term Residents in the EU", Centre for European Policy Studies CEPS: Brussels, Working Document, No. 219/March 2005.

Carrera, S. and A. Wiesbrock (2010), "Whose European Citizenship in the Stockholm Programme? The Enactment of Citizenship by Third Country Nationals in the EU", *European Journal of Migration and Law*, Vol. 12(3), pp. 337–359.

Carrera, S. and A. Wiesbrock (2009), "Civic Integration of Third-Country Nationals. Nationalism versus Europeanisation in the Common EU Immigration Policy", Centre for European Policy Studies, CEPS: Brussels.

Carrera, S. and F. Geyer (2007), "The Reform Treaty & Justice and Home Affairs. Implications for the Common Area of Freedom, Security & Justice", CEPS Policy Brief No. 141, Centre for European Policy Studies, CEPS: Brussels.

Castles, S. (2004), "Why Migration Policies Fail", *Ethnic and Racial Studies*, Vol. 27(2), pp. 205–227.

Castles, S. and M.J. Miller (2003), *The Age of Migration. International Population Movements in the Modern World*, MacMillan: Basingstoke.

Caviedes, A. (2004), "The Open Method of Coordination in Immigration Policy: A Tool for Prying Open Fortress Europe?", *Journal of European Public Policy*, Vol. 11(2), pp. 289–310.

Cornelius, W.A., P.L. Martin and J.F. Hollifield (eds.) (1994), *Controlling Immigration. A Global Perspective*, Stanford University Press: Stanford.

Costello, C. (2009), "*Metock*: Free Movement and 'Normal Family Life' in the Union", *Common Market Law Review*, Vol. 46 (2), pp. 587–622.

Craig, P. and G. de Búrca (2007), *EU Law. Text, Cases and Materials*, Oxford University Press: Oxford, fourth edition.

Currie, S. (2009), "Accelerated Justice or a Step too Far? Residence Rights of non-EU Family Members and the Court's Ruling in Metock", *European Law Review*, Vol. 34(2), pp. 310–326.

De Búrca, G. (1993), "The Principle of Proportionality and its Application in EC Law", *Yearbook of European Law*, Vol. 13, pp. 105–150.

De Búrca, G. and J.H.H. Weiler (2001), *The European Court of Justice*, Oxford University Press: Oxford.

Den Boer, M. and L. Corrado (1999), "For the Record or Off the Record: Comments about the Incorporation of Schengen into the EU", *European Journal of Migration and Law*, Vol.1 (4), p. 397–418.

De Bruycker, P. (2000) (ed.), *Regularisations of Illegal Immigrants in the European Union*, Bruylant: Brussels.

De Hart, B. (2006), "The Marriage of Convenience in European Immigration Law", *European Journal of Migration and Law*, Vol. 8(3), pp. 251–62.

Docquier, F. (2006), "Brain Drain and Inequality across Nations", FNRS, IRES, Université Catholique de Louvain and IZA Bonn, Discussion Paper No. 2440.

Ecotec Research and Consulting (2000), *Admission of Third Country Nationals for Paid Employment or Self-Employed Activity, Ecotec*: Brussels.

Ehlermann, C.D. (1998), "Differentiation, Flexibility, Closer Co-operation: The New Provisions of the Amsterdam Treaty", *European Law Journal*, Vol.4 (3), pp. 246–70.

Eicke, T. (1999), "The Third Country Agreements: The Right to Work and Reside in the First Generation Agreements", in E. Guild (ed.), *The Legal Framework and Social Consequences of Free Movement of Persons in the European Union*, Kluwer Law International: The Hague, pp 89–103.

Elkaïm, G. (2005), "Quelques Remarques du Point de Vue du Négociateur" in F. J. Laferriere, H. Labayle and O. Edström, *La Politique Européenne d'Immigration et d'Asile : Bilan Critique Cinq Ans après le Traité d'Amsterdam*, Bruylant : Bruxelles.

Ellis, E. (1999) (ed.), *The Principle of Proportionality in the Laws of Europe*, Hart Publishing: Oxford.

Emiliou, N. (1996), *The Principle of Proportionality in European Law. A Comparative Study*, Kluwer Law International: The Hague.

Ersbøll, E. (2010), "On Trial in Denmark", in R. van Oers, E. Ersbøll and D. Kostakopoulou (eds.), *A Re-definition of Belonging? Language and Integration Tests in Europe*, Martinus Nijhoff: Leiden, pp. 107–152.

Ersbøll, E. and L.K. Gravesen (2010), "Country Report Denmark", INTEC Project, Centre for Migration Law, Radboud University Nijmegen.

Farrell, H. and A. Héritier (2003), "The Invisible Transformation of Codecision: Problems of Democratic Legitimacy", Report No. 7, Swedish Institute for European Policy Studies (SIEPS): Stockholm.
Favell, A. and R. Hansen (2002), "Markets against Politics: Migration, EU Enlargement and the idea of Europe", *Journal of Ethnic and Migration Studies*, Vol. 28(4), pp. 581–601.
Foblets, M.C. (2009), "The Fragmented Development of EU Immigration and Integration Policy. Which Status for Third-Country Nationals in Europe?", in J. Wouters, L. Verhey, P. Kiiver et al., *European Constitutionalism beyond Lisbon*, Intersentia: Mortsel, pp. 81–109.
Foblets, M.C. and Z. Yanasmayan (2010), "Language and Integration Requirements in Belgium: Discordances Between the Flemish Policy of 'Inburgering' and the Federal Legislators' View(s) on the Integration of Newcomers and Migrants", in R. van Oers, E. Ersbøll and D. Kostakopoulou (eds.), *A Re-definition of Belonging? Language and Integration Tests in Europe*, Martinus Nijhoff: Leiden, pp. 271–306.
Fornerod, A. (2008), "La Langue Française en Droit de la Nationalité et en Droit des Étrangers", *R.F.D.A.*, November-December, p. 1097–1109.
Foster, N. (2006) *Foster on EU Law*, Oxford University Press: Oxford.
Geddes, A. (2000), *Immigration and European Integration. Towards Fortress Europe?*, Manchester University Press: Manchester.
Geddes, A. (1995), "Immigrant and Ethnic Minorities and the EU's 'Democratic Deficit'", *Journal of Common Market Studies*, Vol.33 (2), pp. 197–217.
Gellner, E. (1983), *Nations and Nationalism*, Basil Blackwell: Oxford.
Goedings, S.A.W. (2005), *Labour Migration in an Integrating Europe. National Migration Policies and the Free Movement of Workers, 1950–1968*, Sdu Uitgevers: The Hague.
González-Enríquez, C. and A. Triandafyllidou (2009), "Comparing the New Hosts of Southern Europe", *European Journal of Migration and Law*, Vol. 11(2), pp. 109–118.
Goodwin Gill, G. and J. Mc Adam (2007), *The Refugee in International Law*, Oxford University Press: Oxford, third edition.
Gower, M. (2010), "Immigration: spouses, civil partners and fiancé(e)s", House of Commons Library, Home Affairs Section, Standard Note: SN/HA/862.
Groenendijk, K. (2009), "Forty Years of Free Movement of Workers: Has it been a Success and Why?" in P. Minderhoud and N. Trimikliniotis (eds.) (2009), *Rethinking the Free Movement of Workers: The European Challenges Ahead*, Wolf Legal Publishers: Nijmegen, pp. 11–24.
Groenendijk, K. (2007), "The Long-Term Residents Directive, Denizenship and Integration", in A. Baldaccini, E. Guild and H. Toner (eds.), *Whose Freedom, Security and Justice? EU Immigration and Asylum Law and Policy*, Hart Publishing: Oxford, pp. 429–450.
Groenendijk, K. (2007), "Integration Tests Abroad as a Condition for Family Reunification in the EU?", Immigration Law Practitioner's Association (ILPA), European Update June 2007.
Groenendijk, K. (2006), "Family Reunification as a Right under Community Law", *European Journal of Migration and Law*, Vol. 8 (2), pp. 215–230.
Groenendijk, K. (2006), "Citizens and Third Country Nationals: Differential Treatment or Discrimination?", in J.Y. Carlier, E. Guild & B. Coulie (eds.), *The Future of Free Movement of Persons in the EU*, Collection du Centre des Droits de L'Homme de l'Université Catholique de Louvain, Bruylant, Brussels, pp 79–101.
Groenendijk, K. (2006), "The Legal Integration of Potential Citizens: Denizens in the EU in the Final Years before the Implementation of the 2003 Directive on Long-Term Resident Third Country Nationals" in R. Bauböck, E. Ersbøll, K. Groenendijk and H. Waldrauch (eds.), *Acquisition and Loss of Nationality. Policies and Trends in 15 European Countries*, Amsterdam University Press: Amsterdam, online version of Chapter 10 *at* http://www.imiscoe.org/natac/ , pp. 385–410.
Groenendijk, K. (2005), "Access of Third-Country Nationals to Employment under the New EC Migration Law", in F. Julien-Laferrière, H. Labayle and O. Edström (eds.), *The European Immigration and Asylum Policy: Critical Assessment Five Years after the Amsterdam Treaty*, Brussels: Bruylant, pp. 141–174.
Groenendijk, K. (2004), "Legal Concepts of Integration in EU Migration Law", *European Journal of Migration and Law*, Vol. 6 (2), pp. 111–126.

Groenendijk, K. (2001), "Security of Residence and Access to Free Movement for Settled Third-Country Nationals under Community law", in E. Guild and C. Harlow (eds.), *Implementing Amsterdam, Immigration and Asylum rights in EC Law*, Hart Publishing: Oxford/Portland, pp. 225–240.

Groenendijk, K. (2001), "Long-Term Immigrants and the Council of Europe", in E. Guild and P. Minderhoud (eds.), *Security of Residence and Expulsion. Protection of Aliens in Europe*, Kluwer Law International: The Hague/London, pp. 7–22.

Groenendijk, K. (1999), "Long-Term Immigrants and the Council of Europe", *European Journal of Migration and Law*, Vol. 1 (3), pp. 275–292.

Groenendijk K., R. Fernhout, D. van Dam, R. van Oers and T. Strik (2007), *The Family Reunification Directive in EU Member States. The First Year of Implementation,* Wolf Legal Publishers: Nijmegen.

Groenendijk, K. and E. Guild (2001), "Converging Criteria: Creating an Area of Security of Residence for Europe's Third Country Nationals", *European Journal of Migration and Law*, Vol. 3 (1), pp. 37–59.

Groenendijk, K. E. Guild and R. Barzilay (2000), *Study on the Legal Status of Third-Country Nationals who are Long-Term Residents in a Member State of the European Union, Centre for Migration Law*, Radboud University of Nijmegen, Nijmegen: The Netherlands.

Groenendijk, K, E. Guild and H. Dogan (1998), *Security of Residence of Long-term Migrants. A Comparative Study of Law and Practice in European Countries*, Council of Europe: Strasbourg.

Guèvremont, S. (2009), *Vers un Traitement Équitable des Étrangers Extracommunautaires en Séjour Régulier. Examen des Directives sur le Regroupement Familial et sur les Résidents de Longue Durée,* Wöhrmann Print Service : Zutphen.

Guibernau, M. (2007), *The Identity of Nations,* Polity Press: Cambridge.

Guild, E. (2009), "Free Movement of Workers: From Third Country National to Citizen of the Union" in P. Minderhoud and N. Trimikliniotis (eds.) (2009), *Rethinking the Free Movement of Workers: The European Challenges Ahead,* Wolf Legal Publishers: Nijmegen, pp. 25–38.

Guild, E. (2007), *EU Policy on Labour Migration. A First look at the Commission's Blue Card Initiative*, CEPS Policy Brief No. 145, Centre for European Policy Studies: Brussels.

Guild, E. (2007), "Citizens without a Constitution, Borders without a State: EU Free Movement of Persons" in A. Baldaccini, E. Guild and H. Toner (eds.) *Whose Freedom, Security and Justice?*, Hart Publishing: Oxford, pp. 25–55.

Guild, E. (2005), "Cultural and Identity Security. Immigrants and the Legal Expression of National Identity" in E. Guild and J. Van Selm (eds.) *International Migration and Security. Opportunities and Challenges*, Routledge: Oxon, pp. 101–112.

Guild, E. (2004), *The Legal elements of European Identity: EU citizenship and Migration Law,* Kluwer Law International, European Law Library: The Hague.

Guild, E. (2004), "Who is an Irregular Migrant?" in B. Bogusz, R. Cholewinski, A. Cygan and E. Szyszczak (eds.), *Irregular Migration and Human Rights: Theoretical, European and International Perspectives,* Martinus Nijhoff Publishers: Leiden/Boston, pp. 3–28.

Guild, E. (2004), "Citizens, Immigrants, Terrorists and Others", in A. Ward and S. Peers (eds.), *The European Charter of Fundamental Rights, Politics, Law and Policy*, Hart: Oxford, pp. 231–47.

Guild, E. (2001), *Immigration Law in the European Community,* Kluwer Law International: The Hague.

Guild, E. (2001), "Security of Residence and Expulsion of Foreigners: European Community Law" in E. Guild and P. Minderhoud (eds.), *Security of Residence and Expulsion: Protection of Aliens in Europe*, Kluwer Law International: The Hague/London/Boston, pp. 59–80.

Guild, E, K. Groenendijk and S. Carrera (2009), "Understanding the Contest of Community: Illiberal Practices in the EU?", in E. Guild, K. Groenendijk and S. Carrera (eds.) *Illiberal Liberal States. Immigration, Citizenship and Integration in the EU,* Ashgate: Surrey, pp. 1–25.

Guild, E. and S. Carrera (2008), "The French Presidency's European Pact on Immigration and Asylum: Intergovernmentalism vs Europeanisation? Security vs Rights?", Centre of European Policy Studies (CEPS), 11 September 2008.

Guild, E. and S. Peers (2001), "Deference or Defiance? The Court of Justice's Jurisdiction over Immigration and Asylum" in E. Guild and C. Harlow (eds.), *Implementing Amsterdam. Immigration and Asylum Rights in EC Law*, Hart Publishing: Oxford, pp. 267–290.

Guild, E. and J. Niessen (1996), *The Developing Immigration and Asylum Policies of the European Union. Adopted Conventions, Resolutions, Recommendations, Decisions and Conclusions*, Kluwer Law International, The Hague.

Gümüs, Y.K. (2010), "EU Blue Card Scheme: The Right Step in the Right Direction?" *European Journal of Migration and Law*, Vol. 12(4), pp. 435–454.

Gutmann, R. (1999), *Die Assoziationsfreizügigkeit türkischer Staatsangehöriger: Ihre Entdeckung und ihr Inhalt*, Nomos Verlagsgesellschaft: Baden-Baden.

Hailbronner, K. (2000), *Immigration and Asylum Law and Policy of the European Union*, Kluwer Law International: The Hague.

Hailbronner, K. (1998), "European Immigration and Asylum Law under the Amsterdam Treaty", *Common Market Law Review*, Vol. 35 (5), pp. 1047–1067.

Hailbronner, K. (1995), "Third-country Nationals and EC Law" in A. Rosas and E. Antola (eds.), *A citizens' Europe. In Search of a New Order*, Sage Publications: London/Thousand Oaks/New Delhi, pp. 182–206.

Halleskov, L. (2005), "The Long-term Residents Directive: A Fulfilment of the Tampere Objective of Near Equality?", *European Journal of Migration and Law*, Vol.7 (2), pp. 181–201.

Handoll, J. (2009), "The Metock Case. Union Citizenship, Family Reunion and the Abuse of Rights" in P. Minderhoud and N. Trimikliniotis (eds.) (2009), *Rethinking the Free Movement of Workers: The European Challenges Ahead*, Wolf Legal Publishers: Nijmegen, pp. 173–187.

Handoll, J. (2003), "The Status of Third-Country Nationals Residing on a Long-term Basis", in P. de Bruycker (ed.), *The Emergence of a European Immigration Policy*, Bruylant: Brussels, pp. 269–362.

Harris, N. (2002), *Thinking the Unthinkable, the Immigration Myth Exposed*, IB Tauris: London.

Hedemann-Robinson, M. (1999), "The Area of Freedom, Security and Justice with Regard to the UK, Ireland and Denmark: The Opt-in Opt-outs? Under the Treaty of Amsterdam" in D. O'Keeffe. and P. Twomey (eds.) *Legal issues of the Amsterdam Treaty*, Hart Publishing: Oxford, p. 289–302.

Hix, S. (2001), "Legislative Behaviour and Party Competition in the European Parliament: An Application of Nominate to the EU", *Journal of Common Market Studies*, Vol. 39(4), pp. 663–88.

Hobsbawm, E. (1990), *Nations and Nationalism since 1780,* Cambridge University Press: Cambridge.

Hofhansel, C. (2008) "Citizenship in Austria, Germany and Switzerland: Courts, Legislatures and Administrators", *International Migration Review*, Vol. 42 (1), pp. 163–192.

Hoogenboom, T. (1992), "Integration into Society and Free Movement of Non-EC Nationals", *European Journal of International Law*, Vol. 3 (1), pp. 36–52.

Howard, M. M. (2006) "Comparative Citizenship: An Agenda for Cross-National Research", *Perspectives on Politics*, Vol. 4 (3), pp. 443–455.

Human Rights Watch (2008), "The Netherlands: Discrimination in the Name of Integration. Migrants' Rights under the Integration Abroad Act", Briefing Paper Number 1 May 2008, *at* http://www.hrw.org/backgrounder/2008/netherlands0508/ (accessed 1 December 2010).

Iglesias Sánchez, S. (2009), "Free Movement of Third Country Nationals in the European Union? Main Features, Deficiencies and Challenges of the New Mobility Rights in the Area of Freedom, Security and Justice", *European Law Journal*, Vol. 15(6), pp. 791–805.

Iglesias Sánchez, S. (2009), "Free Movement as a Precondition for Integration of Third Country Nationals in the European Union", in K. Groenendijk, S. Carrera and E. Guild (eds.), *Illiberal Liberal States: Immigration, Citizenship and Integration in the EU*, Ashgate: Surrey, pp. 205–220.

Iglesias Sánchez, S. (2008), "La Aplicación Directa de la Directiva 2003/109/CE a los Nacionales de Terceros Estados que Acrediten Ser Titulares del Estatuto de los Residentes de Larga Duración en otros Estados Miembros de la UE", *Revista de Derecho Migratorio y Extranjería*, Vol. 19, pp. 81–98.

Iglicka, K, P. Kazmierkiewicz and A. Weinar (2005), "Poland" in J. Niessen, Y. Schibel and C. Thompson (eds.), *Current Immigration Debates in Europe: A Publication of the European Migration Dialogue*, Migration Policy Group: Brussels.

Immigration Law Practitioners' Association (ILPA) and S. Peers (2000), "The Amsterdam Proposals. The ILPA/MPG Proposed Directives on Immigration and Asylum", ILPA and Migration Policy Group: London/Brussels.

Ivarsflaten, E. (2008), "What Unites Right-Wing Populists in Western Europe?: Re-Examining Grievance Mobilization Models in Seven Successful Cases", *Comparative Political Studies*, Vol. 41 (1), pp. 3–23.

Jacobs, D. and A. Rea (2007), "The End of National Models? Integration Courses and Citizenship Trajectories in Europe", *Paper Prepared for the EUSA-Conference*, Montreal, 17–19 May 2007.

Jacobs, F.G. (1999), "Recent Developments in the Principle of Proportionality in European Community Law", in E. Ellis (ed.), *The Principle of Proportionality in the Laws of Europe*, Hart Publishing: Oxford, pp. 1–21.

Jacobs, F.G., R. White and C. Ovey (2010), *The European Convention on Human Rights*, Oxford University Press: Oxford, fifth edition.

Joppke, C. (2007), "Beyond National Models: Civic Integration Policies for Immigrants in Western Europe", *West European Politics*, Vol. 30 (1), pp. 1–22.

Joppke, C. (2004), "The Retreat of Multiculturalism in the Liberal State: Theory and Policy", *The British Journal of Sociology*, Vol. 55 (2), pp. 237–257.

Joppke, C. (2003), "Citizenship between de- and re-ethnicization", *European Journal of Sociology*, Vol. 44 (3), pp. 429–58.

Joppke, C. (1998), "Immigration Challenges the Nation-State", in C. Joppke (ed.), *Immigration in Western Europe and the United States*, Oxford University Press: Oxford, pp. 5–48.

Juss, S. (2005), "The Decline and Decay of European Refugee Policy", *Oxford Journal of Legal Studies*, Vol. 25 (4), 749–792.

Katseli, L.T, R.E.B. Lucas and T. Xenogiani (2006), "Effects of Migration on Sending Countries: What do We Know?" OECD Development Centre, Working Paper No. 250.

King, R, G. Lazaridis and C. Tsardanidis (2000), *Eldorado or Fortress Europe? Migration in Southern Europe*, Macmillan: Basingstoke.

Kiwan, D. (2008), "A Journey to Citizenship in the United Kingdom", *International Journal on Multicultural Societies,* Vol. 10, pp. 60–75.

Kocharov, A. (2008), "What Intra-Community Mobility for Third Country Workers?", *European Law Review*, Vol. 33(6), pp. 912–26.

König, K. and B. Perchinig (2005), "Austria", in J. Niessen *et al.* (eds.) *Current Immigration Debates in Europe*. Brussels: Migration Policy Group.

Kostakopoulou, D. (2010), "Introduction" in R. van Oers, E. Ersbøll and D. Kostakopoulou (eds.) *A Re-definition of Belonging? Language and Integration Tests in Europe*, Martinus Nijhoff: Leiden, pp. 1–24.

Kostakopoulou, D. (2010), "Matters of Control: Integration Tests, Naturalisation Reform and Probationary Citizenship in the United Kingdom", *Journal of Ethnic and Migration Studies*, Vol. 36 (5), pp. 829–846.

Kostakopoulou, D. (2002), "Long-term Resident Third-Country Nationals in the European Union: Normative Expectations and Institutional openings", *Journal of Ethnic and Migration Studies*, Vol. 28(3), pp. 443–462.

Kostakopoulou, D. (2002), "'Integrating' Non-EU Migrants in the European Union: Ambivalent Legacies and Mutating Paradigms", *Columbia Journal of European Law*, Vol. 8(2), pp. 181–201.

Kostakopoulou, D. (2001), *Citizenship, Identity and Immigration in the European Union. Between Past and Future,* Manchester University Press: Manchester.

Kovacheva, V. and D. Vogel (2009) "The Size of the Irregular Foreign Resident Population in the European Union in 2002, 2005 and 2008: Aggregated Estimates", *Hamburg Institute of International Economics*. Database on Irregular Migration. Working Paper No.4/2009.

Kruma, K. (2010), "Latvian Integration Policy: Lost in Translation", in R. van Oers, E. Ersbøll and D. Kostakopoulou (eds.), *A Re-definition of Belonging? Language and Integration Tests in Europe*, Martinus Nijhoff Publishers: Leiden, pp. 241–270.

Kruma, K. (2009), "Checks and Balances in Latvian Nationality Policies: National Agendas and International Frameworks", in R. Bauböck, B. Perchinig and W. Sievers (eds.) (2009), *Citizenship Policies in the New Europe*, Amsterdam University Press: Amsterdam, pp. 67–96.

Kruma, K. (2009), "Country Report: Latvia", *EUDO Citizenship Observatory*.

Kruma, K., I. Indans and L. Meijere (2008), "Enacting EU Citizenship in Latvia: the case of noncitizens", *ENACT, Enacting European Citizenship*.

Kyriakou, N. (2010), "National Judges and Supranational Laws on the Effective Application of the EC Law and the ECHR: The Case of Cyprus", June 10 2010, *at* SSRN: http://ssrn.com/abstract=1623560 (accessed 1 December 2010).

Labayle, H. (1997), "Le Traité d'Amsterdam: Un Espace de Liberté, de Securité et de Justice", *Revue Trimestrielle de Droit Européen*, Vol. 4, p. 813–881.

Lahav, G. (2004), *Immigration and Politics in the New Europe. Reinventing Borders*, Cambridge University Press: Cambridge.

Lahav, G. (1997), "Ideological and Party Constraints on Immigration Attitudes in Europe", *Journal of Common Market Studies*, Vol. 35(3), pp. 377–406.

Langrisch, S. (1998), "The Treaty of Amsterdam: Selected Highlights", *European Law Review*, Vol. 23(1), pp. 3–19.

Lanzieri, G. (2009), "Data in Focus", Eurostat: Brussels, *at* http://epp.eurostat.ec.europa.eu/cache/ITY_OFFPUB/KS-QA-09-047/EN/KS-QA-09-047-EN.PDF (accessed 1 December 2010).

Layton-Henry, Z. (1999), "Insiders and Outsiders in the European Union: The Search for a European Identity and Citizenship", in E. Guild (ed.), *The Legal Framework and Social Consequences of Free Movement of Persons in the European Union*, Kluwer Law International: The Hague, pp 49–58.

Le Voy, M. and N. Verbruggen (2005), *Ten Ways to Protect Undocumented Migrant Workers*, PICUM: Brussels.

Le Voy, M, N. Verbruggen and J. Wets (eds.) (2004), *Undocumented Migrant Workers in Europe*, PICUM: Brussels.

Lochak, D. (2005), "L'Intégration Alibi de la Précarisation", *Plein Droit* 59–60.

Loobuyck, P. and D. Jacobs (2006), "The Flemish Immigration Society: Political Challenges on Different Levels", in L. d'Haenens, M. Hooghe, D. Vanheule, H. Gezduci (eds.), *New Citizens, New Policies? Developments in Diversity Policy in Canada and Flanders*, Academia Press: Gent, pp. 105–118.

Martin, D. (2007), "Comments", *European Journal of Migration and Law*, Vol. 9 (1), pp. 141–157.

Mc Adam, J. (2007), *Complementary Protection in International Refugee Law*, Oxford University Press: Oxford.

McGauran, K. (2007), "Germany's Immigration Amendment Act of 2007: Achieving Integration of Foreigners?", *Journal of Immigration Asylum and Nationality Law*, Vol. 21(4), pp. 295–310.

Melis, B. (2001), *Negotiating Europe's Immigration Frontiers*, Kluwer Law International: The Hague.

Michalowski, I. (2010), "Integration Tests in Germany. A Communitarian Approach?" in R. van Oers, E. Ersbøll and D. Kostakopoulou (eds.) *A Re-definition of Belonging? Language and Integration Tests in Europe*, Martinus Nijhoff: Leiden, pp. 185–210.

Michalowski, I. (2009), "Liberal states – privatised integration policies?" in E. Guild, K. Groenendijk and S. Carrera (eds.), *Illiberal Liberal States. Immigration, Citizenship and Integration in the EU*, Ashgate: Surrey, pp. 259–276.

Michalowski, I. (2007), "Modelos de acogida en Alemania, Francia y los Países Bajos: diseño y efectividad de los programas de acogida e integración", in: Fundació CIDOB (ed.), *Políticas y Modelos de Acogida. Una Mirada Transatlántica: Canadá, Alemania, Francia y los Países Bajos*, Documentos CIDOB Migraciones 12 June 2007, pp. 67–92.

Michalowski, I. and A. Walter (2008), "Family Reunification between EC Law and National Integration Policy", in: Anita Böcker et al. (ed.), *Migration Law and Sociology of Law, Collected Essays in Honour of Kees Groenendijk*, Wolf Legal Publishers: Nijmegen, pp 103–120, at 111.

Monar, J. (2010), "The Institutional Balance after the Treaty of Lisbon", Global Jean Monnet/ECSA-World Conference, Brussels, 25–26 May 2010.

Monar, J. (1998), "Justice and Home Affairs in the Treaty of Amsterdam: Reform at the Price of Fragmentation", *European Law Review*, Vol. 23 (4), pp. 320–335.
Monar, J. (1995), "The European Parliament and Immigration Policy: its Positions and Possibilities of Control", in P.M. Twomey and G.D. Korella (eds.), *Towards a European Immigration Policy: Current Situation-Perspectives*, European Interuniversity Press: Brussels, pp. 123–137.
Mowbray, A. (2007), *Cases and Materials on the European Convention on Human Rights*, Oxford University Press: Oxford, second edition.
Mudde, C. (1999), "The Single-Issue Party Thesis: Extreme Right Parties and the Immigration Issue", *West European Politics*, Vol. 22(3), pp. 182–197.
Niessen, J. (2000), *The Management and Managers of Immigration*, Migration Policy Group: Brussels.
Niessen, J, T. Huddleston and L. Citron (2007) (in cooperation with A. Geddes and D. Jacobs), *Migrant Integration Policy Index*, British Council and Migration Policy Group: Brussels.
O'Keeffe, D. (1995), "The Emergence of a European Immigration Policy", *European Law Review*, Vol. 20(1), pp. 20–36.
Oliver, P. (1985), "Non-Community Nationals and the Treaty of Rome", *Yearbook of European Law*, Vol. 5, p. 57–92.
Oosterom-Staples, H. (2007), "The Family Reunification Directive: A Tool Preserving Member State Interest or Conducive to Family Unity?", in A. Baldaccini, E. Guild and H. Toner (eds.), *Whose Freedom, Security and Justice?*, Hart Publishing: Oxford/Portand, pp. 451–488.
Orgad, L. (2010), "Illiberal Liberalism Cultural Restrictions on Migration and Access to Citizenship in Europe", *The American Journal of Comparative Law*, Vol. 58 (1), pp. 53–106.
Özkirimli, U. (2005), *Contemporary Debates on Nationalism. A Critical Engagement*, Palgrave Mcmillan: New York.
Pajares, M. (1999), *La Inmigración en España*, Icaria: Barcelona.
Papagianni, G. (2006), *Institutional and Policy Dynamics of EU Migration Law*, Martinus Nijhoff Publishers: Leiden/Boston.
Pascouau, Y. (2010), "Integration Measures in France: An Evolving Process between Integration and Migration Issues", in R. van Oers, E. Ersbøll and D. Kostakopoulou (eds.), *A Re-definition of Belonging? Language and Integration Tests in Europe*, Martinus Nijhoff Publishers: Leiden, pp. 153–183.
Peers, S. (2010), "Extending EU Long-term Resident Status to Refugees and Persons with Subsidiary Protection Status", *Statewatch Analysis, at* http://www.statewatch.org/analyses/no-114-ltr.pdf
Peers, S. (2009), "Free Movement, Immigration Control and Constitutional Conflict", *European Constitutional Law Review*, Vol. 5 (2), pp. 173–196.
Peers, S. (2009), "The UK Proposals on EU Free Movement Law: an Attack on the Rule of Law and EU Fundamental Freedoms", *Statewatch Analysis, at* www.statewatch.org/analyses/no-72-eu-attack-on-fundamental-rights-08.pdf
Peers, S. (2007), "EU Reform Treaty: Analysis 1: Version 3 JHA Provisions", *Statewatch Analysis* 22 October 2007, *at* http://www.statewatch.org/news/2007/oct/eu-refrom-treaty-jha-anal-1-ver-3.pdf
Peers, S. (2004), "Implementing Equality? The Directive on Long Term Resident Third Country Nationals", *European Law Review*, Vol. 29(4), pp. 437–460.
Peers, S. (2004), "Family Reunion and Community Law", in N. Walker (ed.) *Europe's Area of Freedom, Security and Justice*, Oxford University Press: Oxford, pp. 143–197.
Peers, S. (2000), "The EC-Switzerland Agreement on Free Movement of Persons: Overview and Analysis", *European Journal of Migration and Law*, Vol. 2(2), pp. 127–142.
Peers, S. (1999), "Raising Minimum Standards or Racing to the Bottom? The Commission's Proposed Migration Convention", in E. Guild (ed.), *The Legal Framework and Social Consequences of Free Movement of Persons in the European Union*, Kluwer Law International: The Hague.
Peers, S. (1998), "Who's Judging the Watchmen? The Judicial System of the Area of Freedom Security and Justice", *Yearbook of European Law*, Vol. 18, pp. 337–413.
Peers, S. (1998), "Building Fortress Europe: The Development of EU Migration Law", *Common Market Law Review*, Vol. 35 (6), pp. 1235–1272.

Peers, S. and N. Rogers (2006), *EU Immigration and Asylum Law. Text and Commentary*, Martinus Nijhoff Publishers: Leiden/Boston.

Perchinig, B. (2010), "Country Report Austria", INTEC Project, Centre for Migration Law, Radboud University Nijmegen.

Perchinig, B. (2010), "All You Need to Know to Become an Austrian: Naturalisation Policy and Citizenship Testing in Austria" in R. van Oers, E. Ersbøll and D. Kostakopoulou (eds.) *A Re-definition of Belonging? Language and Integration Tests in Europe*, Martinus Nijhoff: Leiden, pp. 25–50.

Pérez de Nanclares, J.M. (2002), *La Inmigración y el Asilo en la Unión Europea. Hacia un Nuevo Espacio de Libertad, Seguridad y Justicia*, Editorial Colex: Madrid.

Portes, A. (2006), "Migration and Development: A conceptual review of the Evidence", The Centre for Migration and Development, Princeton University, CMD Working Paper # 06-07.

Poulain, M, N. Perrin and A. Singleton (2006), *THESIM: towards Harmonised European Statistics on International Migration*, Presses Universitaires de Louvain: Louvain.

Pratt, S. (2006), "Immigration, Integration and Citizenship: Latest Developments and the EU's Role" in S. Carrera (ed.), *The Nexus between Immigration, Integration and Citizenship in the EU*, CHALLENGE Collective Conference Volume, Centre for European Policy Studies, CEPS: Brussels, pp. 10–13.

Relaño Pastor, E. (2004), "¿Sancionar al Inmigrante o Proteger las Fronteras?: Un Análisis Críticos de la Ley de Extranjería 14/2003, de 20 de noviembre, y la Política de Inmigración Común de la Unión Europea", *Diario La Ley*, AÑO XXV. Número 6017, 13 de mayo de 2004, pp. 1–8.

Rogers, N. (2000), *A Practitioner's Guide to the EC-Turkey Association Agreement*, Kluwer Law International: The Hague.

Rogers, N. and R. Scannell (2005), *Free Movement of Persons in the Enlarged European Union*, Sweet and Maxwell: London.

Rollason, N. (2007), "Citizenship and the Expanding European Union: the Rights of New EU Nationals" in A. Baldaccini, E. Guild and H. Toner (eds.) *Whose Freedom, Security and Justice?*, Hart Publishing: Oxford, pp. 517–28.

Ross, M. (2006), "Effectiveness in the European Legal Order(s): Beyond Supremacy to Constitutional Proportionality?", *European Law Review*, Vol. 31(4), pp. 476–498.

Ryan, B. (2010), "Country Report United Kingdom", INTEC Project, Centre for Migration Law, Radboud University Nijmegen.

Ryan, B. (2009), "The Integration Agenda in British Migration Law", in E. Guild, K. Groenendijk, and S. Carrera (eds.) *Illiberal Liberal States. Immigration, Citizenship and Integration in the EU*, Ashgate: Surrey, pp. 277–298.

Ryan, B. (2008), "Integration Requirements: A New Model in Migration Law", *Journal of Immigration, Asylum and Nationality Law*, Vol. 22(4), pp. 303–316.

Ryan, B. (2007), "The EU and Labor Migration: Regulating Admission or Treatment?" in A. Baldaccini, E. Guild and H. Toner (eds.), *Whose Freedom, Security and Justice? EU Immigration and Asylum Law and Policy*, Hart Publishing: Oxford, pp. 489–515.

Schierup, C.U, P. Hansen and S. Castles (2006), *Migration, Citizenship and the European Welfare State. A European Dilemma*, Oxford University Press: Oxford.

Schnaper, D. (1994), *Community of Citizens. On the Modern Idea of Nationality*. Transaction Publishers: New Brunswick and London.

Schnaper, D. (1991), *La France de l'Intégration. Sociologie de la Nation en 1990*. Gallimard: Paris.

Schout, A. (1998), "The Presidency as a Juggler- Managing Conflicting Expectations", Eipascope, No 2, 1998, p. 2–10.

Schuster, L. and J. Solomos (2002), "Rights and Wrongs across European Borders: Migrants, Minorities and Citizenship", *Citizenship Studies*, Vol. 6(1), pp. 37–54.

Skordas, A. (2006), "Immigration and the Market: The Long Term Residence Directive", *Columbia Journal of European Law*, Vol. 13, pp. 201–229.

Staples, H. (1999), *The Legal Status of Third-country Nationals Resident in the European Union*, Kluwer Law International: The Hague.

Steiner, J. and L. Woods (2009), *EU Law,* Oxford University Press: Oxford (tenth edition).

Tallberg, J. (2003), "The Agenda-Shaping Powers of the EU Council Presidency", *Journal of European Public Policy,* Vol. 10(1), pp. 1–19.

Thym, D. (2008), "Respect for Private and Family Life under Article 8 ECHR in Immigration Cases: a Human Right to Regularize Illegal Stay?" *International and Comparative Law Quarterly,* Vol. 57(1), pp. 87–112.

Toth, J. (2010), "Ethnic Citizenship- Can it be Obtained and Tested?", in R. van Oers, E. Ersbøll and D. Kostakopoulou (eds.), *A Re-definition of Belonging? Language and Integration Tests in Europe*, Martinus Nijhoff Publishers: Leiden, pp. 211–240.

Tridimas, T. (2006), *The General Principles of EC Law*, Oxford University Press: Oxford, second edition.

Tridimas, T. (1999), "Proportionality in Community Law: Searching for the Appropriate Standard of Scrutiny", in in E. Ellis (ed.), *The Principle of Proportionality in the Laws of Europe*, Hart Publishing: Oxford, pp. 65–84.

Tridimas, T. (1996), "The Court of Justice and Judicial Activism", *European Law Review,* Vol. 21 (3), pp. 199–210.

Trimikliniotis, N. (2010), "Country Report: Cyprus", EUDO Citizenship Observatory, January 2010, revised April 2010.

Tryfonidou, A. (2009), "Family Reunification Rights of (Migrant) Union Citizens: Towards a More Liberal Approach", *European Law Journal*, Vol. 15(5), pp. 634–653.

Van Dijk, P. (2001), "Protection of 'Integrated' Aliens Against Expulsion under the European Convention on Human Rights", in E. Guild and P. Minderhoud (eds.), *Security of Residence and Expulsion: Protection of Aliens in Europe*, Kluwer Law International: The Hague, pp. 23–40.

Van Oers, R. (2010), "Citizenship Tests in the Netherlands, Germany and the UK", in R. van Oers, E. Ersbøll and D. Kostakopoulou (eds.). *A Re-definition of Belonging? Language and Integration Tests in Europe*, Martinus Nijhoff: Leiden, pp. 51–106.

Van Oers, R. (2008), "From Liberal to Restrictive Citizenship Policies: the Case of the Netherlands", *International Journal on Multicultural Societies (IJMS)*, Vol. 10, pp. 40–59.

Van Oers, R., E. Ersbøll and D. Kostakopoulou (2010), "Mapping the Redefinition of Belonging in Europe" in R. van Oers, E. Ersbøll and D. Kostakopoulou (eds.). *A Re-definition of Belonging? Language and Integration Tests in Europe*, Martinus Nijhoff: Leiden, pp. 307–332.

Van Simaeys, B. and J.Y. Carlier (1998) "Le Nouvel Espace de Liberté, de Securité et de Justice" in Y. Lejeune (ed.) *Le Traité d'Amsterdam-Espoirs et Déceptions*, Bruylant: Brussels, p. 227–285.

Vasileva, K. (2010), "Statistics in Focus", Eurostat, 45/2010.

Velluti, S. (2007), "What European Union Strategy for Integrating Migrants? The Role of OMC Soft Mechanisms in the Development of an EU Immigration Policy", *European Journal of Migration and Law,* Vol. 9(1), pp. 53–82.

Vermeulen, B.P. and K.M. de Vries (2008), "Citizenship in the Netherlands: Changing Policies and Concepts", *Canadian Diversity/Diversité Canadienne*, Vol. 6(4), pp. 86–90.

Wagner, E. (1998), "The Integration of Schengen into the Framework of the European Union" *Legal Issues of European Integration*, Vol. 25(2), p. 1–60.

Waldrauch, H. (2006) "Acquisition of Nationality" in R. Bauböck, *et al. Acquisition and Loss of Nationality. Policies and Trends in 15 European Countries*, Amsterdam University Press: Amsterdam, extensive online version of chapter 3, at http://www.imiscoe.org/natac/

Walter, A. (2008), *Reverse Discrimination and Family Reunification*, Wolf Legal Publishers: Nijmegen.

Weiler, J.H.H. (1992), "Thou Shalt Not Oppress a Stranger. On the Judicial Protection of the Human Rights of Non-EC Nationals- A Critique" *European Journal of International Law*, Vol. 3, pp 65–91.

Werner, F. (1965), "The Association Agreements of the European Communities: A Comparative Analysis", *International Organization*, Vol. 19(2), pp. 223–249.

Westin, C. (2006), "Sweden: Restrictive Immigration Policy and Multiculturalism", Migration Policy Institute, June 2006.

Wiesbrock, A. (2010), *Legal Migration to the European Union*, Martinus Nijhoff: Leiden.

Wiesbrock, A. (2009), "Discrimination Instead of Integration? Integration Requirements for Immigrants in Denmark and Germany", in E. Guild, K. Groenendijk and S. Carrera (eds.), *Illiberal Liberal States. Immigration, Citizenship and Integration in the EU*, Ashgate: Surrey, pp. 299–314.

Woltjer, A. (2005), "Free Movement of Persons in the European Union- the Evolutive Approach of the Court of Justice EC" in F. Stroink and E. van der Liden (eds.), *Judicial Lawmaking and Administrative Law*, Intersentia: Antwerpen/Oxford, pp. 81–96.

Wray, H. (2009), "The Points Based System: A Blunt Instrument? *Immigration, Asylum and Nationality Law*, Vol. 23(3), pp. 231–251.

Wright, S. (2008) "Citizenship Tests in Europe- Editorial Introduction", *International Journal on Multicultural Societies (IJMS)*, Vol. 10, pp. 1–9.

Ziegler, K.S. (2005), "Integrating Integration?", *European Journal of Migration and Law*, Vol. 7 (2), pp 119–122.

Table of Cases

Court of Justice of the European Union (http://curia.europa.eu)

Case 11/70, *Internationale Handelsgesellschaft mbH v Einfuhr- und Vorratsstelle für Getreide und Futtermittel*, [1970] ECR 1125.
Case 41/74, *Yvonne van Duyn v Home Office*, [1974] ECR 1337.
Case 67/74, *Carmelo Angelo Bosignore v. Oberstadtdirektor der Stadt Köln* [1975] ECR 00297.
Case 30/77, *Régina v Pierre Bouchereau*, [1977] ECR 01999.
Case 53/81, *D.M. Levin v Staatssecretaris van Justitie*, [1982] ECR 01035.
Cases 115, 116/81, *Rezguia Adoui and Dominique Cornuaille v Belgian State* [1982] ECR 01665.
Case 283/81, *CILFIT Srl v Ministero della* Sanità, [1982] ECR 3415.
Joined Cases 35 and 36/82, *Elestina Esselina Christina Morson v State of the Netherlands and Head of the Plaatselijke Politie within the meaning of the Vreemdelingenwet; Sweradjie Jhanjan v State of the Netherlands* [1982] ECR 3723.
Case 267/83, *Diatta v. Land Berlin* [1985] ECR 567.
Case 281, 283-5 & 287/85, *Germany and others v. Commission* [1987] ECR 3203.
Case 12/86, *Meryem Demirel v Stadt Schwäbisch Gmünd* [1987] ECR 1573.
Case 379/87, *Groener v Minister for Education* [1989] ECR 03967.
Case C-192/89, *S. Z. Sevince v Staatssecretaris van Justitie* [1990] ECR I-3461.
Case C-292/89 *R. v. Immigration Appeal Tribunal ex p. Antonissen* [1991] ECR I-745.
Case C-18/90, *Office national de l'emploi v Bahia Kziber* [1991] ECR I-199.
Case C-237/91, *Kazim Kus v Landeshauptstadt Wiesbaden* [1992] ECR I-06781.
Case C-355/93, *Hayriye Eroglu v Land Baden-Württemberg* [1994] ECR I-05113.
Case C-434/93, *Ahmet Bozkurt v Staatssecretaris van Justitie* [1995] ECR I-01475.
Case C-36/96 *Faik Günaydin v Freistaat Bayern* [1997] ECR I-05143.
Cases C-64/96 & 65/96, *Land Nordrhein-Westfalen v. Uecker and Jacquet v. Land Nordrhein-Westfalen* [1997] ECR I-3171.
Case C-98/96, *Kasim Ertanir v Land Hessen* [1997] ECR I-05179.
Case C-348/96, *Criminal proceedings against* Donatella *Calfa*, [1999] ECR I-11.
Case C-416/96, *Nour Eddline El-Yassini v Secretary of State for Home Deparment*, [1999] ECR I-01209.
Case C-1/97, *Mehmet Birden v Stadtgemeinde Bremen* [1998] ECR I-07747.
Case C-340/97 *Nazli v Stadt Nürnberg*, [2000] ECR I-00957.
Case C-413/99, *Baumbast and R v Secretary of State for the Home Department* [2002] ECR I-07091.
Case C-60/00, *Mary Carpenter v Secretary of State for the Home Department*, [2002] ECR I-6279.
Case C-162/00, *Land Nordrhein-Westfalen v Beata Pokrzeptowicz-Meyer* [2002] ECR I-01049.
Case C-171/01, *Wählergruppe "Gemeinsam Zajedno/Birlikte Alternative und Grüne GewerkschafterInnen/UG" and Bundesminister für Wirtschaft und Arbeit and Others*, ECR [2003] I-04301.
Case C-465/01, *Commission of the European Communities v Republic of Austria*, ECR [2004] I-08291.
Joined Cases C-482/01 and C-493/01, *Orfanopoulos and Oliveri v Land Baden-Württemberg*, [2004] ECR I-0000.
Case C-467/02, *Inan Cetinkaya v Land Baden-Württemberg*, [2004] ECR I-10895.
Case C-230/03, *Mehmet Sedef v Freie und Hansestadt Hamburg* [2006] ECR I-00157.
Case C-265/03 *Simutenkov v. Abogado del Estado, Real Federación Española de Fútbol and Ministerio Fiscal* [2005] ECR I-02579.
Case C-373/03, *Ceyhun Aydinli v Land Baden-Württemberg*, [2005] ECR I-06181.

Case C-383/03, *Ergül Dogan v Sicherheitsdirektion für das Bundesland Vorarlberg*, [2005] ECR I-06237.
Case C-540/03 *European Parliament v Council of the European Union* [2006] ECR I-5769.
Case C-212/04, *Konstantinos Adeneler and Others v Ellinikos Organismos Galaktos (ELOG)*, [2006] ECR I-06057.
Case C-97/05, *Mohamed Gattoussi v Stadt Rüsselsheim*, [2006] ECR I-11917.
Case C-291/05, Minister voor Vreemdelingenzaken en Integratie v R.N.G. Eind, [2007] ECR I-10719.
Case C-325/05, Ismail Derin v Landkreis Darmstadt-Dieburg, [2007] ECR I-06495.
Case C-422/05, *Commission of the European Communities v Kingdom of Belgium*, [2007] ECR I-04749.
Case C-242/06, *Minister voor Vreemdelingenzaken en Integratie v T. Sahin*, [2009] ECR I-08465.
Case C-294/06, *Ezgi Payir, Burhan Akyuz and Birol Ozturk v Secretary of State for the Home Department* [2008] ECR I-00203.
Case C-349/06, *Murat Polat v Stadt Rüsselsheim*, [2007] ECR I-08167.
Case C-59/07 *Commission v Spain*, [2007] ECR I-00161.
Case C-92/07, *European Commission v Kingdom of the Netherlands*, [2010].
Case C-127/08, *Blaise Baheten Metock and Others v Minister for Justice, Equality and Law Reform*, [2008] ECR I-06241.
Case C-578/08, *Rhimou Chakroun v Minister van Buitenlandse Zaken*, [2010].
Case C-145/09, *Land Baden-Württemberg v Panagiotis Tsakouridis*, [2010].
Reference for a preliminary ruling from the Raad Van State (Netherlands) lodged on 20 October 2010 – Staatssecretaris van Justitie v M. Singh (Case C-502/10).
Action brought on 25 October 2010 - European Commission v Kingdom of the Netherlands (Case C-508/10).

European Court of Human Rights (http://www.echr.coe.int)

Berrehab v. The Netherlands, no. 10730/84, 21 June 1988, Series A. 126/177.
Case of *Sisojeva and others v. Latvia*, Application no. 60654/00, 16 June 2005.
Affaire *Aristimuño Mendizabal c. France*, Requête no. 51431/99, 17 janvier 2006.
Üner v. the Netherlands [GC], no. 46410/99, 18 October 2006.

Legislative and Policy Acts

This Annex only refers to those legislative and policy acts that have been mentioned across the different Chapters.

EU Level

Adopted Legal Measures

Decision 2004/927/EC providing for certain areas covered by Title IV of Part Three of the Treaty establishing the European Community to be governed by the procedure set out in Article 251 of that Treaty, 22 December 2004, OJ L 396/45.

Decision relating to travel facilities for school pupils from third countries under the Maastricht Treaty, 94/795/JHA: Council Decision of 30 November 1994 on a joint action adopted by the Council on the basis of Article K.3.2.b of the Treaty on European Union concerning travel facilities for school pupils from third countries resident in a Member State, OJ 1994 L 327.

Directive 2009/50/EC of 25 May 2009 of the Council on the Conditions of Entry and Residence of Third-country Nationals for the Purposes of Highly Qualified Employment, OJ 2009 L 155/17, 18.6.2009.

Directive 2008/115/EC of the European Parliament and of the Council of 16 December 2008 on common standards and procedures in Member States for returning illegally staying third-country nationals, OJ 2008 L 348/98.

Directive 2005/71/EC of 12 October 2005 of the Council on a Specific Procedure for Admitting Third-country Nationals for the Purpose of Scientific Research, OJ 2005 L289/15, 3.11.2005.

Directive 2004/114/EC of 13 December 2004 of the Council on the Conditions of Admission of Third-country Nationals for the Purposes of Studies, Pupil Exchange, Unremunerated Training or Voluntary Service, OJ 2004 L375/12.

Directive 2004/38/EC of the European Parliament and of the Council of 29 April 2004 on the right of citizens of the Union and their family members to move and reside freely within the territory of the Member States, OJ 2004 L158/77.

Directive 2003/109/EC of 25 November 2003 of the Council concerning the Status of Third-country Nationals who are Long-term Residents, OJ 2004 L 16/44, 23.1.2004.

Directive 2003/86/EC of 22 September 2003 of the Council on the Right to Family Reunification, OJ 2003 L 251/12, 3.10.2003.

Directive 2001/40/EC of the Council of 28 May 2001 on the mutual recognition of decisions on the expulsion of third-country nationals, OJ 2001, L 149/34.

Directive 73/148 EEC of 21 May of 1973 on the abolition of restrictions of the movement and residence within the Community for nationals of Member States with regard to the establishment and the provision of services, OJ 1973 L 173/14.

Directive 68/360 EEC of 15 October of 1968 of the Council on the abolition of restrictions of movement and residence within the Community for workers of Member States and their families, OJ 1968 L 257.

Council Directive 64/221/EEC of 25 February 1964 on the co-ordination of special measures concerning the movement and residence of foreign nationals which are justified on grounds of public policy, public security or public health, OJ 056, 04.04.1964, P.0850–0857.

Regulation (EC) No. 862/2007 of the European Parliament and of the Council of 11 July 2007 on Community Statistics on Migration and International Protection and repealing Council Regulation (EEC) No. 311/76 on the Compilation of Statistics on Foreign Workers, OJ 2007 L 199/23.

Regulation (EC) No 562/2006 of the European Parliament and of the Council establishing a Community Code on the rules governing the movement of persons across borders (Schengen Borders Code), 15 March 2006, OJ 2006 L 105/1.
Regulation (EC) No 883/2004 of the European Parliament and of the Council of 29 April 2004 on the coordination of social security systems, OJ 2004 L 166.
Council Regulation (EC) No 859/2003 of 14 May 2003 extending the provisions of Regulation (EEC) No 1408/71 and Regulation (EEC) No 574/72 to nationals of third countries who are not already covered by those provisions solely on the ground of their nationality, OJ 2003 L 124.
Council Regulation (EC) No 539/2001 of 15 March 2001 listing the third countries whose nationals must be in possession of visas when crossing the external borders and those whose nationals are exempt from that requirement, OJ 2001 L 81/1.
Regulation No 1408/71 of the Council of 14 June 1971 on the application of social security schemes to employed persons, to self-employed persons and to members of their families moving within the Community, OJ 1971 L149.
Regulation (EEC) No. 1612/68 of the Council of 15 October 1968 on freedom of movement for workers within the Community, OJ 1968 L 257/2.
Regulation (EEC) No. 38/64 du Conseil du 25 mars 1964 relatif à la libre circulation des travailleurs à l'intérieur de la Communauté, OJ 1964 965/64.
Regulation (EEC) No. 15/61 relatif aux première s mesures pour la réalisation de la libre circulation des travailleurs à l'intérieur de la Communauté, OJ 1961 1073/61.

Initiatives

Proposal for a Directive of the European Parliament and of the Council on the conditions of entry and residence of third-country nationals for the purposes of seasonal employment, COM (2010) 379 final, Brussels, 13.7.2010.
Proposal for a Directive of the European Parliament and of the Council on conditions of entry and residence of third-country nationals in the framework of an intra-corporate transfer, COM (2010) 378 final, Brussels, 13.7.2010
Proposal for a Council Directive on a Single Application Procedure for a Single Permit for Third-country Nationals to Reside and Work in the Territory of a Member State and on a Common Set of Rights for Third-country Workers Legally Residing in a Member State, COM (2007) 638 final, Brussels, 23.10.2007.
Proposal for a Council Directive on the Conditions of Entry and Residence of Third-country Nationals for the Purposes of Highly Qualified Employment, COM (2007) 637 final, Brussels 23.10.2007.
Proposal for a Council Directive Amending Directive 2003/109/EC to Extend its Scope to Beneficiaries of International Protection, COM (2007) 298 final, Brussels, 6.6.2007.
Proposal for a Council Directive on the Conditions of Entry and Residence for the Purpose of Paid Employment and Self-Employment Activities, COM (2001) 0386 final, Brussels, 11.7.2001.
Proposal for a Council Directive concerning the status of third-country nationals who are long-term residents, COM (2001) 127 final, OJ 2001 C 240/79.
Commission proposal for a Convention on the admission of third-country nationals, 30 July 1997 OJ 1997 C 337/9.

Non Legally Binding Measures

European Commission

Commission Report, First Annual Report on Immigration and Asylum (2009), COM (2010) 214 final, 6.5.2010.

Commission Communication on Delivering an Area of Freedom, Security and Justice for Europe's Citizens: Action Plan Implementing the Stockholm Programme, COM (2010) 171 final, Brussels, 20 April 2010.
Commission Communication, Europe 2020, a Strategy for Smart, Sustainable and Inclusive Growth, COM (2010) 2020, 3.3.2010.
Commission Communication, on guidance for better transposition and application of Directive 2004/38/EC on the right of citizens of the Union and their family members to move and reside freely within the territory of the Member States, COM (2009) 313 final, 2.7.2009.
Commission Communication, An Area of Freedom, Security and Justice Serving the Citizen, COM (2009) 262 final, Brussels, 10.6.2009.
Commission Report, On the Application of Directive 2003/86/EC on the Right to Family Reunification, COM (2008) 610 final, 8.10.2008.
Commission Communication, A Common Immigration Policy for Europe : Principles, Actions and Tools, COM (2008) 359 final, 17.6.2008.
Commission Communication, Third Annual Report on Migration and Integration, COM (2007) 512 final, 11.9.2007.
Commission Communication, Circular Migration and Mobility Partnerships between the European Union and Third Countries, COM (2007) 248 final, 16.5.2007.
Commission Communication, Policy Plan on Legal Migration, COM (2005) 669 final, 21.12.2005.
Commission Communication, The Hague Programme: Ten Priorities for the next Five Years. The Partnership for European Renewal in the Field of Freedom, Security and Justice, COM (2005) 184 final, 10.5.2005.
Green Paper on an EU Approach to Managing Economic Migration, COM (2004) 811 final, 11.1.2005.
Commission Communication, First Annual Report on Migration and Integration, COM (2004) 508 final, 16.7.2004.
Commission Communication, Study on the Links between Legal and Illegal Migration, COM (2004) 412 final, 4.6.2004.
Commission Communication, Area of Freedom, Security and Justice: Assessment of the Tampere programme and Future Orientations, COM (2004) 401 final, 2.06.2004.
Commission Communication on Immigration, Integration and Employment, COM (2003) 336 final, 3.6.2003.
Commission Communication, on a Community Immigration Policy, COM (2000) 757 final, 22.11.2000.
Commission Decision of 8 July 1985 setting up a prior communication and consultation procedure on migration policies in relation to non-member countries, OJ 1985 L 217/25.
White Paper on the Completion of the Internal Market, COM (1985)310 final, 14.6.1985.
Commission Communication, Guidelines for a Community Policy on Migration, COM (1985) 48 final, Bulleting of the European Communities, Supplement 9/85, 7.3.1985.

Council of the EU

Council Resolution of 4 December 1997 on measures to be adopted on the combating of marriages of convenience, OJ 1997 C382/01.
Council Resolution of 4 March 1996 on the status of third-country nationals residing on a long-term basis in the territory of the Member States, OJ 1996 C 80/2.
Council Resolution of 20 June 1994 on Limitations of Admission of Third-country Nationals to the Territory of the Member States for Employment, OJ 1996 C 274/3.
Report of the Ministers of Immigration to the Council 3 December 1991.

Council/Presidency Conclusions

Council of the European Union, The Stockholm Programme: An Open and Secure Europe Serving and Protecting Citizens, 5731/10, Brussels, 3 March 2010.

European Council Conclusions, Brussels, 11 December 2009.
Council of the European Union, European Pact on Immigration and Asylum, 13440/08, Brussels 24 September 2008, adopted on 16 October.
Brussels European Council Conclusions 4/5 November 2004, 14292/1/04, Brussels, 8 December 2004.
Tampere European Council Conclusions, 15 and 16 October 1999.

European Parliament

Report on Strategies and Means for the Integration of Immigrants in the European Union, A6-0190/2006, 17 May 2006, Rapporteur: Stavros Lambrinidis.
Report on the Links between Legal and Illegal Migration and Integration of Migrants, A6/0136/2005, 3 May 2005, Rapporteur: Patrick Gaubert.
European Parliament Resolution on the Communication from the Commission on Immigration, Integration and Employment, OJ 2004 C92E/390.
Report on the Communication from the Commission on Immigration, Integration and Employment, A5-0445/2003, 1 December 2003, Rapporteur: Claude Moraes.
Report on the Commission Communication on an Open Method of Coordination for the Community immigration policy, COM (2001)387, A5-0224/2003, 16 June 2003, Rapporteur: Ana Terrón i Cusí.
Legislative resolution embodying Parliament's opinion on the proposal for a Council Act establishing the Convention on rules for the admission of third-country nationals to the Member States (COM(97)0387C4-0681/97 – 97/0227(CNS)), OJ 1999 C150/196.

Agreements between the Union and Other States

Decision of the Council and of the Commission of 17 November 2009 on the conclusion of a Partnership and Cooperation Agreement establishing a partnership between the European Communities and their Member States, of the one part, and the Republic of Tajikistan, of the other part; OJ 2009 L350/1.
Council and Commission Decision of 26 February 2009 concerning the conclusion of the Stabilisation and Association Agreement between the European Communities and their Member States, of the one part, and the Republic of Albania, of the other part, OJ 2009 L 107.
Stabilisation and Association Agreement between the European Communities and their Member States, of the one part, and Bosnia and Herzegovina, of the other part, signed 16 June 2008.
Stabilisation and Association Agreement between the European Communities and their Member States, of the one part, and Serbia, of the other part, signed 29 April 2008.
Stabilisation and Association Agreement between the European Communities and their Member States, of the one part, and Montenegro, of the other part, signed 15 October 2007, OJ 2010 L 108/3.
Euro-Mediterranean Agreement establishing an Association between the European Community and its Member States, of the one part, and the Republic of Lebanon, of the other part, OJ 2006 L143/2.
Euro-Mediterranean Agreement establishing an Association between the European Community and its Member States, of the one part, and the People's Democratic Republic of Algeria, of the other part, OJ 2005 L 265/2.
Stabilisation and Association Agreement between the European Communities and their Member States, of the one part, and the Republic of Croatia, of the other part, OJ 2005 L 26/3.
Euro-Mediterranean Agreement establishing an Association between the European Communities and their Member States, of the one part, and the Arab Republic of Egypt, of the other part, OJ 2004 L304/39.

Stabilisation and Association Agreement between the European Communities and their Member States, of the one part, and the former Yugoslav Republic of Macedonia, of the other part, OJ 2004 L 84/13.
Agreement establishing an association between the European Community and its Member States, of the one part, and the Republic of Chile, of the other part, OJ 2002 L352/3.
Euro-Mediterranean Agreement establishing an Association between the European Communities and their Member States, of the one part, and the Hashemite Kingdom of Jordan, of the other part, OJ 2002 L129/03.
Decision of the Council, and of the Commission as regards the agreement on Scientific and Technological cooperation of April 4 2002 on the conclusion of seven agreements with the Swiss Confederation, OJ 2002 L 114/1.
Euro-Mediterranean Agreement establishing an association between the European Communities and their Member States, of the one part, and the State of Israel, of the other part, OJ 2000 L 147/3.
Partnership Agreement between the members of the African, Caribbean and Pacific Group of States on the one part, and the European Community and its Member States, on the other part, signed in Cotonou on June 23, OJ 2000 L317/3.
Euro-Mediterranean Agreement establishing an association between the European Communities and their Member States, of the one part, and the Kingdom of Morocco, of the other part, OJ 2000 L 70/2.
Council and Commission Decision of 31 May 1999 on the conclusion of the Partnership and Cooperation Agreement between the European Communities and their Member States, of the one part, and the Republic of Azerbaijan, of the other part, OJ 1999 L 246 of 17.09.1999.
Council and Commission Decision of 31 May 1999 on the conclusion of the Partnership and Cooperation Agreement between the European Communities and their Member States, of the one part, and the Republic of Armenia, of the other part, OJ 1999 L 239 of 09.09.1999.
Council and Commission Decision of 31 May 1999 on the conclusion of the Partnership and Cooperation Agreement establishing a partnership between the European Communities and their Member States, of the one part, and the Republic of Uzbekistan, of the other part, OJ 1999 L 229 of 31.08.1999.
Council and Commission Decision of 31 May 1999 on the conclusion of the Partnership and Cooperation Agreement between the European Communities and their Member States, of the one part, and Georgia, of the other part, OJ L 205 of 04.08.1999.
Council and Commission Decision of 12 May 1999 on the conclusion of the Partnership and Cooperation Agreement between the European Communities and their Member States, of the one part, and the Kyrgyz Republic, of the other part, OJ 1999 L 196 of 28.07.1999.
Council and Commission Decision of 12 May 1999 on the conclusion of the Partnership and Cooperation Agreement between the European Communities and their Member States, of the one part, and the Republic of Kazakhstan, of the other part, OJ 1999 L 196 of 28.07.1999.
Euro-Mediterranean Agreement establishing an association between the European Communities and their Member States, of the one part, and the Republic of Tunisia, of the other part, OJ 1998 L97/2.
Council and Commission Decision of 28 May 1998 on the conclusion of the Partnership and Cooperation Agreement between the European Communities and their Member States, of the one part, and the Republic of Moldova, of the other part, OJ 1998 L 181 of 24.06.1998.
Council and Commission Decision of 26 January 1998 on the conclusion of the Partnership and Cooperation Agreement between the European Communities and their Member States, of the one part, and Ukraine, of the other part, OJ 1998 L 049 of 19.02.1998.
Council and Commission Decision of 30 October 1997 on the conclusion of the Partnership and Cooperation Agreement between the European Communities and their Member States, of the one part, and the Russian Federation, of the other part, OJ 1997 L 327 of 28.11.1997.
European Economic Area Agreement signed in Porto on 2 May 1992, OJ 1994 L1.
Council Regulation (EEC-Algeria) No 2210/78 of 27/9/78, OJ 1978 L 263.

Council Regulation (EEC-Morocco) No 2211/78 of 27/9/78, OJ 1978 L 264.
Council Regulation (EEC-Tunisia) No 2212/78 of 27/9/78, OJ 1978 L 265.
Additional Protocol and Financial Protocol signed on 23 November 1970, annexed to the Agreement establishing the Association between the European Economic Community and Turkey and on measures to be taken for their entry into force - Final Act – Declarations Signed on 23 November 1970, OJ 1972 L 293/4.
64/732/EEC: Council Decision of 23 December 1963 on the conclusion of the Agreement establishing an Association between the European Economic Community and Turkey, OJ 1964 217/3685.

National Level

Four Case Studies

Spain: Legislation

Ley Orgánica 2/2009, de 11 de diciembre, de reforma de la Ley Orgánica 4/2000, de 11 de enero, sobre derechos y libertades de los extranjeros en España y su integración social, BOE 12 diciembre de 2009.
Instrucción DGI/SGJR/04/2009, Spanish Ministry of Labour and Immigration.
Instrucción DGI/SGRJ/04/2008, Spanish Ministry of Labour and Social Affairs.
Real Decreto 240/2007, de 16 de febrero, sobre entrada, libre circulación y residencia en España de ciudadanos de los estados miembros de la Unión Europea y de otros estados parte en el acuerdo sobre el espacio económico europeo, (BOE núm. 51, de 28 de febrero), en su redacción dada por el Real Decreto 1161/2009, de 10 julio (BOE núm. 177, de 23 de julio).
'Convenio entre el Reino de España, la República Francesa y el Principado de Andorra, relativo a la entrada, circulación, residencia y establecimiento de sus nacionales' hecho "ad referendum" en Bruselas el de diciembre de 2002 (BOE núm 153, de 27 de junio de 2003).

Spain: Other Relevant Documents

Ministerio de Trabajo e Inmigración (2010), *Extranjeros con Certificado de Registro o Tarjeta de Residencia en Vigor y Extranjeros con Autorización de Estancia por Estudios en Vigor a 31 de Diciembre de 2009*, Ministerio de Trabajo e Inmigración: Madrid.
Sentencia 117/07 del Juzgado Contencioso administrativo número 3 de Santander, 26 abril 2007.

Italy: Legislation

Circolare n. 7589 del 16 novembre 2010 Ministero dell'Interno.
Decreto 4 giugno 2010 Modalita di svolgimento del test di conoscenza della lingua italiana, previsto dall'articolo 9 del decreto legislativo 25 luglio 1998, n. 286, introdotto dall'articolo 1, comma 22, lettera i) della legge n. 94/2009. (10A07303) (GU n. 134 del 11-6-2010).
Legge 15 luglio 2009, n. 94, Disposizioni in materia di sicurezza pubblica. (09G0096), Gazzetta Ufficiale n. 170 del 24-7-2009.
Decreto legislativo 8 gennaio 2007, n.3 Attuazione della direttiva 2003/109/CE relativa allo status di cittadini di Paesi terzi soggiornanti di lungo periodo, Gazzetta Ufficiale N. 24 del 30 Gennaio 2007.
Decreto Legilslativo 25 luglio 1998, n. 286, Testo unico delle disposizioni concernenti la disciplina dell'immigrazione e norme sulla condizione dello straniero.
(Supplemento ordinario n.139 alla Gazzetta Ufficiale n.191 del 18.08.1998).

Italy: Other Relevant Documents

ISTAT (2010), *Italia in Cifre 2010*, Istituto Nazionale di Statistica: Roma.

Sweden: Legislation

Aliens Act (2005:716) Issued: 29 September 2005, with amendments: up to and including Swedish Code of Statutes 2009:16.

Sweden: Other Relevant Documents

Statistics Sweden (2009), *Tables on the Population in Sweden 2008*, Statistiska centralbyrån.

Latvia: Legislation

Cabinet Regulations 7 July 2009.

Law "Long-term resident status of the European Community in Latvia" which was enacted on 21 July 2006, OG no. 107, 07.07.2006.

Immigration Law in force since 01 May 2003, with its amendments up to 22 April 2010.

Other Member States

Austria

Federal law concerning the execution of aliens police operations, the issue of documents to aliens and the granting of entry authorization, Federal Law Gazette I No. 100/2005.

Bundesgesetz über die Gewährung von Asyl, BGBl. I Nr. 100/2005.

Settlement and Residence Act, Federal Law Gazette I No. 100/2005.

Niederlassungs - und Aufenthaltsgesetz, BGBl. I Nr. 100/2005.

Belgium

Loi relative à certains aspects de la condition des étrangers et instituant le Code de la Nationalité belge, 28 JUIN 1984, Dossier numéro : 1984-06-28/34.

Bulgaria

Law on the Foreigners in the Republic of Bulgaria, Prom. SG. 153/23 December 1998, last amendments dated SG 103/29 December 2009.

Cyprus

Cyprus Supreme Court, Case No 673/2006, *Cresencia Cabotaje Motilla v Republic of Cyprus*, 21 January 2008.

Cyprus Immigration Act as amended in 2007, 8(I)/2007.

Czech Republic

Act No. 326/1999 Coll., Foreigner´s Residence Act.

Denmark

Act no. 572 of 31 May 2010.

Act no. 379 of 25 April 2007.

Aliens Act No. 243 of 27 March 2006, Lovtidende A, 9 June 2006.

Estonia

Aliens Act (Välismaalaste seadus) (1993), RTI, no 44.

Finland

Finnish Aliens Act 301/2004 (Ulkomaalaislaki) as amended by the Act 358/2007.

France: Legislation

Code de l'entrée et du séjour des étrangers et du droit d'asile

Version consolidée au 1 juillet 2010.

Arrêté du 1 décembre 2008 relatif à l'évaluation dans leur pays de résidence du niveau de connaissance, par les étrangers, de la langue française et des valeurs de la République et aux formations prescrites dans ces domaines conformément aux articles R.311-30-1 à R.311-30-11 du code de l'entrée et du séjour des étrangers et du droit d'asile, JORF 5 décembre 2008.

Décret no 2008-1115 du 30 octobre 2008 relatif à la préparation de l'intégration en France des étrangers souhaitant s'y installer durablement, JORF 1 novembre 2008.

Loi no 2007-1631 du 20 novembre 2007 relative à la maîtrise de l'immigration, à l'intégration et à l'asile, JORF n°270 du 21 novembre 2007.

Loi n. 2006-911 du 24 juillet 2006 relative à l'immigration et l'intégration, NOR: INTX 0600037L, Journal Officiel de la République française, 25 juillet 2006.

Ordonnance n°2004-1248 du 24 novembre 2004 relative à la partie législative du code de l'entrée et du séjour des étrangers et du droit d'asile. NOR: INTX0400217R, Journal Officiel de la République française, 25 novembre 2004.

Loi n. 2003-119 du 26 novembre 2003 relative à la maîtrise de l'immigration, au séjour des étrangers en France et à la nationalité, NOR: INTX 0300040L, Journal Officiel de la République française, 27 novembre 2003.

France: Other Relevant Documents

Présentation du projet de loi relatif à l'immigration, à l'intégration et à la nationalité, Ministère de l'immigration, de l'intégration, de l'identité nationale e du développent solidaire, Paris, 1 April, 2010.

Haut Conseil à l'intégration (2009), *Faire Connaitre les Valeurs de la République*, April 2009.

Germany

German Federal Administrative Court (BVerwG), judgment of 30 March 2010, case 1 c 8.09.

Residence Act of 30 July 2004 (Federal Law Gazette I, p. 1950), last amended by the Act of Implementation of Residence and asylum – Related Directives of the European Union of 19 August 2007 (Federal Gazette I, 1970).

Verordnung über die Durchführung von Integrationskursen für Ausländer und Spätaussiedler (Integrationskursverordnung-IntV), 13.12.2004.

Greece

Law 3879/2010 modifying Law 3386/2005 and Presidential Decree 150/2006.

Presidential Decree 150/2006, Official Journal 160/A 31.7.2006.

Law 3386/2005, "Entry, residence and social inclusion of third country nationals in Greek territory", Articles 67–69, Official journal 212/A 23.8.2005.

Hungary

Act II of 2007 on entry and residence of third country nationals.

Government Decree No. 114 of 2007, 24 May on implementation rules to the Act II of 2007.

Ireland

Immigration, Residence and Protection Bill 2010.

Lithuania

Law on the Legal Status of Aliens of 29 April 2004 No. IX-2206 as amended by 22 July 2009 – No XI-392.

Luxembourg

Loi du 23 octobre 2008 sur la nationalité luxembourgeoise (publiée au Mémorial A - N° 158 du 27 octobre 2008).

Loi du 29 août 2008 portant sur la libre circulation des personnes et l'immigration, Journal Officiel du Grand-Duché de Luxembourg, A-No. 138, 10 septembre 2008.

Règlement grand-ducal du 5 septembre 2008 portant exécution de certaines dispositions relatives aux formalités administratives prévues par la loi du 29 août 2008 sur la libre circulation des personnes et l'immigration, Journal Officiel du Grand-Duché de Luxembourg, A-No. 138, 10 septembre 2008.

Malta

L.N. 278 of 2006, Immigration Act (CAP. 217) Status of Long-term Residents (Third Country Nationals) Regulations, 2006.

The Netherlands

LJN: BN3934, Rechtbank Rotterdam , 08/4934.

LJN: BJ3776, Rechtbank's-Gravenhage, zittingsplaats Rotterdam, Awb 08/42722.

Hague District Court (Amsterdam session) 3 June 2009, LJN: BI8797

Royal Decree of 29 December 2008, Staatsblad 605.

Decree on Aliens of 2000 (Vreemdelingenbesluit 2000; "the Vb 2000") as amended by Royal Decree of 29 September 2004 (Staatsblad 2004, p. 496).

Besluit Inburgering (Royal Decree on Integration).

Wet inburgering in het buitenland, Wib (Civic Integration Abroad Act).

Wet inburgering nieuwkomers: Newcomers Integration Act.

Wet inburgering: Integration Act.

Portugal

Lei n.o 23/2007 de 4 de Julho, Aprova o regime jurídico de entrada, permanência, saída e afastamento de estrangeiros do território nacional, Diário da República, 1.a série—N.o 127—4 de Julho de 2007.

Romania

Law amending the Government Emergency Ordinance No. 194/2002 regarding the Legal Status of Aliens in Romania, Official Gazette of Romania, Section I, No. 1116/November 27, 2004, entered into force 1 January 2007.

Slovakia

Act on Residence of Foreigners 48/2002, official journal 23/2002, p. 518 as amended by Act 8 November 2005, official journal 558/2005.

United Kingdom

Home Office. UK Border Agency. July 2009. *Earning the Right to Stay. A New Points Test for Citizenship.*

Home Office (Border and Immigration Agency) (2007), "Marriage Visas: Pre-entry English Requirements for Spouses", Consultation Paper, December 2007.

Journal Articles

International Herald Tribune, *Swiss Referendum Favours Wider Economic Ties to EU*, 9 February 2009.
Il Corriere della Sera, *L'Idea della Lega Nord: "Permesso di Soggiorno a Punti. Via chi Sbaglia"*, 7 October 2008.
El País, *De la Vega confirma el pacto con París en inmigración*, 5 July 2008.
El País, *París renuncia al contrato de integración para satisfacer a España*, 1 July 2008.
Eurostat News release, STAT/05/48, 8 April 2005.

Biography

Dr Diego Acosta Arcarazo was born in June 1980 in Madrid, Spain. He studied law at the Universidad Autónoma in Madrid spending a semester at the Université Libre in Brussels (Belgium) and at the PUC University in Rio de Janeiro (Brazil). He then pursued his studies obtaining a Masters in European Law (Stockholm University) and a DEA in Public International Law (Florida International University in Miami and Autónoma University in Madrid). He then obtained a PhD in European Law (King´s College London). He has interned for the United Nations (New York) and the European Parliament (Brussels). He has also worked for the Spanish Embassy (Bogotá, Colombia), as an assistant researcher for the Miami European Union Centre (Miami) and the Swedish Institute for European Policy Studies (Stockholm) and as a visiting lecturer and tutor at Kings College, Birkbeck College and BPP in London and in the Sergio Arboleda University in Bogota, Colombia. Dr Acosta is currently a Lecturer in Law at the University of Sheffield (United Kingdom). He has been invited to give several conferences in the last few years in different universities around the world on the subject of immigration, such as McGill in Montreal, the University of Miami and the University of Barcelona. He has had several articles published on the area and is currently involved in various research projects on immigration.

Index

www.ingramcontent.com/pod-product-compliance
Lightning Source LLC
LaVergne TN
LVHW011119300926
849160LV00008B/448